C000240903

PAIN AND RETRIBUTION

PAIN AND RETRIBUTION

A Short History of British Prisons,
1066 to the Present

DAVID WILSON

REAKTION BOOKS

For Frances Crook – my generation's Elizabeth Fry

Published by Reaktion Books Ltd
33 Great Sutton Street
London EC1V 0DX, UK
www.reaktionbooks.co.uk

First published 2014
Copyright © David Wilson 2014

Printed and bound in Great Britain
by TJ International, Padstow, Cornwall

A catalogue record for this book is available from the British Library
ISBN 978 1 78023 283 6

Contents

Introduction

A number of themes guide this historical account of British prisons. First, I use the contemporary criminological idea that prison has always had to acknowledge and then satisfy the demands of three 'competing audiences': the public, which would include politicians, the media and commentators about prisons, as well as the general public; prison staff; and finally, prisoners themselves.[1] The relative ascendancy and power of these three groups varies at different points in the narrative, but the need to appeal to them is used as a device to create a link both between different historical eras and between issues that emerge over the course of the period under discussion. This is a history that sees continuities, not breaks with the past.

Ultimately I will argue that it is the failure of prison as an institution to be able to satisfy all three of these audiences at the same time that leads to it being seen to be in 'crisis', and therefore regarded as a failure – albeit a failure that continues to prosper in terms of the numbers who are sent there and the money that we spend in keeping them locked up. This will not be the last irony that will appear in the pages that follow.

And, having given my game away in the first two paragraphs, I should also acknowledge that I know that some readers might prefer their history to be written in a linear fashion, doggedly moving from one year to the next, with the relevant Acts of Parliament dutifully ticked off and stacking up, one on top of each other. However, I have allowed myself the luxury of jumping back and forth between the distinct periods being described at different points in my narrative so as to throw more light onto the issues under discussion, and to show how these issues might be understood or interpreted by my three competing audiences across the centuries. In doing so, I hope that I will be able to show that despite what we believe, or at least what we are told to believe, prisons haven't really changed much at all. Nor have I felt the need to dutifully recount – or even acknowledge – each relevant Act of Parliament that might have been applied to prisons or those who are sent there. To have done so would have been to write a book dealing with the history of sentencing policy or of the law, rather than one specifically about prisons and prisoners.

As I hope these opening paragraphs reveal, my interest is in prison as an institution. By this I mean that I am not just concerned with who gets imprisoned, but with what happens to these people when they are incarcerated; and, more broadly, why the prison seems to have retained such a hold on our collective psyche and imagination. In doing so I will regularly use the descriptions 'the penal system' and 'penal policy', which technically would include (at least) probation, but I will concentrate throughout on prisons – what they look like and how they are organized and managed. I want you to walk with me on the prison's landing, meet some of the people who are being locked up there, note the remarkable absence of monsters and discuss all of this with the prison's staff. I do briefly describe the origins of the probation service and more recent attempts to 'punish in the community', but this is a history which charts the rise and rise of a very different form of punishment – one which takes place behind the walls of an institution. At various points in time these institutions have been called 'gaols', 'jails', 'penitentiaries' or 'prisons'. I discuss this change of nomenclature in the text, and what the different labels mean about what happened within those walls.

At different places in the narrative I discuss policing and especially the politics of law and order. Both throw light onto who gets sent to prison and what happens to them when they are locked up, because the simple reality is that our prison system is the ultimate expression of our criminal justice process, which is usually determined by these two procedures. The politics of law and order come more to the fore as we move closer to the present day and seems to dominate contemporary discussions about prison. I wonder if this might simply be the result of the fact that fewer and fewer criminologists are actually able to conduct research within prisons; thus they are forced to analyse the institution of prison from a policy perspective instead of from their knowledge of what actually happens within the 'belly of the beast'.[2] Indeed, one well-known and respected criminologist who regularly writes about punishment recently told me that he had actually never been inside a prison. Where I can, I try to actually describe prisons and prisoners, as opposed to policies *about* prisons and prisoners.

Second, while I use a great number of official sources to guide the narrative (because these are all too readily available in print, and are collected almost fetishistically in our university libraries), given that very few people have ever visited a prison – and get most of their information about imprisonment from television and films – I have tried to prioritize the voices of prisoners. This has not been an easy task, and while I use prisoners' autobiographies and accounts of their times inside throughout, these voices are obviously more plentiful in the contemporary period. Before the 1960s accounts were almost inevitably written by atypical prisoners such as Oscar Wilde, or by campaigners such as Charles Dickens, who made it their business to find out about what happened within the penal system. Thus I do not claim that what I have produced is a 'history from below' – if that is actually ever possible – although I do believe that it is important to try to reflect how prison has been experienced by those who get locked up, even if they might be described as 'celebrities', rather than simply describing what is claimed for prison and how it is run, or what those with the power to make these claims and explanations argue that it achieves. Why should their claims be treated any more seriously than the claims of prisoners, or indeed of prison staff?

Prison staff – of various grades, backgrounds and disciplines, and, like prisons, often described in different ways – appear throughout the narrative, although they are but one of my main interests in what follows. Even so, especially in the latter portions of the book, I try to use the voices of basic-grade prison officers (please note that the title 'warder' was abolished in 1922) to throw some light onto the themes which have preoccupied the narrative, and to provide some insight into how these officers make sense of their responsibilities given that they have become one of the 'audiences' that seeks to legitimize prison. After all, it is a very odd choice of career to deprive people of their liberty and to spend all of your working days locking them up.

A third theme that will reappear throughout the narrative will be my attempt to understand why prison – no matter what role it performs, and despite the fact that it is perpetually seen as in 'crisis' by the tabloid press – has remained so popular within our historic and recent public policy, with the exception of one long, glorious, unusual period of sustained decarceration. Clearly, decarceration – the opposite of incarceration – has not characterized our recent approach to prisons; quite the reverse. So throughout I will attempt to use the history of our prisons to throw some light onto our current prison numbers. As I write, Britain has more people locked up in our prisons than at any point in its history, with more women, men, young people, old people and people who have ethnic minority backgrounds behind bars than ever before. Astonishingly, we have more life-sentenced prisoners in Britain than the whole of Western Europe combined. When did we start to diverge in our penal policy from our European neighbours, a process described as 'English exceptionalism', which has seen us incarcerate more of our citizens than the French, the Germans, the Norwegians, Swedes, Finns and Italians? In this respect at least, we remain exceptional.

These goals for my gaols notwithstanding, throughout the narrative I will outline the four main justifications for why we have used prison, both in the past and more recently, and explain what it is that we hope to achieve when we send someone to jail, and how this might have changed over time. Briefly, these goals are deterrence (both of the individual offender and of those in society more generally who might be contemplating committing crime); incapacitation; retribution; and finally rehabilitation.

The main focus of the book is the period from 1877 to the present day, and I will largely, but not exclusively, describe prisons in England and Wales. However, I have also included chapters about prisons in pre-modern Britain, the foundation of Millbank, the first state prison in England, and developments prior to 1877. And, while there are separate penal (and legal) systems in England and Wales and in Scotland, I will make reference throughout to prisons in Scotland, especially as the narrative moves closer to the present day, which has seen something of a divergence in penal policies between Scotland and the rest of Britain. In the course of researching this book it also became increasingly obvious to me that there is a desperate need for a separate book about the history of Scottish prisons, but that task must wait for another occasion.[3] I will also briefly allude to prisons and prisoners in Europe, despite my geographic focus, and will describe some recent and fascinating developments in the USA in a concluding section.

Throughout I have tried to keep academic references to a minimum, but have included these by way of endnotes where they help to explain my argument. In this way, I hope that the reader's attention isn't too distracted from the text, while those who want to follow up on my sources have a means of doing so. I should also acknowledge that I have conducted a limited number of interviews with serving and former prisoners and prison staff of various grades, serving in different institutions, to help shape the text.

Above all, this history reflects my own personal experiences of having managed prisons, and of visiting prisons – sometimes on official business, either for HM Prison Service, for the Council of Europe or for the Howard League of Penal Reform – in Britain and in other parts of the world. So, too, it reflects my decision to resign from the prison service. Indeed, nowadays I am as much identified by my responsibilities for and my role within the Howard League for Penal Reform as I am for having been a prison governor. I also chair the charity the Friends of Grendon and I am vice chair of New Bridge, which was set up in 1956 to create links between offenders and the community. On a daily basis, as a professor of criminology at Birmingham City University, I also teach undergraduate and postgraduate students about crime and punishment. I regularly present documentaries about crime and punishment on television and the radio.

These various roles and experiences have obviously had a direct impact on what I think about prisons and prisoners, and how they are presented within the print and broadcast media. As such, it would be wrong of me to claim that this history is neutral and dispassionate. Rather, it is formed by my own desire to learn from the past and to see how this can help us to make sense of prisons today and in the future. I want to use this history to understand why we continually and increasingly use prison as a sentencing option given that it is a costly, counterproductive failure. Ultimately, in the pages that follow, I try to explain why it is perfectly possible to have 'less crime, safer communities and fewer people in prison'. This phrase is one that will occur in other places in the text.

Copied from a MS. in the British Museum (Roy. Mss. 16 F. 2) by James West.

This drawing represents the Tower about the year 1418. When Charles Duke of Orleans, and his youngest brother, John Count of Angoulesme, were taken prisoners at the Battle of Agincourt Oct.r 25 1415. The Duke is represented sitting in the interior of the White Tower, writing his poems. He is also represented looking out of his chamber window; he appears also on the Bulwarks, welcoming some faithful adherent, who has recently arrived from his beloved France.

Charles of Orléans imprisoned in the Tower of London c. 1415, in an illuminated manuscript of the late 15th century.

ONE

Grand Castles and Thieves' Holes

They are surely most dismal places.
James Boswell on a visit to Newgate, 3 May 1763

Prisons, as we have come to know them, were an invention of the nineteenth century. Much of what we now associate with prisons – such as, for example, the separation of male inmates from female ones, and young offenders from adults; the provision of work and education; and, above all, a term of imprisonment being used as a sentencing decision, and therefore as a punishment in itself – were developments that were only gradually established over time in an often uneven, messy, chaotic process of transformation. These changes were largely undertaken by the Victorians and so prison, as the institution that we would now know and recognize, came into being around the same time as postage stamps, music halls, trains, cameras and the flushing toilet.

This is not to imply that prisons did not exist before the nineteenth century. However, the roles that these places performed and the ways in which they were organized internally were markedly different in the prisons that would gradually become established by the end of the nineteenth century and at the beginning of the twentieth century, as was the nature of imprisonment.

These earlier places of confinement – grand and forbidding castles or, at the other end of the spectrum, what the Scots called 'thieves' holes' – were largely custodial in function. In other words, their role was to hold on to the prisoner until he or she could be dealt with in some other way, such as being exiled, transported to another part of the world, mutilated, executed or required to pay compensation for the damage that he or she had done. The killing of an earl in medieval Scotland, for example, required compensation of sixteen cows to be paid to the departed peer's family.[1] The goal was to get rid of the prisoner as quickly as possible (so as to cut down on costs), and a long-forgotten Scottish phrase captures this objective perfectly – the task of prison was to have the prisoner 'clenzit or conviktt'. In other words, freed or hanged.

In this chapter I will consider some of the many spaces that were used as prisons, and how prisoners located in these spaces were treated. It will become ever more apparent how different these prisons were in usage to what we have come to expect of prisons today. Even so, there are some surprising continuities. I have also chosen to use two iconic places as case studies – the Tower of London and Newgate Gaol – largely because these different prison spaces (one of which still survives) have seeped into our collective imaginations and have almost become what we understand to be the quintessential prisons. Finally I will address the role of the Church and various clerics in the early history of the prison.

Grand Castles: The Tower of London

The Tower of London is one of the most visited historic monuments in the world, and most people associate it with the Crown Jewels, perhaps with ravens, and with imprisonment, torture and executions. It formally dates from 1066 and the need of William the Conqueror to establish and then flaunt his authority within London, the capital and most important urban area of his new kingdom, which he had recently won through warfare. The Tower was William's showpiece: a symbol of his power, control and domination. From the outset it was intended as both a Norman symbol of state authority and an object of fear. It was designed to be an imposing, impregnable fortress and, until the nineteenth century, it achieved that purpose and was only rivalled in London by St Paul's Cathedral in terms of height and scale.

Despite its association with imprisonment, the Tower was not built as a prison and its role as such, as with most castles, was incidental to its main functions. Even so, it acted as a state prison from 1100 – when it locked up its first recorded prisoner, Ranulf Flambard – until 1820, and thereafter at times of national emergency, such as when it imprisoned its last two prisoners, Rudolf Hess and the spy Josef Jakobs. Hess was Hitler's deputy and was imprisoned at the Tower for four days in May 1941, and Jakobs was shot there in August 1941 in the rifle range that stood in the Outer Ward.

Since the Tower was not built as a prison, it had no specially designed accommodation in which to incarcerate its inmates. Prisoners therefore lodged in whatever space was available. High-ranking prisoners were usually kept in parts of the royal residences that the Tower maintained. There was some rationalization of prisoner accommodation for the first time under the tenure of Sir William Waad, who was made lieutenant of the Tower in 1605. A list from 1641 suggests that Cradle, Salt, Broad Arrow, Constable, Martin, Well, Beauchamp, Bell, Bloody, Coldharbour and Lanthorn towers could all accommodate prisoners – in some degree of comfort. Contrary to popular thinking, there was no dungeon, nor a large prison block filled with manacled prisoners.[2]

For most of the Tower's history as an important but incidental state prison, there were two types of confinement. The first was close confinement, whereby the prisoner was secured in his quarters and subject to strict security with no visitors allowed; the second, confinement within the tower's precincts. Conditions in these latter circumstances were not at all grim. A list of possessions that the Privy Council agreed to send to the imprisoned Earl of Castlehaven in 1630, for example, included such luxuries as a 'bed of crimson taffeta', '12 peeces of tapestry neare suitable as they may bee' and 'three turkie carpets', as well as bedding for a servant.[3] Arrangements such as these had been created much earlier in the Tower's history; King John Balliol of Scotland – who spent three years in the Tower after being captured after the Battle of Dunbar in 1296 – was allowed out of the Tower to go hunting and could travel up to 21 miles outside of London. He was also accompanied in the Tower by a number of servants, and so rooms had also to be found for two squires, a huntsman, a barber, a chaplain, assistants, grooms, a tailor, a laundress, pages and the king's pack of ten hunting dogs.

The medieval king that we know most about, at least in relation to the time that he spent in the Tower, is John II of France (1319–1364), who was also known as John the Good. He was captured at the Battle of Poitiers in 1356 by Edward, Prince of Wales – the 'Black Prince' – and finally arrived at the Tower in April 1360. He was lodged, along with his son and a number of servants, in the White Tower, where he stayed in some considerable style. He arrived with five wagons filled with possessions: one for himself; another for his son; one wagon holding materials for his chapel and one for his kitchen; and finally one which held musical instruments. He made a number of trips outside of the Tower, and held a feast for Edward III and Queen Philippa of Hainault at the Tower at his own expense. John's ransom was fixed at the eye-watering sum of half a million pounds sterling, and he was allowed to return to France to arrange for its collection, leaving his second son – the Duke of Anjou – as a hostage in Calais. When he discovered that his son had escaped and that he was unable to raise the ransom, he chivalrously returned to captivity in England, where he died in 1364.

Not every prisoner was as chivalrous as John the Good and, partly as a result of the fact that the Tower was not specifically designed to hold prisoners, there were a number of escapes. Ranulf Flambard, for example, the bishop of Durham and probably the Tower's first ever prisoner, escaped in 1101 after a length of rope had been smuggled into the Tower in a barrel of wine. Flambard laid on a banquet for his guards, and after they had eaten and drunk to insensibility he climbed down the rope and made his way to France, leaving his captors snoring heavily behind him. In 1534 Alice Tankerville managed to persuade one of her guards to help her to escape, although both were quickly recaptured and then executed. Almost 200 years later, in 1716, Winifred Maxwell had more luck when she organized the escape of her husband – the Jacobite William, Earl of Nithsdale – by disguising him as a woman and then smuggling him out of the Tower with the rest of her entourage. Winifred remained in the cell and pretended to have a conversation with her escaped husband so as to distract the guards from what she had just been able to accomplish.

These various incidents, albeit separated by several centuries, also draw our attention to the abilities of the 30–40 guards who were paid to keep undesirable Londoners out of the Tower and the prisoners inside. Since the Tower had not been designed as a prison, it needed to rely on the professionalism of its staff to make conditions secure. The Tower's guards were first issued with an uniform during the Tudor period, and became established as 'yeomen warders', similar to the royal bodyguard known as the 'Yeomen of the Guard'. In turn they were under the command of the porter, otherwise known as the chief yeoman warder, and the yeoman gaoler. Often prisoners might be lodged within the yeoman warder's own accommodation and, almost inevitably, relationships would develop between them. Even so, the yeomen warders were personally responsible for the security of their prisoners and it was not unusual for them to be disciplined as a result of escapes. A deputy lieutenant of the Tower made this speech to his yeomen warders in 1722 that some might still find good advice today:

> There is no faith to be given to prisoners, and I advise all officers
> to do their duty with regularity, as well as civility, and to keep to

the letter of the orders without relaxing, for if you deviate a little from them, they are never satisfied till you give more and more liberties, till at last, you must either become criminal or in ceasing to gratify them, they fall out with you as an ill-natured man and tyrannical in your office.[4]

The guards were also at least partly responsible for some of the myths and exaggerations that circulated about the Tower, especially in relation to its role as a site of torture and execution. In reality the Tower was merely a point of departure for most of those who were about to be executed (most often on Tower Hill, or at Tyburn), and it has been calculated that there were only 112 executions of prisoners formerly lodged at the Tower and only seven within it, excluding the execution of some eleven spies during the First World War and of Josef Jakobs in 1941.[5] The Tower's role as a site of torture has also been exaggerated. However, some prisoners, especially during the sixteenth and seventeenth centuries, were subjected to torture, as this was a means to gather information that might later be used against them, although torture was not and has never been recognized as a means of gathering intelligence under English law. Even so, the guards who inflicted this torture were acting on the orders of the highest levels of government and while their intention was not in the first instance to punish these prisoners, the torture is likely to have been experienced as such.

There were three methods of torture employed: the rack; the 'Scavenger's Daughter', a set of neck and wrist irons that forced the prisoner into various contorted positions; and the much simpler method of simply manacling the prisoner by his wrists and suspending him off the floor. The most common method was the rack, which was last used in 1640 and decommissioned by 1675. Essentially it was a bed on which the prisoner lay prior to being pulled in different directions by his hands and feet. A Shakespearean scholar called Isaac Reed located a rack in the stores of the Tower in 1799, and provides a near-contemporary description:

It consists of a strong iron frame about 6 feet long, with 3 rollers of wood within it. The middle one of these, which has iron teeth at each end, is governed by 2 stops of iron, and was, probably, that part of the machine which suspended the powers of the rest, when the unhappy sufferer was sufficiently strained by the cords etc to begin confession.[6]

We know that the rack was used on Guy Fawkes and legend has it that he only confessed after ten days of interrogation, several of which may have been spent on the rack. We also know that the first woman to be 'racked' was the writer Anne Askew in 1546. Askew had been arrested for distributing Protestant literature and for resolutely refusing to accept an arranged marriage to a Catholic farmer called Thomas Kyme. She was brought to the Tower from Newgate to be interrogated by a succession of clerics, but refused to recant her convictions and was eventually burned at the stake in Smithfield in July 1546. The story of her life and execution touched the public's imagination and quickly became the stuff of legend.[7] However, given that torture could only be ordered by the Privy Council, it was rare. Between 1540 and 1640 there were only 48 cases of torture that received official sanction, although of course we cannot rule out the possibility that other cases of torture were unofficially sanctioned.[8]

Myths and Exaggerations

All of this rather raises the question of how these myths about the Tower, and especially what happened within it, began to circulate and then gained lasting popularity. Clearly, given that torture was a private matter being undertaken on behalf of the state, and which may have involved state secrets being divulged, there would have been few witnesses present who could later describe what had actually occurred. This absence opened up the opportunity for the imagination to take hold, especially after capital punishment specifically, and imprisonment more generally, became enclosed behind the prison's walls. It might also often have been in the state's interest to exaggerate its abilities to gain confessions from those it saw as a threat to its power. The state wanted to present itself as invincible. This was not lost on the yeomen warders, especially when the Tower became a dark tourist attraction and money could be made from exaggerating or embellishing what had actually occurred behind the Tower's walls, away from the public's gaze. After all, the Tower had always acted as a showpiece, so why not make money out of this role?

The practice of showing the Tower to visitors had been established during the reign of Elizabeth I (r. 1558–1603). Visitors paid the yeoman warders to guide them around the site, often paying a little more money to see different parts of the Tower once entry had been afforded. In 1639 it cost Lady Judith Barrington 11 shillings to visit the Tower; less than 30 years later it cost General Patrick Gordon 33 shillings; but by 1729 there were fixed prices to view the mint, jewel house, menagerie and armouries. In 1838 a temporary ticket office was constructed, and this was replaced thirteen years later by a purpose-built office, which conveniently had lavatories attached. The cost at this time to gain entry was sixpence, a significant price reduction from that paid by Lady Barrington or General Gordon. This helped to encourage more people to pass through the Tower's gate. By 1839, 80,000 visitors were visiting the Tower each year. In 1875 free admission on Mondays, Saturdays and official holidays was introduced, which allowed visitor numbers to increase further to more than half a million per year.[9]

But what was it that visitors wanted to see and hear about? Some indication of this can be gleaned from the fact that a miniature rack was made for public display around 1850 in response to visitor interest, even though the rack itself had fallen out of use in 1640. Victorian artist George Bernard O'Neill lavishly painted a yeoman warder regaling children with stories around an execution block, and a photograph from 1895 exists of another guard showing a group of visitors the 'scaffold site', even though no permanent scaffold site actually existed.[10] This idea of the Tower's bloody past was also seized upon by Victorian writers, especially William Harrison Ainsworth, who published *The Tower of London: A Historical Romance* in 1840. In this novel, based on the story of Lady Jane Grey, the Tower becomes a setting for tragic events and foul play. It was also Ainsworth who perpetuated the myth that the Tower had dungeons, and that it boasted a scaffold with the soil underneath 'dyed with the richest and best blood in the land'. Dark tourism had clearly found its first home.[11]

But what generally should we conclude from this case study of the Tower of London as a prison? The answer is, first, that it was not designed as such, and that even if it acted in this capacity on occasion, it was often ill-equipped to perform that role. As a result, there were a number of escapes. Second, many of the prisoners who were lodged in the Tower lived there in considerable comfort. They often had the power, influence and money to be able to purchase a standard of living that the vast majority of people could never have achieved. This would not have been lost on the public at large, and perhaps in all of this we might glimpse the beginnings of a more general resentment about what prisoners – who, by the fact of their imprisonment, are seen as having transgressed – have access to or possess which those who have not transgressed do not. Nor was there any attempt to regulate the prisoner's day by providing work or education, for it is clear that the role that the Tower played when imprisoning was purely custodial. It simply held the prisoner securely until he or she could be dealt with in some other way. A more contemporary description might be 'incapacitation'. There is no sense that the prisoner was sentenced to a term in the Tower as a form of punishment in itself, even if a small number might have been subjected to torture when located there (which common sense suggests would have been experienced as a form of punishment).

Finally, it is clear that the Tower was a powerful symbol of state control and authority – a symbol that became all the more potent because few people actually knew what went on behind the Tower's walls. This absence of public scrutiny allowed a number of myths about the Tower to gain popularity, and these were in turn later recycled back to the public when the Tower became a site of dark tourism in the nineteenth century. The public clearly wanted their prisons to be bloody, hellish places of torture and torment. None of this applied to the Tower of London.

A Few More Grand Castles, and Some Other Prisons

As far as lodging prisoners was concerned, there were many other castles which performed similar roles to the Tower. In Scotland, for example, political prisoners or religious dissenters could be located in Edinburgh, Stirling, Doune, Dunnottar and Blackness castles, as well as on the island stronghold of the Bass Rock, from which no prisoner ever escaped. These were effectively state prisons. Blackness, a castle near Edinburgh, was built in the shape of a ship, and in the sixteenth century housed such celebrated prisoners as Cardinal Beaton, Lord Hay of Yester and the Earl of Morton, who had been accused of various offences but who had failed to appear before a council of his peers to answer these charges. At this time, the generic term used for imprisonment in Scotland was 'warding', and so Lord Hay promised that he would 'enter himself in ward in Blakness Castle . . . under pain of 10,000 merks'.[12]

A prisoner of some standing or importance might be warded within a castle, but more run-of-the-mill offenders were warded in thieves' holes, private lodgings, their own homes or increasingly in tolbooths. These were originally booths at a fair where tolls were collected, but gradually they developed into permanent structures in which a court might meet and offenders could be imprisoned. There were tolbooths in Glasgow, Perth and Dundee, but Edinburgh's is perhaps the best known. The old tolbooth of the capital had been built in 1480, but was ordered to be demolished in 1561 (although this did not actually happen), by which time it consisted of an 'iron room' – where prisoners awaiting execution were shackled – a jailer's house and a thieves' hole (which suggests that this term might have been used generically simply to describe a bare room). A new tolbooth was subsequently erected, which provided accommodation for the Lords of Session and Town Council, and part of St Giles' Cathedral was also partitioned off and converted into a prison, which was also called the tolbooth.

We know comparatively little about thieves' holes, although the name probably explains exactly what they were. Henry Graham, who published his *The Social Life in Scotland in the Eighteenth Century* in 1899, provides us with a glimpse of what they may have been like:

> The receptacle for prisoners in a village was a 'thieves' hole', a little hut with a damp earthen floor, with hardly a glimmer of light from the tiny opening, through which the snow drifted and the wind swirled in mad career through the room, and out again, under and above the ill-fitting doors – through a hole in which the wife of the constable, intent on other avocations, thrust the food for the inmates. A small country town had for its residence for prisoners a vile thatched room, perhaps fourteen feet long,

Edinburgh's Tolbooth (St Giles' Cathedral), *c.* 1803–17, etching.

dark, filthy, and fireless, and in winter perishingly cold, where for months untried prisoners waited till the circuit court opened to hear their case; while for security they were sometimes loaded with chains and fastened to an iron bar or bedstead.[13]

Whether a prisoner was warded within a castle, a thieves' hole or a tolbooth, the main function of this warding – as in the Tower of London – was custodial. Being warded was not a punishment of the court, but rather a means of keeping the prisoner secure until a punishment could be imposed, as is clearly expressed in Graham's description. While the goal was to get rid of these prisoners as quickly as possible, this did not always happen: some might be warded for a considerable period of time. Sir James Macdonald, for example, was a prisoner at Edinburgh Castle from 1604 until his eventual escape eleven years later, and the Earl of Orkney was warded for six years before being executed in 1615.

From 1648 onwards, prisoners could also be transported as a punishment in Scotland. This punishment was liberally used after the Jacobite rebellion of 1745, when around 800 prisoners were transported to America between March 1747 and November 1748. The governor of South Carolina, for example, is reported to have bought 'thirty Highland rebels at £30 apiece'. Many of these Jacobites had been imprisoned in England as well as in Scotland, which reflects something of the growing connection between imprisonment on both sides of the border – a trend which would ebb and flow over time, with some periods being characterized by a closeness of penal approach across Britain, while others are more clearly different and distinct from each other. Of note is the fact that of the 58 Jacobites who escaped from prison, only thirteen managed to do so from an English gaol, which suggests either that English prisons were of a superior and more secure design than their northern counterparts, or that there were lingering Jacobite sympathies among Scottish jailers.[14]

The Church as Prison

As the story of part of St Giles's Cathedral in Edinburgh being used as a tolbooth reveals, there were other buildings that could be used as prisons. Even today, the website of the cathedral acknowledges this historic function. However, it is probably less well known that the steeples of churches in towns such as Edinburgh, Perth, Inverness and Dundee were converted to serve as prisons and were often considered more secure than the local tolbooths. Indeed, it has been suggested that St Giles's only stopped being used as a tolbooth because of complaints by parishioners that prisoners kept dropping pebbles on their heads. An unnamed Caithness man with debts of £1,400 was imprisoned in the vault of the steeple of an Inverness church for seven years, and had to petition the local magistrates to be moved to the tolbooth. He described how he was living with

> the greatest severity . . . and affliction . . . not having the use
> or benefit of the least fire, or little candlelight allowed me . . .
> tho' ever so sick and unwell. The said vault being so cold and
> obnoxious to the health . . . that it is a wonder . . . that a person
> of my age has continued alive so long in it.[15]

These stories should remind us of the importance of the role played by clerics and by the Church as an institution in enforcing morality and in disciplining and punishing those who transgressed. Professor Andrew Coyle notes that minor offenders – those, for example, who might simply have drunk alcohol to excess, or had sex outside of marriage – could find themselves fastened by the neck to the wall of a church by an iron collar. These collars were also known as 'jougs', and it is likely that this is where the modern slang of being 'in the jug' as a reference to prison comes from.[16] We should also remember that adultery was made a capital crime in Scotland in 1563, and that at this time there was a 'stool of repentance' in every church. As the location of this stool indicates, punishment, when it came, was meant to be public. It is also clear that, especially in the sixteenth century, the Church was both a site for and a dispenser of punishment, but that over time there was a gradual move away from offences against religious morality – which were punished by the Church – to offences against secular authority, which were to be punished by the state.

This earlier role of the Church and of clerics in the history of punishment and prisons also provides us with some balance when we begin to consider the work of others who were religiously motivated, and their role within the history of prisons and 'penitentiaries'.[17] And, as I hope will be revealed, the various themes that we have so far described in this chapter will become the necessary background to our final case study of Newgate Gaol.

An Ordinary Gaol: Newgate

I have described Newgate as an 'ordinary' gaol, but only so as to draw attention to the fact that unlike the Tower, it did not lock up kings and queens, earls, lords or ladies, but a very different type of prisoner. Nor was it built as a fortress, which would have been important to the state at times of crisis, such as during a war. Even so, as a prison Newgate was often at the heart of important historical events in London – from the Peasants' Revolt in the summer of 1381 to the Gordon Riots of 1780 – and later developments within the gaol make it central to our understanding of what prisons had been like before they were developed in the nineteenth century.

Newgate was also a favourite place for writers and artists to visit, as well as those whom we might now call commentators on prisons specifically

Newgate Prison, London, from Thomas Bayly, *Herba parietis; or, the Wall Flower as it Grew out of the Stone Chamber Belonging to the Metropolitan Prison of London Called New Gate* (1650).

Newgate c. 1724.

and crime and punishment more generally. Dickens famously visited Newgate in 1836 and Gustave Doré in 1872, when he etched a view of prisoners walking around the circle of the 'press yard', which Van Gogh would later turn into an iconic image of incarceration. Newgate was also the prison where the writers Christopher Marlowe, Ben Jonson and Daniel Defoe were locked up – Jonson on a capital charge. He therefore had to plead the 'benefit of clergy' to escape hanging.[18] This penal loophole required the prisoner to be able to read in Latin Psalm 51, the solemn *Miserere Mei*, with its plea 'Have mercy upon me, O God.' This allowed the literate to escape their sentences, and so became known as the 'neck verse'. (The literate have always been unusual in prisons.) Other more familiar pieces of language escaped over the prison's walls too and entered into common usage, such as 'pulling your leg' and being 'left in the lurch' – phrases that are still in use today, but which were once related to the

Newgate after 1780 (George Dance's design).

process and mechanics of capital punishment, given that the 'lurch' was the wagon that would carry the prisoner to the gallows, and there the hangman might have to 'pull his leg' to make certain he had actually died. Successive Newgate chaplains to the condemned – called the 'Newgate ordinary' – almost single-handedly invented the 'true crime' genre.[19] And in 1842, even a king wanted to visit the gaol, so as to be able to discuss prison reform with Elizabeth Fry, who had transformed part of the prison.

In short, Newgate and what happened inside its walls seeped into public consciousness so that it became iconic of not only what a prison actually was, but of what could be done inside that space if there was organization and the will to do so. Newgate became a theatre where the social dramas that beset England could be played out; a place where heroes, heroines and villains could be created; and where the public, in ways that would disappear when imprisonment became a more private affair, could shape, comment upon and conclude as they wished about what was right and what was wrong. After all, people could pay to go inside Newgate to look at the gaol and its prisoners, and the streets surrounding it were often clogged with queues of Londoners waiting to gain entry. The description 'ordinary' hardly does any of this justice.

To begin with some basic history, as the historian Kelly Grovier describes, there were really four distinct phases in the development of Newgate.[20] It is not certain when the prison was first established, but the original structure lasted until 1423, when it was replaced by

'Whittington's Gaol', as in Richard (Dick) Whittington, Lord Mayor of London. This structure was in turn burned down in the Great Fire of London in 1666, and the building that took its place made way in 1770 for the final version of Newgate, which was designed by George Dance the Younger. This was subsequently knocked down in August 1902, but not before George Woolfe, who had murdered his girlfriend, was hanged there on 6 May of that year, becoming the last of the 1,169 people to be executed at the prison after the gallows had been moved to Newgate from Tyburn in 1783. The Central Criminal Court – also known as the 'Old Bailey' – now stands on the old prison site.

The original Newgate was probably built on the orders of Henry II in the twelfth century. This original structure was enlarged in 1218; converting one of the turrets into a cell cost the Royal Exchequer £100. However, we also know that in 1253 Peter de Rivallis – Treasurer of the King's Wardrobe – was rewarded for his services to Henry III by being given residence within Newgate, reflecting the fact that the accommodation that was available was of mixed use. As Grovier acknowledges, there is therefore a 'blurred ambivalence' about accommodation within Newgate: some of the space within the gaol was desirable and sought after, while other areas must have been cramped and reserved for those

Newgate after 1780 (George Dance's design).

Newgate main entrance, from Henry Mayhew's *The Criminal Prisons of London, and Scenes of Prison Life* (1862).

who were to be incarcerated. This mix of the desirable with the disgraceful did not disappear quickly, and even as late as the eighteenth century some lodgings within the prison 'continued to command some of the highest rents in all of London and were available only to the most affluent prisoners'.[21]

The rebuilt Newgate – after the Great Fire of London – was completed by 1672, and consisted of a gatehouse with two imposing towers that

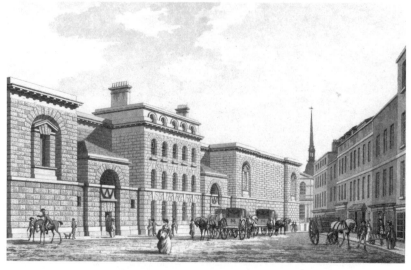

Newgate, after 1780 (George Dance's design), print dated 1799.

View of the Inside of Newgate, 1809.

flanked Newgate Street. A number of outward-facing statues stood on its facade, symbolizing Justice, Mercy, Truth, Liberty, Peace, Plenty and Concord. Given that the stench of the prison got so bad at times that local businesses were forced to close down, especially when the weather was warm, these stone figures clearly represented an ideal that was rarely realized.[22] This would not be the last time in the history of our prisons when what was officially claimed for a prison, or for the prison system, was at some distance from what was actually achieved. In 1724 one Batty Langley – whose brother was a turnkey at the gaol – was able to gain entry to Newgate as a result of this family connection and describe the interior. Stating that he would not depart 'one Tittle from the naked Truth', he described how the prison had five different levels: one below ground and four above. There was a distinction between masters' (the more upmarket area which could command the highest fees), commons' and women's 'wards' (a reference to 'warding', as opposed to having any medical overtones), and these wards were in turn subdivided between felons and debtors. The debtors were located in an area that was nick-named 'Tangier' – a contemporary allusion to pirates who had taken captives on the Barbary Coast – and those located in this area were known as 'tangerines'.[23]

New prisoners arriving at the gaol would enter through a door in the archway in Newgate Street, and were then taken to the Condemned Hold, which was located near the keeper's house. This was where they

The Burning and Plundering of Newgate & Setting the Felons at Liberty by the Mob, contemporary print of 1780.

would be 'clamped' – put in irons – although debtors could have these removed if family or friends were able to pay the keeper's fees for doing so. Those arrested on criminal charges were kept in chains for the duration of their sentence, although through a process known as 'easement' they could have heavy chains replaced by lighter ones. It was of course in the keeper's financial interests to have a newly received felon in as heavy a set of chains as possible, as these made it much more difficult for the prisoner to escape, and then later their easement would become a source of income.

In fact, everything within the gaol was a way of generating revenue. Gaols were mini businesses: semi-private enterprises that extracted money out of the misery of those that got locked up. Ability to pay determined whether or not a new entrant to Newgate would be assigned room in the masters' or commons' wards and, once allocated, they were thereafter expected to pay a 'garnish' to the steward – usually a tenured inmate – to buy everything from candles to coal and food. On the masters' side, Hall Ward and the press yard were regarded as the most luxurious. Prisoners were also expected to pay for other amenities such as mattresses and bedding, and perhaps a table and somewhere to sit. Batty advises that Hall Ward also had south-facing windows which allowed for excellent ventilation – a real luxury given the smell of bodies crowded together in an environment with inadequate drainage. If one had the money, it was also possible to hire other prisoners to act as servants to do everything from cleaning one's clothes and accommodation to kindling the fire. Finally there was a drinking cellar where brandy and wine could be purchased, and immediately above this was an interview room where prisoners could meet their family and friends, or their lawyers. Visits could only be made through the keeper and these, of course, cost money too – one shilling and sixpence per visit.[24]

Even paying the keepers of Newgate a fixed salary – something introduced in 1734 – and then later giving them accommodation and a liquor allowance did little to curb their interest in making money out of their charges. A keeper known as William Pitt, for example, was able to extort almost £4,000 in a matter of months from prisoners who had been sent to Newgate in the aftermath of the Jacobite Rebellion.[25] It is little wonder that the keeper of Newgate became a stock villain in ballads, plays and novels of the period.

Accommodation on the commons' side was of a very different kind. The destitute, or those who were troublesome, were located on the second floor of the gaol known as the 'Bilbows', or in a basement dungeon known as the 'Stone Hold', which seems to have been in a state of permanent darkness. Langley described the latter as 'paved with stone, on which the prisoners lie without any Beds, and thereby endure great Misery and Hardship'.[26] Few women were ever located on the masters' side of the gaol, although there was a cell reserved for them known as 'My Lady's Hold', which Langley did not think impressive. Almost every woman was assigned to the women's ward, which was located on the third floor, near the chapel. For a fee of sixpence (payable to the turnkey), male inmates were allowed to visit their female peers. This de facto prostitution was sometimes welcomed by the women involved, not just because it allowed them to make a little money in an environment where everything that was needed to live had to be bought, but also because a woman who had been convicted of a capital offence could avoid execution by 'pleading the belly'; in other words, by being pregnant. Indeed, the mother of the fictional Moll Flanders (who in Defoe's novel is born in Newgate) pleaded her belly for a reprieve prior to being transported to

America. This plea was only rendered obsolete by the Sentence of Death (Expectant Mothers) Act of 1931.

There was even money to be made out of executions, and one of those who could make the most was the Newgate ordinary – the official chaplain to the condemned. This figure was also sometimes known as 'the great Bishop of the Cells', and if the trial judge had the leading role in the first half of the drama of the execution, it was the chaplain who presided over the finale. God and the gallows went together very happily and the scaffold, as much as the courtroom, was the stage on which a narrative of exhortation and repentance was played out before the public, who flocked in their thousands to watch these spectacles of death. It has been calculated that a Londoner growing up in the 1780s could by the 1840s have attended some 400 executions outside of Newgate and watched 1,200 people die.[27] In these public rituals of execution, both the condemned and the clerical had a role to play. Harry Potter, our foremost historian of the death penalty, has even described the chaplains who presided over executions as 'high priests and impresarios', and Grovier notes that because the ordinary had unrivalled access to the condemned prisoner, 'these moonlighting clergymen routinely trebled or quadrupled their paltry salary by divulging and embellishing the condemned's version of events.'[28]

In particular the public became fascinated by accounts of the lives of the condemned and of the crimes that they had committed. These were first published in 1705 as the 'Tyburn Calendar' – in this context a 'calendar' simply referred to prisoners who were scheduled to appear at court – and then eventually as the 'Newgate Calendar', even though prisoners did not actually need to have spent time at Newgate to appear in the calendar. By the end of the eighteenth century, the Newgate Calendar was one of the most popular books in the country and, as a publishing phenomenon, it owed much to the reportage and creativity of the Newgate ordinary. This was 'true crime', and writing it was eagerly taken up by the ordinary not just because there was money to be made from these stories, but because they could be used for a moral purpose. In short, the Newgate Calendar was filled with stories of the condemned pleading with the reading public not to behave as they might have done, and often confessing to their sins before God (or not, as the case might be – which was where the creativity of the ordinary came in). The message within the Newgate Calendar was clear: don't stray too far from the scriptures as a guide for living your life. Even the final words of the about-to-be-hanged, before being 'launched into eternity', were therefore deliberately harnessed to re-establish and reassert the moral authority of the state and of God.

We should, of course, question this moral authority in a state where a system of laws and punishments known as the Bloody Code ensured that the death penalty was available for some 225 offences, which led to some 7,000 men and women losing their lives between 1770 and 1830.[29] The Newgate ordinaries were much less vocal about the fact that the vast majority of those who were being executed were poor and marginalized, or that hanging itself was a slow and usually painful way to kill someone. Luckily other religious leaders were far more willing to address questions of justice.

Elizabeth Gurney was born in Norwich in 1780, and was the eldest daughter of a wealthy Quaker banking family. In 1800 she married Joseph Fry – also a Quaker – and the couple moved to London, where they proceeded to have eleven children. However, it was the visit of Stephen Grellet, a French friend and missionary who had briefly visited Newgate, and the stories that he told of what he had found, that convinced Fry that she had to do something to alleviate the conditions within the prison for the women who were locked up there. She arranged to visit the prison herself in 1813 and was appalled by the squalid, cramped conditions that she found. There were 300 women crammed into a space designed to house 50; some women, who were clearly insane, howled in pain; many others were drunk;

Mrs Fry reading to the Prisoners in Newgate, in the Year 1816, engraving, 1863.

and the smell and hopelessness of it all – especially the fact that babies and children were being brought up in these conditions – depressed Fry greatly. As she was later to write to Grellet, so as to convince him that she was not exaggerating, 'All I tell thee is a faint picture of the reality: the filth, the closeness of the room, the ferocious manners, and the abandoned wickedness which everything bespoke are quite indescribable.'[30]

Within three years she had established a small school in the women's quadrangle in a space that had been cordoned off from the rest of the yard, and went out of her way to ensure that those who attended had food, clothes, books and, of course, Bibles. In due course, other Quakers attracted by Fry's example came to Newgate to lend a hand. The school that she established was merely the prelude to other reforms that she prompted within the gaol. Fry adopted a principle of divide and rule, dividing the female prisoners by age and offence into groups of twelve, with each group supervised by a matron. Each group read from the Bible, sewed and prayed. This very quickly changed the prison's culture, and Fry and her matrons provided a positive role model for the prisoners to emulate. Her success convinced those in charge of Newgate to give Fry more power, and she was able, for example, to have alcohol banned on the women's side of the gaol. She was also a passionate opponent of the Bloody Code, and while Fry noted that all that most women cared about before being executed was their appearance, carefully choosing 'the dress in which she shall be hanged', she also remarked that the crimes that these women were being hanged for were petty in comparison 'to the crime of the Government towards themselves'.[31] She also set up the first ever national women's association, the British Ladies' Society for Promoting the Reformation of Female Prisoners.

Fry's success was partly dependent on the fact that she was not only prompted by penal reform but was reacting to ideas that had started to circulate at the time both in Europe and in England, especially through John Howard, the High Sheriff of Bedfordshire. As such she was reflecting the spirit of the age. That she became widely celebrated as the 'angel of prisons' and even as a 'living saint' was in part a consequence of this zeitgeist which had begun to focus on justice and the law, crime and punishment, the role of the state, and prisons. So great was Fry's celebrity as a penal reformer that Frederick William IV, king of Prussia, visited her in Newgate on 31 January 1842.

However, there was one crucial difference between how this European interest in prisons manifested itself and how it was applied in England.

Mather Brown, *John Howard*, 1789, oil on canvas.

While Beccaria, Montesquieu and even Voltaire wrote about justice and the need for reform within what we would now call the criminal justice system, Fry and Howard applied their ideas in a practical way. Though they wrote books, like their European counterparts, they were just as likely to be found actually in a prison, measuring the cells that people were being locked up in, counting the fees that had to be paid to the keepers and turnkeys, and sharing – albeit briefly – the environment which they would then go on to describe. And, as we have seen, Fry made practical changes to the regime at Newgate. Howard and Fry travelled extensively to visit prisons, both in this country and abroad, and Fry is even reported to have stayed overnight in Newgate. So committed was Howard – who had himself been a prisoner-of-war and as a consequence had once found himself incarcerated in France – to visiting prisons that his most recent biographer has described him as 'curious', although a much better description might be 'obsessed'.[32] Howard died on a visit to a prison in Ukraine, which is where he is buried.

These experiences undoubtedly gave both Howard, and especially Fry, greater credibility when they argued for changes to be made within prisons – we might even use the contemporary description of Fry's contribution to Newgate as 'action research' – although we should not become too carried away in our claims of what was actually achieved. Change takes time, especially where prisons are concerned, and while Fry pushed penal reform forward into the public consciousness and occasionally on to the policy agenda, the advocacy of would-be reformers also began to prompt reactions against what they were arguing. The Revd Sidney Smith, writing in the *Edinburgh Review* in 1822, for example, argued that he wanted removed 'all the looms of Preston Jail and substitute nothing but the treadmill', and Sir Walter Scott noted in his journal in February 1828:

> The philanthropy of Howard, mingled with the ill-usage of his son, seems to have risen to a pitch of insanity . . . I do not, however, see the propriety of making them dandy places of detention. They should be places of punishment, and that can hardly be if men are lodged better, and fed better than when they were at large.[33]

In these comments we can begin to see the origins of the need for prison to appease competing audiences, both in terms of what role prison should serve, and concerning what should happen within prison, although these debates would become more vital as the nineteenth century progressed. For the moment, we can conclude that while Newgate – unlike the Tower of London – was built as a gaol, there was still no concept of being sent there as a sentence of the court, and the continuing reality of transportation prevented prisons from moving too quickly on to the policy agenda and being seen as a responsibility of the state. This development would come soon enough, and when it did, the debates that Howard and Fry had started about how best to manage prisons, what sort of regimes should be put in place there and how one might prevent prisoners from committing further crimes when they were released would become matters of great public interest and political action. The prison was about to become a penitentiary.

TWO

Prisons, Penitentiaries
and the Origins of
the Prison System

[Prisons] rid us of a . . . formidable class of wild beasts
– the incorrigible criminals. It is surely not at all necessary
that a penal colony should be a paradise?
Hugh Miller, 1856

For a relatively obscure development in our social history, there is in fact a great deal written about the origins of the state penal system in England and Wales, even if there has been comparatively little written about the origins of that system in Scotland. A surprising number of books, book chapters, monographs and articles exist about this subject, and more often than not – in a conscious allusion to the French philosopher Michel Foucault's *Discipline and Punish: The Birth of the Prison* – these begin by comparing the 'unreformed' local jails of the late eighteenth century encountered in chapter One, administered by the county magistracy through private and semi-private contractors, with the new 'reformed' prisons – the 'penitentiaries' – of the early and mid-nineteenth century. These had been – to use a more contemporary phrase – designed, financed and managed by the state, a process completed by the Prisons Act of 1877, when the state gained control over the entire penal system both in Scotland and in England and Wales.

The root of the word 'penitentiary' is 'penitent' – literally one who feels regret for one's sins, who is repentant and seeks forgiveness. This clearly also reflects the ideas of Fry and Howard, and a more general belief at the time that sending someone to prison – where he/she would be locked up in a cell and where they might have to work, or be separated from other prisoners – would allow time for reflection about the crimes they had committed. In this way, the Church, through the prison's chaplain – one of the Victorian triumvirate of prison officials (along with the medical officer and the governor) – maintains a formal role in ministering

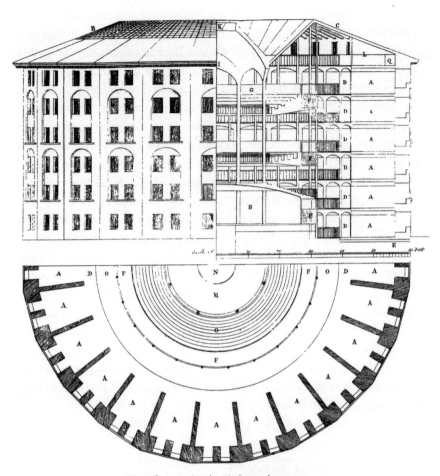

Plan of Jeremy Bentham's Panopticon, 1791.

to offenders, and crime retains its association with sin. In one sense this was also a very optimistic view about what prisons – the penitentiaries – could achieve with those who had committed crime; an optimism partly inspired by the work of Fry.

It is not too hard to understand why the penitentiary has attracted so much attention. For traditional Whig historians, for example, this was merely another form of progress, which had been facilitated by great men and women such as Elizabeth Fry and John Howard. Indeed, even today both Fry and Howard have a continuing hold on our public consciousness – the latter through the Howard League for Penal Reform and the *Howard Journal of Criminal Justice*, and the former through appearing on our £5 bank-notes. However, for revisionist historians, sociologists and criminologists, darker forces are at work, and in a series of sophisticated analyses the penitentiary emerges merely as another way in which the state gained control over the masses at a time when different work and social habits needed to be inculcated in order to support the new industrial marketplace. This is not to imply that the penitentiary exists in these analyses as simple allegory. We know a great deal about the daily routines of the penitentiary, especially the controversies over the 'silent' or 'separate' systems, the thoughts of their governors (and some of the other staff), the development of penal architecture, what type of diet, clothing, work and exercise was taken by the prisoners, how they were punished and the various political machinations that formed the penitentiaries' background.

Some of the most sophisticated revisionism has centred on the philosopher Jeremy Bentham's plan for a prison – the Panopticon – which was never actually built. This is significant, for there is a tendency within this historiography to be more concerned with the abstract and theoretical, as opposed to the daily life and routines of incarceration as experienced by those who were subjected to it. Since history is often a search for sources, and dominated by the powerful, it is usually much easier to describe and theorize about architectural plans, idiosyncratic proposals like Bentham's and parliamentary debates than it is to give voice to the prisoners, the recipients of all this attention. How did they

Jeremy Bentham, 1829.

respond to the penitentiary? What were their thoughts and observations to this new type of discipline and control? Were they passive recipients of the penitentiary, or did they resist?

The historian and Canadian politician Michael Ignatieff does indeed promise us that he is concerned with prisoners' 'resistance', but this is rarely described, and when it is hardly develops beyond a series of one-off episodes with little theoretical underpinning.[1] Even Philip Priestley's *Victorian Prison Lives* – which has the distinction of being one of the few works in this historiography to actively seek out the voices of those who were incarcerated – is dominated by the lives of wealthier and atypical prisoners who felt that their experiences were worth recording and were able to get publishing deals. Priestley does not use his material to generate a broader theoretical understanding of what his subjects' descriptions might have meant in relation to the penitentiary, and the state's control over their lives.[2]

This observation is not meant to be unduly critical, for it is quite clear that there are various obstacles in developing a broader theoretical perspective. Even in our own time, when it is commonplace – almost required – for offenders and ex-offenders to produce autobiographies, and where a generation of ethnographic research has only just begun to leave a mark on the penological record, prisoners have rarely found a voice in governmental or academic discourse about prisons and imprisonment. Given that their views, thoughts, observations and writing are rarely considered important enough to warrant any serious discussion in relation to our own penal problems, perhaps it is hardly surprising that the occasional glimpses one sees or hears of Victorian prisoners never gets developed beyond the level of interesting antiquarianism.

However, the problem here is not so much to do with sources, as difficult as these are, as it is a failure to use penological theory historically; to allow social historians to dominate how we interpret the origins and development of the penitentiary and state penal system. This is not to imply some kind of crude academic turf war, but rather to suggest that new insights emerge in relation to this subject-matter by applying penological theory from our own day to the past. In this respect it has been encouraging to read Norval Morris's source-based fictional account of life on Norfolk Island, and his attempts to use his story as a platform to discuss contemporary penal reform.[3] Thus, after a simple narrative description of the Panopticon and Millbank, the first national penitentiary, I want to move our history forward by detailing and then constructing an analysis of events at Millbank around the theme that I have previously introduced about prison needing to be 'legitimate'. In other words, it must be seen as just by three different and often competing audiences: the public (including politicians and commentators), prison staff and prisoners themselves.

I am consciously attempting to allow Millbank to emerge from out of the shadows of both the Panopticon and HMP Pentonville, which was to replace Millbank in 1842 and to stand as the main example of what prison was about at this point in our history. The former has never really deserved the attention that it has received, and while the latter has been well served by a variety of histories – most obviously that written by Ignatieff – Millbank has all too often been dismissed simply as a 'failure', and usually a failure of architecture. Yet, both from the pre-Victorian era and from our own time, we know all too well that prisons can transcend their architectural roots and succeed as places that lock people up. How else can we explain our enduring use of ships as places of confinement? More was at stake in Milbank's failure than the complexity of its design, and perhaps we would do well to remember a contemporary penal maxim most persuasively given voice by Lord Justice Woolf in his inquiry into the disturbances at HMP Strangeways and elsewhere in 1990: prisons only run with the consent of the prisoners, and problems occur when that consent is withdrawn.[4]

Let us consider how Millbank was viewed by our three audiences – the public, prison staff and crucially, prisoners. Clearly there are difficulties in relation to sources, and at the outset I should acknowledge that much of what is described about Millbank is taken from one source – Arthur Griffiths's *Memorials of Millbank and Chapters in Prison History* (1875). Griffiths was far from being an impartial observer, and as a penal administrator in the late Victorian period – he was appointed deputy governor of Millbank in 1872 – he had many axes to grind, and took almost every opportunity to do so. However, in grinding these axes various incidents emerge that deserve greater scrutiny than have previously been accorded to them, and which allow us an insight into life within the prison at this point in time.

In relation to the public audience of the penitentiary, I use the work of Charles Dickens (1812–1870) for three particular reasons. First, Dickens was a regular visitor to prisons throughout his life, and a friend of several prison governors. He used the materials from these visits in his journalism and throughout his novels, most obviously in *The Pickwick Papers*, *David Copperfield*, *A Tale of Two Cities*, *Oliver Twist* and especially *Little Dorrit*.

Second, Dickens was the most popular author of his day, with his own public readings attracting mobs of working people. As one commentator has suggested:

> Dickens's most important gift to the working classes was the role he played in making them articulate. He provided a fund of allusions, characters, tropes, and situations that could be drawn upon by people who were not trained to express themselves on paper.[5]

Finally, and perhaps more importantly, Dickens knew only too well about life inside, and without doubt we can trace much of his interest in prisons back to his father's own incarceration in February 1824 for debt in the Marshalsea in Southwark, London. His father's imprisonment resulted in Dickens having to work in a blacking factory, a set of circumstances which is fictionalized most clearly in *David Copperfield*. Insolvency as a more general theme dominates his writing, especially *Little Dorrit*. The extent to which Dickens internalized this experience can only be guessed at, and of course Dickens always seems to work best in the abstract – in theory – and a search for any consistent articulated practical philosophy about imprisonment or any other issue in his work is almost doomed to fail.[6] However I can think of no more insightful understanding about what it means to be imprisoned to those who are deprived of their liberty than the exchange in *Little Dorrit* between Arthur Clennam and William Dorrit, whose release has been delayed for a few hours:

> 'It is but a few hours, sir,' Clennam cheerfully urged upon him.
>   'A few hours, sir,' he returned in a sudden passion. 'You talk very easily of hours, sir! How long do you suppose, sir, that an hour is to a man who is choking for want of air?'

Thus perhaps in selectively using Dickens we can go some way in attempting to give voice to the prisoners of the early to mid-Victorian period, as well as understanding how the prison was imagined by the era's bestselling novelist.

Alba

Here I need to mention Scotland. For, despite the fact that Howard and Fry both visited Scottish jails on a number of occasions – and Howard even managed to convince the Lord Provost of Edinburgh to hold a competition (which was won by Robert Adam) to build a new prison – as one Scottish historian puts it, 'no voice seems to have been raised in Scotland in the cause of reform.'[7] This is not quite accurate, and we should note in particular the work of William Brebner, who has been dubbed 'the founding father of the Scottish Prison System'.[8] Brebner was in charge of the Glasgow Bridewell, where he introduced the 'separate system' before it became more popularly associated with penal conditions in Philadelphia. He also founded a House of Refuge for newly released prisoners and a training school for staff, and formalized their rates of pay and hours of attendance. So influential was he in Scotland that prior to his death in January 1845, he was simultaneously in charge of two prisons in Glasgow and the General Prison in Perth – where all prisoners serving over nine months were sent – as well as acting as the superintendent of Lanarkshire prisons. Staff that Brebner trained became governors of the prisons at Lanark and Ayr in 1835, Dumfries in 1838, Dundee in 1839 and Hamilton, Dumbarton, Cupar, Inverness and Kirkcudbright in 1840.

Muirhead Bone, 'The Old Jail, Glasgow', detail, from the series *Etchings of Glasgow* (1899).

In the decade before Brebner's death, many of the smaller local prisons in Scotland were closed, and the Prison Act of 1839 replaced the old local burgh structure north of the border with a centralized system under the control of a general board of directors of prisons. In this respect, the Prisons Act of 1877 – which saw the centralization of English and Welsh prisons under the control of a prison commission – was merely aping developments that had been in progress in Scotland for decades. There may have been fewer public debates about prison conditions in Scotland than there would be in England – and fewer prisoners – but this should not be taken to imply indifference to the reforms advocated by such men as Brebner, and may indeed have reflected a more generalized and popular acceptance.[9] However, this absence of public comment and debate in Scotland means that the focus of this chapter is on England and Wales.

The Panopticon and Millbank

Before proceeding further, and as a way of setting the scene, it might be of use to provide some historical detail about the Panopticon and its failure, the eventual founding of Millbank and the progress that it made in its early years. For reasons of space this short history only takes us up to 1842 with the founding of HMP Pentonville, but later developments, incidents and how the prison was organized within Millbank are described in subsequent sections, when we consider questions of legitimacy. Finally it should be noted that the prison was pulled down in 1893, although we do not have to accept one historian's conclusion that only 'two good things came out of Millbank: after its destruction, its sixteen acre site was used for housing the poor, and its levelling provided work for some of London's unemployed.'[10]

The Panopticon and Millbank originate from the same place, in that both are inextricably linked to the American Declaration of Independence and the coming of war in 1776. At a stroke this brought the transportation of offenders – and others – to a halt, and therefore posed a not insignificant problem to the authorities as to what they should do with those who broke the law but would not be executed. Indeed, this issue of what to do when transportation came to an end had to be resolved by politicians later in the century, too.

The scale of this problem can be understood when one considers that it has been calculated that between 1718 and 1775 some 30,000 people were transported to America, and that transportation to Botany Bay would

Pentonville prison, interior view, c. 1840s, from the *Illustrated London News*.

not begin until 1787.[11] In the meantime, influenced by the extraordinary popularity of John Howard, and indeed encouraged by him, Sir William Blackstone and Sir William Eden introduced the Penitentiary Act in 1779, which made it possible to substitute imprisonment for transportation in one of the two proposed state-run penitentiaries. This act basically synthesized everything that was believed at that time about what should be done with prisoners, in that they would be subjected to solitary confinement, have regular religious instruction, be required to work (but not for profit), would have to wear a uniform, and be subjected to a coarse diet. The minimum sentence would be six months for women and twelve months for men, with a maximum sentence of seven years. A commission of three people, including Howard himself, was set up to investigate the best sites for the erection of the penitentiary buildings, but by 1780 this had collapsed through internal disagreement. In 1781 a second commission chose sites at Wandsworth and Battersea, and an architectural competition was advertised to turn the philosophy of the act into reality. This was won by William Blackburn. Nonetheless a change of government in 1782 saw these plans shelved, and a new transportation act passed which would pave the way for Botany Bay.

Despite this failure at a national level to make the penitentiaries a reality, there was a flurry of prison-building at the local level, which helped to keep the issue of incarceration in public and parliamentary discourse. Various individuals came to dominate that discourse in one way or another, and one of the most fervent was Jeremy Bentham, who never ceased to advocate on behalf of his unique design for the penitentiary – the Panopticon, or 'all seeing eye', the plans for which he published in 1791. Robin Evans provides the best description of the form that the Panopticon would take:

> The Governor was billeted with his family in a well-fenestrated cylindrical kiosk inside a much larger rotunda. The kiosk looked out across an intermediate space onto a circle of 192 cells four storeys high. All light for the kiosk filtered into the middle of the rotunda through large windows in these encircling bank of cells. Hence the prisoners, themselves brightly illuminated, would be unable to see into the darkness of the kiosk, much as the people out in the street cannot see into a house window. The privilege of those within this protected core – the governor, his family, assistants and visitors – was to observe the prisoners without themselves being seen to spy on them.[12]

Bentham thought of every aspect of design in his plans – from blinds, shutters, lamps and speaking tubes to the type of uniform that the prisoners would wear so as to guarantee their humiliation. Nothing seemed to escape his gaze. He even suggested that the prisoners should not just have their hair cut off, but also their eyebrows, and that they should be subjected to semi-permanent tattooing. After all, uniforms could be discarded, and hair and eyebrows would grow again, but the tattoos – and thus their humiliation – would last for much longer. The important point to grasp here is that inspection – which also featured in the designs for Millbank and Pentonville – was elevated as the guiding principle of the Panopticon above all others, and that in essence what was being proposed was a model community where, as Evans has described it, 'Christian redemption was replaced with a comprehensive materialistic psychology' that would 'grind rogues honest' through work.[13] Everything about its design and organization was centred on oversight and overhearing as a means of establishing omnipotence – especially the omnipotence of Bentham.

Bentham was not without influence, and so a sympathetic parliamentary committee gave him money to buy a site at Millbank in 1797. The government would eventually compensate him for all his efforts to the tune of £23,000 in 1813. However, the Panopticon's eventual downfall was not so much brought about by the uniqueness of its design than by the fact that Bentham wanted both to be the governor and, crucially, to own the prison himself. Thus the Panopticon would be in private hands, outside of the government's control, and it was this that eventually allowed the Holford Committee to reject the Panopticon in 1811 and to recommend that the government build a much larger penitentiary, capable of holding 1,200 prisoners, on the site that had been bought at Millbank.

George Holford was responsible for overseeing the design, construction and opening of Millbank between 1812 and 1822, although the first prisoners were actually received in June 1816. Holford championed the jail against its many critics, and stuck resolutely to the principles that were at the heart of the prison, most especially its polygonal layout and a penal regime that was devoid of the treadmill – which had been designed by William Cubitt in 1818. Holford also published two poems on behalf of the prison: 'The Convict's Complaint' and 'The Convict's Thanks'. The latter of these was supposed to have been written by a prisoner who had been sent to Millbank, and who wanted to thank 'those who planned the

Millbank Penitentiary, London, print of c. 1829 and courtyard view, 1890.

silent cells', a reference to the fact that when they were initially received the prisoners were separated from each other, and could only graduate to work in groups through their good behaviour.

The prison was originally designed by William Williams, but his design was revised by Thomas Hardwick, and when it was completed the buildings alone covered seven acres, making it the largest prison in Europe. Evans again provides us with the best description of its design features, and here the similarities to and differences from the Panopticon should be noted:

> At its centre was a circular chapel and around this was a hexagonal range of buildings containing offices of the central administration: governor, chaplain, surgeon and master manufacturer. Extending out from the hexagon were six nearly identical pentagons, four for men, two for women, each one a semi-autonomous prison with its own staff of ten overseen by a taskmaster who acted as resident deputy to the governor. What looked on the plan like small circular booths in the middle of the pentagons were in fact three storey surveillance towers within which were the taskmaster's bedroom, his parlor where he took his meals with an assistant, and, on the ground floor, a warders' mess where information was received and given.[14]

Griffiths advises us that 'the early discipline of the prisoners at Millbank, as designed by the committee, was based on the principle of constant inspection and regular employment', although it is also clear that Griffiths was no supporter of the regime. Indeed, he found it too lax, and criticized 'the free and easy system of management', commenting that 'the whole place appears to have been like a big school'.[15] We do not need to accept this judgement, but it should be noted that almost from the start the prison was dogged by difficulties. For example, in the spring of 1816 cracks appeared in some of the pentagon walls, and putting these right brought the total cost of the jail to a staggering £458,000. Prisoners rioted about their food allowance in 1817, and between 1822 and 1824 30 prisoners died from diarrhoea, which resulted in the whole prison population being evacuated. A parliamentary commission recommended further changes to the design of the prison, and to its regime, to promote 'cheerfulness'.[16] Nonetheless, there were riots in September 1826 and again in March 1827; various warders were assaulted and in one incident the infirmary warder's cat was found hanged with the following notice attached to its neck:

> You see your cat is hung And
> you have been the corse of it
> for your Bad Bevior to those
> around you. Dom yor eis, yoo'l
> get pade in yor torn yet.[17]

Relationships developed between male and female prisoners, who were not at this time rigorously segregated, and between female prisoners and warders. In a chapter that Griffiths labels 'General Misconduct', various plots to kill the governor and chaplain are revealed. They survived, but many of the prisoners did not; in what Griffiths labels a 'suicide epidemic', they began to take their own lives. From 1837 the Reverend Daniel Nihil was appointed as chaplain and governor to take over from Captain Ben Chapman, who had governed Millbank since 1823, but his tenure was dogged by a series of escapes, staff indiscipline and unrest. In 1842 Pentonville opened and Millbank became a holding and classification centre for those prisoners awaiting transportation to Australia. The prison changed its role again in 1877 when it became a female prison, and was eventually closed in 1893.

Crisis? What Crisis?

Two consistent phenomena have dominated prisons in our own time. The first is inexorable growth, in terms of the number of prisoners, prisons and penal penalties; and the second is the idea that the penal system, which would include probation, is in some form of crisis. Two contemporary criminologists, Michael Cavadino and James Dignan, in what they describe as a 'radical pluralist account', analyse the penal crisis from the standpoint of there being a 'crisis of legitimacy', using the sociological definition of legitimacy as power that is perceived to be morally justified. Thus this crisis results not from overcrowding or poor conditions – as real as these might be – but from what people believe and feel, and from the moral reactions of people within and outside the penal system to the material situation. As such, they believe that the penal crisis of our own day is essentially a moral crisis, and stems from the need of the penal system to make itself legitimate to three different groups of people: the public, which includes politicians and penal commentators; penal staff; and penal subjects – most obviously prisoners, but also those serving community penalties. Thus 'failing to satisfy the sense of justice of these different audiences leads to the alarming visible "symptoms" of the crisis: political problems, industrial relations problems, malaise among prison and probation staff, and disorder among prisoners.'[18]

If we were to use this radical pluralist account of the penal crisis, and reapply it historically, how would we reinterpret Millbank and the various reactions to it? Does this reinterpretation offer us different insights into how the prison worked, the incidents that are described above and why it ultimately failed? And, perhaps more crucially, can we see something more positive in the behaviour of the prisoners given the fact that they were for the first time being incarcerated by the state in what Griffiths describes as 'essentially an experiment – a sort of crucible into which the criminal elements were thrown, in the hopes that they might be changed or resolved by treatment into other superior forms'?[19]

In particular I will concentrate on three aspects of life within Millbank – food, disorder (including riots and escapes) and suicide – and my reasons for choosing these three issues as opposed to others are explained below. However, as a general rule, examples are used where there are the greatest number of sources, although it should be acknowledged that it has not always been possible to find evidence to illustrate how each audience viewed these three aspects, and that one audience's opinion will inevitably dominate another's concerning some issues.

Food

Food is a very emotive subject in prison, whether we are describing historical or more recent penal conditions. This is especially true in long-term prisons, with one contemporary prisoner describing how 'it was surprising how important a place food held in our lives. Meal times broke up the day, marked the passage of time, and were a kind of focal point, something to look forward to.'[20] In short, food becomes one of the most important determinants of whether or not prisoners have had a good or a bad day. My identification of long-term prisoners is a particular reminder that prison culture can be described as being 'indigenous' or 'importationist', with the former implying that culture evolves to suit the specific and unique circumstances of prison life, cut off from the outside world, while the latter is more evident in local prisons where sentences are shorter, with prisoners coming and going, and who literally 'import' their culture from the outside into the jail.

Some evidence of the continuing centrality of prison food to the life of the prisoner comes from one life-sentenced prisoner's views about what he gets to eat. Tom Shannon commented that at HMP Maidstone 'if you saw the food arriving here as a producer you would stand proud. If you saw it on the hot plate, you would weep. Something very mysterious happens to the food.'[21] There is much more going on here than simply concerns about the quality of food, for the very nature of the institution and its treatment of the prisoners is being questioned.

Yet for the public audience this issue is seen very differently. Thus, for example, there are usually howls of complaint when the local media get hold of what is on the prison's Christmas menu, which is usually compared very favourably with what is to be served in homes for the sick or elderly, and there are even political dimensions to this issue.

So let us again consider events at Millbank, where there was a mutiny over the bread in the spring of 1818. At one Sunday Service – which was attended by the Chancellor of the Exchequer – the male prisoners threw loaves at the chaplain, and the female prisoners started to chant 'give us our daily bread' and 'better bread, better bread'. This led to the Chancellor of the Exchequer speaking to the prisoners and promising to raise the matter of food with the Secretary of State. No changes were immediately forthcoming; this led to a riot that was only quelled with the aid of the Bow Street Runners. The bread was not withdrawn, but the governor was eventually forced to resign.[22]

The public interpreted all of this rather differently from the prisoners, and Griffiths advises us, for example, that the prison was popularly known as 'Mr Holford's fattening House', and that 'there need be no fear of escapes; all that was needed was a proper guard to prevent too great a rush of people in.'[23] Partly in response to this perception, the prison's dietary scale was changed to appease public opinion, so that the prisoners were allowed soup but no solid food. 'This soup was made of ox heads, in the proportion of one to every one hundred prisoners', and while it cannot be proved this can perhaps account for why almost half the prison's population was sick in 1823, and why ultimately 30 prisoners died. Despite this, the Reverend Daniel Nihil was still complaining as late as 1840 of the 'extreme sauciness of the prisoners with regard to their victuals'.[24]

Nihil's comments may reveal a lingering sensitivity as to how what the prisoners ate was viewed by the wider Victorian public, who, judging by the fiction of the period, ate a great deal and often. It has been estimated that in *The Pickwick Papers*, for example, there are 35 breakfasts, ten luncheons and 32 dinners, and that some form of drink is mentioned on no less than 249 occasions. Peter Ackroyd has suggested that food for Dickens represented security and well-being, and that in his fiction 'food can be a register . . . for something very close to the need for love' and 'a proper measurement of human pride and social respectability'.[25] It should also be remembered that those imprisoned for debt, such as Dickens's father, were able to have food brought into jail for them, and that they could purchase food and drink from the jailer. Consider this example from *Little Dorrit*, which describes Clennam following Amy into the Marshalsea, and her preparation of supper for her father:

> She had brought the meat home that she should have eaten herself, and was already warming it on a gridiron over the fire, for her father, clad in an old grey gown and a black cap, awaiting his supper at the table . . . she filled his glass, put all the little matters on the table ready to his hand, and then sat beside him as he ate his supper. Evidently in observance of their nightly custom, she put some bread before herself, and touched his glass with her lips; but Arthur saw that she was troubled and took nothing. Her look at her father, half admiring and proud of him, half-ashamed for him, all devoted and loving, went to his inmost heart.

Clearly this is about love – the love that Amy has for her father, and that Clennam has for Amy – but it is also about respectability. There is not enough food for Amy to eat, but she tries not to draw attention to this fact for fear that it may offend her father in front of a guest. It is also a passage that serves to illustrate how prisons were less closed than they were to become at Millbank. After all, Clennam is a visitor to the jail, and Amy does not need to stay within the prison at all. She does so out of love for her father, but every day leaves the jail to go to work, and returns each night when her work is done. The contrast with Millbank could not be starker, for there no food could not be brought into or bought in the jail; there was no wine, and all that the prisoners had to eat was what was provided to them by the state. Families did not live with those who had been convicted and visitors could not enter prisoners' cells. Indeed, perhaps one could go as far as to say that the biggest change between prisons run under contract to the local magistrates and those run by the state was that state prisons became a more closed and secret world. As such they were a territory that would become the preserve of the imagination, and therefore of journalists and novelists.

Dickens seems first to have become interested in writing about prisons in November 1835, a fact that Ackroyd describes as 'intriguing'. However, at around that time the question of how prisons should be run was a frequent topic of discussion in newspapers. William Crawford's *Report on the Penitentiaries of the United States*, which advocated that prisoners should be kept separate from one another so as to prevent 'contamination', had been published in 1834. Dickens was much against this, but it may explain his interest in prisons that seemed to prompt a visit to Newgate, which appears in his *Sketches by Boz*. This is an illuminating piece of descriptive journalism, largely concentrating on the condemned cells (which would feature in *Oliver Twist*), but very little is said about the food that the prisoners ate, beyond the fact that 'on the table was a sufficient provision of a kind of stewed beef, and brown bread in pewter dishes'. Clearly Dickens did not want to make capital out of what was being eaten by the prisoners, and so, for example, the phrases 'sufficient provision' and 'a kind of stewed beef' are consciously intended to deflect any criticisms that the prisoners were being well or even overfed, and may even have engendered some sympathy in the reader. Indeed, this is obviously what is intended with his description of the condemned man's last night, dreaming of a reprieve and of walking with his wife in a 'pleasant field, with the bright blue sky above them'. However, as so often happens with Dickens, he is quick to prompt contradictory emotions, and so, for example, he describes the young offenders that he meets as 'fourteen villainous little faces we never beheld. There was not one redeeming feature among them – not a glance of honesty, not a wink expressive of any thing but the gallows and the hulks, in the whole collection'.

Disorder

Prison is about maintaining order and control, specifically control over the lives of the prisoners. While it is the sentence of the court that deprives people of their liberty, it is the purpose of prison to translate that sentence – that loss of liberty – into a practical reality. As such, the lives of the prisoners are carefully regulated in virtually every respect: when they get up in the morning and when they go to bed, how much exercise they take, where and how often they work, what visits and letters they receive, and what relations they are able to establish with each other and with the prison's staff. There are inevitably many ways in which prisoners can rebel against this control, but assaults on staff, riots and escapes are the most serious forms of rebellion. That is why today's HM Prison Service has set targets for itself in relation to the number of assaults that take place in prison and the number of escapes that occur per year, and why a great deal of public money is spent in training prison staff to deal with riots and other forms of mass disorder.

Millbank experienced several riots during its early years, and we have already drawn attention to disturbances brought about by changes in the dietary scale. Griffiths reports further disturbances in late 1826, which resulted in a greater use of solitary confinement, and in March 1827 recorded that 'Pentagon 6 is in uproar. As Captain Chapman hurries to the scene he is saluted with the crash of glass, interspersed with loud cries of triumph and of encouragement.'[26] This disturbance seems to have continued for several days, and the prisoners wrote to the parliamentary commission about their grievances. This incensed Griffiths even over half a century later, and he writes that since 'these letters afford curious evidence of the importance prisoners arrogated to themselves, it may be interesting to publish one in extenso.' We are left with an interesting source to reveal the cause of the disturbances, at least from the point of view of the prisoners. And what does this letter reveal? It alleges three instances of staff brutality: 'who gave Mr Bulmer authority to strike a lad named Quick almost sufficient to have broken his arm?'; 'who gave Mr Pilling the same authority to smite a lad to the ground, named Caswell, with a ruler, the same as a butcher would a bullock?'; the third incident involved Mr Pilling again, 'assisted by that villain Turner (we cannot give him a better term – we wish we could)'. All of this led the prisoners to conclude that 'we do not wish to be too severe, but unless Pilling and Turner are removed from the establishment, and that shortly, we will fight as long as there is a drop of blood in us'. So as to counterbalance their view of Mr Pilling, whom they argue takes 'a delight in aggravating the cause with a grin, or a jeer of contempt', they identify '3 good men in the Pentagon – Messrs Newstead, Rutter and Hall'.

Clearly these prisoners had not been persuaded that the prison was treating them fairly, or that relationships with staff were good, and there were further incidents throughout the next few months, culminating in an assault on the machine-keeper called Mullard. The response of the government was to allow prisoners at Millbank to be flogged, and to send some of the ringleaders to the hulks. This proved only to be a temporary solution, and by 1830 – despite claims by the governor that events had quietened down – it was recommended that the prisoners should be separated from each other, and that the problems were not caused by the likes of Messrs Bulmer and Turner, but from 'indiscriminate association'.[27] In all of this, the parliamentary commission was merely echoing a fashionable view as to how to maintain order and reform prisoners, and this view would become all the more dominant with the publication of William Crawford's *Report on the Penitentiaries of the United States*. Put simply, this favoured separating prisoners from one another, and since Crawford was appointed just two years later as one of the first two prison inspectors – along with the Revd Whitworth Russell – he was in a very good position to see the 'separate system' incorporated not just into Millbank but other prisons too.

Dickens was squarely against the separate system, a fact that Griffiths drew attention to by quoting from the notes that Dickens had published of his visit to the Eastern Penitentiary in Philadelphia in 1842. Ackroyd provides further details about this visit, written up in *American Notes*, and quotes Dickens as describing the circumstances of the prisoners: 'I looked at some of them with the same awe as I should have looked at men who had been buried alive and dug up again.' Ackroyd also tells us of a dinner party hosted by Dickens some four years later to which he had invited Alexander Maconochie, who between 1840 and 1844 had governed Norfolk Island in the Pacific. What is of note is that Maconochie had instituted a regime for the prisoners who had been transported there based on a system of rewards, known as the 'marks system', rather than a regime of separation.[28] Dickens's opposition to the separate system, and indeed to the idea of the penitentiary, is most strongly put in *David Copperfield*, in which a visit to Pentonville is described. In contrast to what he had written in *Sketches by Boz* about his visit to Newgate, here Dickens spares no rhetorical flourish, and so even the food that the prisoners eat is invoked by Copperfield as evidence of how the separate system is wrong:

> It being then just dinner-time, we went, first into the great kitchen, where every prisoner's dinner was in course of being set out separately (to be handed to him in his cell), with the regularity and precision of clock work. I said, aside to Traddles, that I wondered whether it occurred to anybody, that there was a striking contrast

between these plentiful repasts of choice quality, and the dinners, not to say of paupers, but of soldiers, sailors, labourers, the great bulk of the honest, working community; of whom not one man in five hundred ever dined half as well. But I learned that the 'system' required high living.

Inevitably, on their visit Copperfield and Traddles meet the villain Uriah Heep, 'a certain number Twenty Seven, who was the Favourite, and who really appeared to be a Model Prisoner'. Here was the clinching argument against Pentonville – the fact that Heep was regarded as having been reformed through a regime of separation.

What the staff made of the separate system, which was introduced at Millbank under the leadership of the Revd Daniel Nihil, is largely a matter for conjecture. However, it is quite clear that there was unrest among the staff because of how prisoners at Millbank were being treated (although not necessarily because of the separate system per se), especially as Nihil seemed to take the prisoners' side against the warders. Griffiths – who was no supporter of the separate system – provides us with a variety of examples. Thus we are informed that during a disturbance (the separate system was no guarantee of order) in which 'several prisoners were most turbulent and needed summary repression, [Nihil] takes a very old warder to task for his unnecessary severity', and Griffiths suggests that the prisoners were 'too much disposed to give themselves ideas, and quite absurdly puffed up with an idea of their own importance'. As such the warders were 'masters . . . only in name, and one of them complains . . . rather bitterly that he is worse off than a prisoner'. Griffiths thought that the 'condition of these officers was hardly to be envied', and that the 'warders had to choose between becoming hypocrites' or losing their jobs.[29]

What really irked Griffiths was the fact that Millbank was from the beginning controlled by a parliamentary committee, and as a governor from the later Victorian period he found this distasteful. For example, he comments that 'the supreme authority in the Penitentiary was vested in the Superintending Committee', and goes further, suggesting that as a consequence the prison was 'a huge plaything; a toy for a parcel of philanthropic gentlemen, to keep them busy during their spare hours'.[30] Griffiths wanted prisons to be in the hands of prison governors and warders with a minimum of interference from outside. Any evidence that demonstrated that outside interference led to the prison being poorly managed helped him to make his case.

Escapes served this purpose while at the same time allowing Griffiths to distance himself from the separate system. Thus Nihil's inability to prevent one prisoner, Pickard Smith, from escaping led him to ask the Secretary of State to have the prisoner removed from the penitentiary. Not unnaturally, the Secretary of State thought that it would bring discredit to the penitentiary if 'prisoners were transferred on account of its inability to secure them', although Nihil felt that

> the peculiarity of our system hardly appears to be considered as an objection to his continuance here. The principle of the Penitentiary was that it was not merely a place of safe custody and punishment, but a place of reformation; and, therefore, if it failed in this latter objective in any instance, a power was reserved of sending away the prisoner as incorrigible for fear of his interfering with the progress of the system among other prisoners.

Here was a failure of the system which allowed Griffiths to reflect that 'in our modern days escapes are of rarer occurrence'.[31]

Suicides

Escaping over the wall is clearly one way in which a prisoner can rebel against the regime of a prison, but there are other forms of escape. Suicide can also be seen as an extreme reaction to the circumstances that prisoners find themselves in after they have been imprisoned. This might strike us as too damning a conclusion, but as Alison Liebling – the most authoritative penologist on suicide in prisons from our own day – suggests, in terms that could equally be applied to Millbank,

> the apparent motivation for prison suicide appears to be fear or loss; fear of other inmates, of the consequences of one's crime, of imprisonment, and loss of a significant relationship, such as lack of communication or divorce. Shame, guilt and mental disorder play a relatively minor role.[32]

It is difficult to find definitive figures about suicide at Millbank. However, it was clearly a problem, for Griffiths informs us that there was an 'epidemic of suicides', although he saw these as 'feigned . . . their last idea was to succeed'. We should not ignore the fact that he might simply have been describing what is now known as 'self-harm', which again makes it difficult to quantify the extent of suicide within Millbank. He suggests, for example, that

> a woman with a piece of linen tied tightly round her neck, and nearly producing strangulation; men, one after another, found suspended but always cut down promptly, and proved to be un-hurt in spite of pretended insensibility; cases of this kind occurred so frequently, that I should fill many pages were I to recount a tithe of them.

He suggests that suicide began in the prison with the arrival of William Major in October 1824, who declared 'I'd sooner be hanged like a dog than stay in the Penitentiary.' Not unnaturally, the governor had Major's knife and scissors removed, but the prisoner informed him that 'I'd do anything to get out of this place; kill myself or you.' For this outburst Major was placed in solitary confinement, but three weeks after his release he was found hanging in his cell, although he was revived. Griffiths suggests that this was not a serious attempt, but other prisoners also attempted suicide at this time, including one Combe, Catherine Roper and Lewis Abrahams – 'a gloomy, ill-tempered man' who succeeded in taking his own life.[33] While Liebling resists forming a general theory of prison suicides today, she concludes that they represent a 'cry of pain, not just a cry for help . . . they are acknowledging (and communicating) their own resourcelessness; their failure to cope'.[34] This conclusion also seems apt for Millbank.

Failing Prison and the Need for a System

So why did Millbank – the first national penitentiary – fail? The short answer is that it failed because it was unable to convince any of the audiences that it needed to satisfy that it could actually operate successfully. It could not make the public, the prison's staff or the prisoners feel or believe that it was legitimate. Thus its failings were much more than simple errors of architectural design. For different reasons, each audience was left with the distinct impression that Millbank had failings that it could not overcome. The public might have focused on how much the prisoners got to eat in comparison with the 'deserving poor', or the fact that prisoners were able to escape, or the separate system introduced under Nihil, which seemed cruel and led to people taking their own lives. Others might have considered it a failure because of the simple fact that those prisoners who were released did not seem to have changed to any great extent.

There were clearly different grades of staff working at Millbank, and it is easier to talk with confidence about the views of the governors than of the warders. Millbank for Griffiths had been a 'toy', a 'huge play thing' for politicians to 'busy their spare hours', and while these claims were written several years after the period described, there does at least seem to have been some evidence of governors leaving the jail because of political interference. The opinions of the warders are more difficult to determine, especially as those who emerge from the sources only do so by virtue of being quoted by Griffiths. However, he does at least present evidence of staff being dismissed or disciplined, and provide some insight into their feelings that the balance of power was in favour of the prisoners.

The prisoners, experiencing new levels of carceral attention, cut off from the rest of the world, responded at first by believing that politicians would listen to their grievances. For someone like Griffiths, this merely demonstrated how amateurish politicians were in bothering to listen to prisoners at all, and how the prisoners then became 'puffed up'. However, there is no overwhelming evidence to suggest that politicians really interfered too much on behalf of prisoners, as the example of Pickard Smith demonstrates. It would seem that prisoners developed other techniques to counter the influence of the penitentiary, which are not so dissimilar to those used by prisoners today: disorder of various forms, escape and, in extreme cases, suicide. In short, they withdrew their consent to be governed.

However, while Millbank as a prison may indeed have failed, this did not seem either to discourage politicians from building more prisons or to encourage them to return the penal system to the local magistracy. If Millbank was an experiment, as Griffiths claimed, we should see that experiment as having two parts: the first involving the routines and regime of Millbank specifically; and the second concerned with the state taking responsibility for the penal system as a whole. While the first part of the experiment may have failed, there was enough confidence in what had been achieved to expand the state's carceral influence and control, culminating in the Prison Act of 1877. Yet lessons had also been learned from the experiences of Millbank: parliamentary influence was to be kept to a minimum in relation to the internal organization of jails, and prison became further separated from its public audience. The end result was that the prison became more secret; more closed; a world within a world. It would take a very special prisoner to make it visible once more and to try to engage a public audience's sympathies for those who were locked up.

THREE

The Prisons Act of 1877 and the Gladstone Report of 1895

This too I know and wise it were
If each could know the same
That every prison that men build
Is built with bricks of shame,
And bound with bars lest Christ should see
How men their brothers maim.

Oscar Wilde, 'The Ballad of Reading Gaol', 1897

The formal origins of our penal system date from the Prisons Act of 1877. At a stroke this Act meant that responsibility for the control and direction of prisons became the responsibility of the state – the failure of the 'experiment' at Millbank notwithstanding. As a result, from that date onwards prisons gained a central importance in our public policy, an importance which they have retained. The Act of 1877 – partly in response to the end of transportation to Australia twenty years earlier (which meant that prisoners returned to the community after their sentence had ended) – saw the transfer of every aspect of prison administration to the Secretary of State. This is turn led to the appointment of a prison commission to administer that responsibility, with Lt Col. Edmund Frederick Du Cane acting as its first chairman.[1] Du Cane personally came to embody almost everything about how prisons were run until his retirement in 1895.

Under Du Cane prisons became places of punishment, and their role within public policy was to symbolize the state's general deterrence of crime and offenders. In terms of policy approach the Act of 1877 can be seen as a continuation of another piece of government legislation, the Prison Act of 1865, which characterized prisons as being for 'hard labour, hard fare and a hard bed'. It is difficult to overstate Du Cane's impact, and one historian has concluded that he 'outwitted politicians, terrified his subordinates, and sowed dragon's teeth among the ranks of the increasingly formidable higher civil service'.[2]

The Act, as it applied to England and Wales, received royal assent on 12 July 1877, and the Prisons Act (Scotland) on 14 August of that year. Both came into force on 1 April 1878. Scotland's first chairman of its prison commission was Thomas Lee, the Sheriff of Perth, but he did not have the same force of character as Du Cane. Indeed, Lee's legal background contrasted markedly with Du Cane's military career, and while Alexander Burness McHardy – who would become chairman between 1896 and 1909 – was a military man and a protégé of Du Cane, Scotland's prison commissioners, and Scottish prisons more generally, have always tended to reflect the culture of the broader criminal justice system, rather than the regimen and structures of the military.

While the Prisons Act, as it applied to England and Wales, was in many ways a point of departure from the past, in Scotland it can best be seen as a logical extension of the centralizing forces that had been at play for the previous 40 years. Centralization and rationalization continued. When Lee took over as chairman of the Scottish Prison Commission, he had responsibility for 56 county jails and the General Prison at Perth. A year later he had reduced the numbers of prisons to 42, and by 1888 there were only fifteen left, although new prisons had been built at Barlinnie and Dumfries in 1882 and Peterhead in 1886. Aberdeen and Inverness prisons would open in 1890 and 1901 respectively.

However, even in England and Wales, Du Cane would not have things all his own way. In 1895 the Gladstone Committee – chaired by Herbert Gladstone, son of William Ewart Gladstone – made radical suggestions about how prisons should be run that would fundamentally end the punishment and deterrence that had come to characterize prisons under Du Cane. It is not entirely clear why Prime Minister Herbert Asquith initiated the inquiry chaired by Gladstone, although there had been a string of hostile newspaper articles about prisons in the press through-out 1893, many of them directed at Du Cane's militaristic and autocratic style. In any event, the Gladstone Committee's report suggested that 'recidivism', not punishment and deterrence, 'is the most important of all prison questions, and it is the most complicated and difficult'.[3] Whereas prisoners under Du Cane had all been treated alike – with the first-time young offender dealt with in exactly the same way as the repeat adult recidivist – the Gladstone Committee recognized that every pris-oner was an individual. In an oft-quoted passage, the *Gladstone Report* suggested that:

We think that the system should be made more elastic, more capable of being adopted to the special cases of individual prisoners; that prison discipline should be more effectually designed to maintain, stimulate, or awaken the higher susceptibilities of prisoners, to develop their moral instincts, to train them in orderly and industrial habits, and whenever possible to turn them out of prison better men and women, both physically and morally, than when they came in.[4]

The key point to grasp here is that in a little under twenty years the fundamental aims of why people were being sent to prison changed, and that the Gladstone Committee's report, which shaped the Prison Act of 1898, ushered in a variety of developments supported by the new chairman of the prison commissioners, Sir Evelyn Ruggles-Brise. This would include the development of the borstal system for young offenders, removing them from the influence of adult offenders; the improvement of educational facilities in prison; gradual changes to the rule that prisoners should be 'silent', especially when they worked in association; the end of the 'separate' system; changes to the prisoners' diet; and even the introduction of concerts and lectures.

Here we should note that the Elgin Committee's report of 1900 was far more important to future developments to prisons in Scotland, even if many similar initiatives to those introduced into English and Welsh prisons as a result of the Gladstone Report were also introduced into Scottish prisons about this time. Even so, this should not be taken too far and, as I have indicated, how prisoners experienced and responded to these changes (or experienced prison during the time of Du Cane's chairmanship) has been largely ignored. However, one prominent prisoner during this period – Oscar Wilde, who was imprisoned between 1895 and 1897 – perhaps summed up how most prisoners felt at this time in 'The Ballad of Reading Gaol', in which he wrote

> That every prison that men build
> Is built with bricks of shame,
> And bound with bars lest Christ should see
> How men their brothers maim.

Let us consider the forces that created the Prisons Act of 1877, and how these forces had an impact on what happened to those people who got locked up in the later Victorian period. In so doing we will see how the various competing audiences that we have already encountered continued to shape how prisons would develop, and begin to understand how what we would now call the politics of law and order had an impact even on Victorian prisons. Indeed, the 1860s and '70s were dominated by moral panics – especially about so-called 'ticket-of-leave men' leaving prison – and, even as the Prison Act of 1898 was becoming law, London was gripped by fear of a new type of criminal: 'hooligans'.[5]

The End of Transportation

Between 1750 and 1900 there were a number of broad historical developments that are crucial to our understanding of the nature of both punishment and how the state thought it best to respond to crime. One of these was the move away from prisons being run as a business by entrepreneurial gaolers towards having the state act as gaoler through a sentence of imprisonment, within an increasingly centralized system of prisons. Another involved those responsible for administering this system eventually being used as 'experts' by the courts. There was a gradual move away from punishment that was public (and therefore visible) to punishment – including execution – that took place behind the prison's walls. However, perhaps the most important development

'Prison Ship, in Portsmouth Harbour', from *Fifty Plates of Shipping and Craft Drawn and Etched by E. W. Cooke* (1828).

Henry Rushbury, *Debtors' Prison, York*, 1933, drypoint.

over this period was an end to transportation – the physical removal of offenders from Britain – which was replaced with their incarceration in state-run prisons. In this way imprisonment therefore became a punishment in itself and, correspondingly, prisons and what happened there moved on to centre stage. This was a process that took time. After all, it is clear that for a number of pragmatic reasons, usually financial, the state preferred to transport those who were deemed as having broken the law. For as long as they supported this approach, prisons and the building of new prisons came a poor second in terms of developments within public policy.

Of course, offenders had been exiled or banished throughout the Middle Ages, but perhaps we can see the more formal beginnings of transportation as a state policy in the Transportation Act of 1718, which was partly formulated in response to the first Jacobite Rebellion. A sentence of transportation was usually for seven or fourteen years, but could also sometimes be imposed for life. Indeed, even if it was only for seven years, it was practically difficult and usually beyond the means of the person who had been transported to return to Britain. In other words, people who were transported tended to stay where they had been transported to, although in fiction Dickens has Abel Magwitch return to London from New South Wales in 1829 to meet up with Pip in *Great Expectations*. However, it was to the American colonies that most people were transported in the eighteenth century and, as has been discussed, between 1718 and 1775 almost 30,000 people were sent there to serve their sentences, usually to

Fleet Prison – Poor Debtors' Cell, c. 1840s, wood engraving.

toil in the cotton and tobacco fields. The Declaration of Independence in 1776 effectively ended this policy, and so the state needed to find a suitable alternative for those who would previously have been sentenced to transportation.

The temporary expedient that was adopted was to house those sentenced to transportation in old, rotting ships – known as 'the hulks' – and then to make the prisoners work at dredging rivers or labouring in the Royal Dockyards. In effect the state was administering a system of imprisonment, but rather than continuing in this direction – for example, by building prisons on dry land – and thus formalizing this approach, the Transportation Act of 1784 signalled the government's preference for removing offenders overseas. However, a new penal colony had to be found, and by May 1787 six transport ships, together with two warships and three store-ships, took 736 convicts – 48 of these 'First Fleeters' died en route – and arrived in January 1788 in Botany Bay.[6] By the end of the Napoleonic Wars the numbers being transported to Australia increased from 1,000 to 2,500 people per annum, and reached a peak in the 1830s when 5,000 people were being transported overseas each year.[7] Around 165,000 offenders would eventually be transported to Australia.

The numbers being transported began to peak for a variety of reasons, including opposition from the colonies themselves, and the fact that there were those in Britain who started to question whether or not transportation was actually a punishment. Indeed, we should remember that Magwitch was revealed as Pip's benefactor in *Great Expectations*, after having made his fortune in New South Wales. A Select Committee on Transportation, under the chairmanship of Sir William Molesworth, came to the conclusion that this policy should end, and a series of penitentiaries should be built to deal with offenders. The ubiquitous Revd

A view of the Bradford 'Old Dungeon', 1860s, lithograph.

Fleet Prison, after Thomas Rowlandson, 1808.

Sidney Smith wrote to the prime minister in 1826 satirizing a sentence of transportation:

> Translated into common sense [it] is this: 'Because you have committed this offence, the sentence of the Court is that you shall no longer be burdened with the support of your wife and family. You shall be immediately removed from a very bad climate and a country overburdened with people to one of the finest regions of the earth, where the demand for human labour is every hour increasing, and where it is highly probable you will ultimately gain your character and improve your future. The Court has been induced to pass this sentence upon you in consequence of the many aggravating circumstances of your case, and they hope your fate will be a warning to others.[8]

One wonders what Smith actually wanted a formal system of punishment to do, especially if he did not want the offender to 'gain' his 'character and improve [his] future'. Even so, he overestimates the benefits and downplays the many disadvantages of being transported. The First Fleeters, for example, were transported in quarters which had no light and were

Women at work in Brixton prison, c. 1860, from Henry Mayhew's *The Criminal Prisons of London, and Scenes of Prison Life* (1862).

poorly ventilated, crammed four to a space equivalent to that of a modern king-sized bed, even though the journey itself would take 252 days across 15,000 miles of ocean. They had also been cheated out of meat, bread and medicine by Duncan Campbell, the crooked contractor who had been responsible for providing provisions to the fleet.[9] From later in the century, correspondence exists showing how sick Scottish convicts under sentence of transportation were moved back and forth between various Scottish jails and the governor of Millbank, who complained bitterly that the prisoners were unfit for the rigours of the journey. There are a series of reports of ill-treatment and even the deaths of Scottish prisoners sent south to await transportation. In 1848, for example, the doctor at Millbank complained that Patrick McGinty – who had been sent south from Glasgow – was in 'the last degree of Emaciation and debility', and that 'very great danger would attend his removal'. Indeed, the governor of Millbank was moved to write to the Sheriff of Edinburgh:

> I cannot avoid expressing my regret that convicts should be sent to this establishment under circumstances which oblige me from motives of humanity to act in violation of the regulations framed for my guidance.[10]

This is not to deny that many of those who were transported did indeed prosper in the countries to where they had been forcibly exiled, and no doubt they also wrote letters to those friends and family members that they had left behind, perhaps more often than not putting a brave face on their circumstances. All of this would undoubtedly feed into the climate of debate – the daily, popular, public chatter – about transportation and its benefits or drawbacks. And, given that few transported prisoners ever returned home, who could really deny or confirm what transportation was actually like? Whatever the reality, when transportation ended, new solutions to the problem of what should be done with offenders loomed large in the public policy agenda, and the prison – and what happened within our prisons – moved into public view. In particular the public had to get used to a new phenomenon: the newly released prisoner returning to the community that had previously punished him by sending him to prison.

Moral Panic and the Ticket-of-leave Men

Moral panic is that strangest of phenomena – a concept that has been able to seep out of the academy and become part of everyday usage. We have got used to journalists in particular happily applying the term, and even advertisers have been quick to see the commercial advantages of suggesting that their product is 'edgy' – and therefore desirable – by generating a moral panic about what it is that they are trying to sell, or promote.[11] The difficulty with all of this application is that we have tended to lose sight of what was originally meant by the label 'moral panic' – and its associated 'folk devils' – and allowed the concept to float far too far from its academic moorings.

Originating from the late Stanley Cohen's *Folk Devils and Moral Panics* (1972), which was concerned with two youth groups in mid-1960s England called the 'Mods' and the 'Rockers', a moral panic was created by sensationalized and exaggerated media reporting about fights between these two groups over a Bank Holiday at a seaside resort, and then in turn by the reaction of the police and the courts – which paradoxically created an 'amplification of deviance', so that other young people wanted to become Mods or Rockers. In other words, a moral panic is created by relatively intense media coverage about a specific event or group of people, but for a defined period of time; this coverage is exaggerated both in terms of the scale of those involved and the harm that they could inflict; those that are involved are portrayed and became 'folk devils'; and finally there is an emphasis that the people, group or behaviour that comes under scrutiny is connected in some way to deeper issues and problems that are affecting society.[12]

With the gradual move away from transportation in the 1850s and '60s, and then its eventual and formal end in 1868, what happened to prisoners inside our gaols became a subject of popular interest and debate. In particular people wanted to believe that when a prisoner was released back into the community after having served a term of imprisonment, they were less likely to reoffend in the future; that they had been deterred from committing more crime because of the punishment that they had received; or, alternatively, that their time spent inside had given to them the education, skills or opportunity for reflection that would reform and rehabilitate them.

The focus of this popular interest was centred on the ticket-of-leave men and a particular form of crime called 'garrotting', or sometimes more popularly 'putting the hug on', which quickly became commonly associated with them. Tickets-of-leave had been introduced in 1853, and were in effect a Victorian form of parole. Prisoners were released early on a licence – their 'ticket-of-leave' – which was approved and signed by the Secretary of State, and which gave details about the prisoner and informed them that this licence could be revoked for misconduct.[13] Soon the popular press wanted to know what prisoners had to do to earn these tickets-of-leave, and some began to suggest that the prisoners either pulled the wool over the eyes of prison officials – such as the chaplain – to convince them they had changed, so as to get out early; or that they were being given an easy time in gaol that compared far too favourably with the lives of hardworking people in the community, and that they therefore were not punished enough.

Matters came to head with the 'garrotting panic' that swept through London in the winter of 1862. In effect garrotting was a form of street robbery that involved choking the victim. It was usually perpetrated by two or three robbers acting in concert against their hapless target. The sociologist Geoffrey Pearson suggests that this technique may actually have been perfected by prison guards who worked on the hulks,[14] but whatever its origin – and many newspapers were quick to claim that the crime was 'foreign' to the English character – the media were awash with stories of garrotting ticket-of-leave men destroying the very fabric of British society. The Times, for example, claimed that this was a new variety of crime – the 'modern peril of the streets' – which had created something like a 'reign of terror' in London, to the extent that 'whole sections of a peaceable city community were on the verge of arming themselves against sudden attack'. The paper concluded that: 'Our streets are actually not as safe as they were in the days of our grandfathers. We have slipped back to a state of affairs which would be intolerable even in Naples.'

The magazine Punch went further and carried scores of cartoons purportedly reflecting the reality of life in London as a result of the garrotters. One such cartoon, entitled 'Going out to Tea in the Suburbs – A Pretty State of Things for 1862', has three young women (the 'pretty state', so to speak) anxiously going off for tea, surrounded by six heavily armed guards keeping watch for any ticket-of-leave men who might be ready to pounce. Another, 'A Suburban Delight', has a rather prosperous-looking gentleman out at night and about to walk down an alley. Two armed, shady-looking characters suggest to this gentleman:

Dark Party (with a ticket-of-leave, of course). Ay, yer pardon, Sir
– But if you was a-goin down this Dark Lane, p'raps you'd allow
Me and this here Young Man to go along with yer – cos yer see
there haint no Perlice about – and we're so precious feared
o'bein' garotted!

It is interesting that *Punch* concentrates on the perceived threats to
the suburbs, and also specifically questions the inability of the police to
prevent these threats, which is presumably why the three young women
had to hire their own personal bodyguards. Given the absence of the
'Perlice', *Punch* suggested vigilante action and produced a range of cartoons
suggesting an ever more outlandish array of preventative gadgets to eliminate the possibility of being garrotted. One such device, for example,
was a large spiked collar which had to be worn round the neck so as to prevent a garrotter from being able to get his arms around his intended
victim's throat. Another was an 'anti-garrotte overcoat' which flowed
extravagantly outwards and would thus prevent any ticket-of-leave man
from being able to get close enough to the wearer of the coat to be able
to garrotte him or her.

Politicians quickly responded to this public anxiety and, partly reflecting suggestions in the press, they soon came up with a solution: bringing
back flogging, which had only been abolished in 1861. Sir George Grey,
the home secretary, warned that this would be a panic measure and was
roundly criticized for being the 'garrotter's friend'. Instead many more
politicians were willing to listen to rabble-rousing populists such as
Colonel John Sidney North, who suggested that anyone not willing to
flog an offender was a 'wretched old woman for his leniency'; again touch-
ing on how prisoners were fed, he reminded the House that

These rascals had their roast meat, pudding, ale and porter – things
which no honest labourer on the Hon. Gentlemen's estates could
get . . . The country was justly indignant at the manner in which
these ruffians were treated.[15]

The Garrotter's Act became law on 13 July 1863 and would remain
on the statute book until judicial corporal punishment was ended in 1948.
The act authorized up to 50 strokes of corporal punishment, in addition
to any other punishment that was awarded for those convicted of robbery, and a royal commission was established to look more closely at

transportation and what happened to prisoners once they were released from gaol.

However, it would be wrong to see the passing of the Garrotter's Act wholly as a reaction to panic – even though there was actually comparatively little increase in violent crime over the winter of 1862 – and so too we might interpret the undoubtedly populist comments of Colonel North as also aimed at attempting to find the proper balance about how society should respond to those convicted of crime in an era when it was no longer possible to transport then to Australia.

We should also remember that this debate came at a time when it was becoming increasingly clear that public executions were no longer producing a general deterrent effect (if they had ever done so), and that it was only a matter of time before these perverted ceremonies would have to be moved behind the prison's walls – an issue I consider further below when discussing the execution of Trooper Charles Thomas Wooldridge. Far from being deterred, the public attended an execution with a variety of intentions and emotions which might range from simple enjoyment to an opportunity to commit crime, or actively advocating on behalf of the about-to-be-executed. None of this suggested that the state had control over this process, and if a public execution was intended to convey to the population the 'majesty of the Law' then increasingly it did no such thing. So by 1868 hanging ceased to be a public spectacle and instead had become a private ritual over which the state had far greater control.

With transportation ended and public executions no longer producing the desired deterrent effect, this twin-track approach had to change, especially in the face of more optimistic arguments which suggested that it might be possible to reform the offender. Gatrell has described how the gallows and transportation, as opposed to what some Victorians dismissed as the approach of the 'humanity mongers', were 'opposing emotional repertoires'.[16] Each vied for ascendancy in the public policy debate about what should be done with prisoners, with the former pessimistic about human nature, and therefore in favour of deterrence, while the latter was far more optimistic. Pessimism won. Moving executions inside the prison's walls was therefore not so much about humanity, civilization or 'progress' as much as being a way of camouflaging the state's violence within a growing and increasingly professional bureaucracy of punishment.

So in the winter of 1862 there was indeed what we might now call a moral panic about the ticket-of-leave men and a particular form of crime – garrotting. What this reveals is that issues related to prison and what happened to offenders when they were sent there were beginning to be taken seriously in our public policy, and that decisions had to be made about what prison was for and who should be responsible for our prison system. The Prisons Act of 1877 grasped both those nettles: prison was for punishment, and punishment was a state responsibility. The matter was resolved; or so it seemed.

Reading Gaol

Reading Gaol has a long history, and one local historian even traces its origins back to 1537, when there seems to be a record of a blacksmith being publicly flogged and then thrown into the prison.[17] Just like Newgate, it is clear that the prison went through several reincarnations, with a 'new' gaol – sometimes known as the 'first' Reading Gaol – built in 1785 and opened in 1786. This version of the prison lasted until 1842. Rather confusingly, two years later the next 'new' gaol was built, close to the railway station at a cost of £40,000. In appearance it was a cross between HMP Pentonville and Warwick Castle. This is the Reading Gaol of Wilde's poem, and when it was completed in 1844 it quickly became the focal point of the town. It must have created quite an impression on Victorian visitors to Reading, with its four turrets and castellated Gothic-style outer wall.

The gatehouse of the new prison also had a flat roof and was designed to accommodate public executions, the last of which took place in 1862. To the right of the gatehouse was a four-bedroomed house for the governor, and to the left another for the chaplain, which suggests something

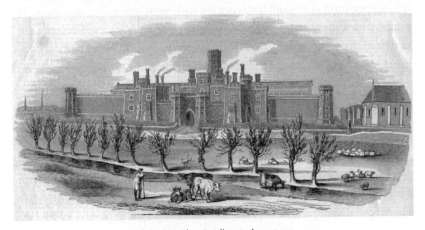

The New Gaol, at Reading, 19th century.

of the status that these roles attracted within Victorian society. The four turrets could also accommodate staff.[18]

The gaol had 250 cells divided into five wings, with women occupying E Ward, which had 32 cells – two of which were reserved for those under punishment. The prison modelled its interior on HMP Pentonville; in other words, there was a radial design, with the five wings spreading outwards in a circle from a central point, like spokes in a wheel. Each cell was 13 feet long by 7 feet wide and 10 feet high ($396 \times 213 \times 305$ cm). They were simply furnished, with a stool, table and some shelves, and a hammock suspended from iron fastenings in the wall which served as the prisoner's bed. A gas light illuminated the walls, which were covered with four notices concerning prison rules and diet; particulars of the prisoner; the nature of their offence; and morning and evening prayers. Every cell had a Bible.[19] Prisoners were only allowed to leave their cells for chapel services, exercise or visitors. Meals were brought to the cells. When the new gaol opened there was also integral sanitation within each cell, although this was removed in the 1860s when a harsher climate of public opinion – partly prompted by the ticket-of-leave men and the Prison Act of 1865 – thought that such luxuries merely pampered, rather than reforming prisoners. Indeed, one of the first prisoners would hardly have attracted much public sympathy: Abraham Boswell was sentenced to six months of hard labour for the attempted rape and indecent assault of a two-year-old child. After integral sanitation was removed, prisoners had to 'slop out' their waste into a central sluice.

As for the regime within the prison, the governor favoured the separate – as opposed to the silent – system, which literally meant that prisoners would not come into contact with each other. The design of the prison aided this goal. Prisoners were kept apart from each other, both as part of their punishment and from a fear that crime could be passed on from one person to another, almost as if it was some sort of disease. Even when the prisoner went to the chapel, they would have to wear a hood – a 'Scottish cap' – which prevented them from being identified or from recognizing anyone else, and they would have to sit in a specially designed individual cubicle so that the only person they could see would be the chaplain. Chaplains inevitably exercised considerable power in Victorian prisons, and occupied that place in debates about punishment and reform which would eventually be inherited by psychologists and psychiatrists. There was also a great deal of silence in the separate system – all the better, it was believed, for the prisoners to recognize the wrongs that they had committed, come to terms with their offending and change their ways. The penitent in the penitentiary, as it were. This was the type of regime into which Oscar Wilde was incarcerated, and I use Wilde as my major source not just because of his sheer eloquence in describing the conditions of late Victorian prisons, but also because other sources of this quality are simply not available.

Wilde and 'The Ballad'

The circumstances of Wilde's imprisonment are well known, and I recount them here – and reproduce some stanzas from 'The Ballad of Reading Gaol' – only to throw light on to how prison was experienced by those who were imprisoned. Given that Wilde's ballad is about an execution, in private, behind the gaol's walls, what he writes also provides us with a glimpse of the reality of state executions when they could no longer be viewed by the public. In this sense Wilde lifts the veil on the development of this secret and ritualized violence and, uniquely it seems to me, writes about all of this from the perspective of a serving prisoner in a prison on execution day, rather than from that of the various officials – governor, chaplain or executioner – who had to administer this type of justice.

Wilde was sentenced to two years of hard labour on 25 May 1895 at the Old Bailey, following his conviction at the conclusion of his second trial on charges of indecency and sodomy. The trial had arisen after Wilde had unsuccessfully attempted to sue the Marquis of Queensberry (of boxing's Queensberry's Rules fame) for libel. Queensberry was the father of Wilde's lover Lord Alfred Douglas, who was known as 'Bosie'. Clearly disapproving of their relationship, Queensberry went to the Albemarle Club on 18 February to confront Wilde. Wilde was not in the club, and so Queensberry left his card, on which he wrote 'For Oscar Wilde, Posing Somdomite' – clearly boxing had taken its toll on Queensberry's ability to spell 'sodomite'.[20] Wilde sued for libel, but Queensberry successfully defended this charge and so in April 1895 a warrant was issued for Wilde's arrest, which was executed at the Cadogan Hotel. He was then remanded in custody at Holloway, but released on 7 May after the jury failed to reach a verdict in his first trial. A retrial was ordered for 22 May, which was to last for three days.

Wilde was found guilty at this second trial. He was taken briefly to Newgate before being transferred back to Holloway and thereafter sent to HMP Pentonville. It was here that Wilde would have been introduced to the rigours of the 'separate' system, with its isolation and silences, infrequent visits and no letters. His day was enlivened only by visits from the chaplain, picking oakum – unravelling the twine of old tarred ropes that had been salvaged from ships – and sewing mailbags. Wilde suffered stomach problems and when he was transferred to HMP Wandsworth on 9 July he was reweighed and it was discovered that he had lost 22 lb (10 kg). This transfer itself owed much to Lord Haldane, one of the prison commissioners, who had visited Wilde in Pentonville and who had arranged for him to have some books, much to the governor's displeasure. He may have been transferred to Wandsworth because the prison's chaplain – the Revd W. D. Morrison – was a well-known opponent of the separate system. However, if it was expected that the prison's clerics would have offered him some solace and support, Wilde's supporters hadn't considered that the deputy chaplain of Wandsworth would write to the newspapers in September 1895 complaining that Wilde had smelled of semen. In fact, this smell, it was later discovered, was disinfectant.[21]

There were concerns for Wilde's mental as well as his physical health and he was eventually placed in Wandsworth's infirmary. Several investigations failed to find any psychiatric problems. Even so, Haldane again intervened and had Wilde moved to Reading Gaol on 21 November. He was transferred by train, and had to endure several passers-by on the station platform making fun of him. Wilde writes in De Profundis – the only work that he wrote while in prison ('The Ballad of Reading Gaol' was written after his release) – of how humiliating he had found this experience.

> From two o'clock till half past two on that day I had to stand on the centre platform at Clapham Junction in convict dress and handcuffed, for the world to look at. I had been taken out of the hospital ward without a moment's notice being given to me. Of all possible objects I was the most grotesque. When people saw me they laughed. Each train as it came in swelled the audience. Nothing could exceed their amusement. That was, of course, before they knew who I was. As soon as they had been informed they laughed still more. For half an hour I stood there in the grey November rain surrounded by a jeering mob.

This public humiliation that Wilde experienced is worth considering further. The prison uniform and the handcuffs that he wore were clearly symbols that the Victorians understood as denoting shame and punishment, although this punishment was now increasingly hidden from their view. The bureaucratization that the Prisons Act of 1877 had ushered in served to put a social distance between the public and the prisoner, so that the prison – and, by association, the prisoner – became a source of disgust and revulsion. This had not always been the case, especially when the public had felt more able to visit prisons and prisoners, and when there had therefore been a greater connection between what happened behind and in front of the prison's walls.

All prisoners would surely have felt much the same as Wilde, although we might also presume that he experienced a greater sense of shame given his previous public profile and celebrity. Used to being feted, he was now reduced to being a 'grotesque' 'object'. There is also something very current about this passage, given that we seem to be endlessly debating such issues as 'punishment in the community', which involves offenders being identified in some way as offenders. In Wilde's observation that he was moved 'without a moment's notice', we can hear echoes of prisoners' complaints from our own day of being 'ghosted' – moved speedily and anonymously – out of establishments, with no opportunity to say goodbye to fellow inmates.

Wilde was allocated Cell 3 on the topmost of the three landings on C wing; in other words, Cell C.3.3. At this time the prison held 170 prisoners, including thirteen women on E ward. The regime at the gaol was similar to that at HMP Pentonville. The separate system was enforced within Reading with some relish by the governor – Colonel Isaacson – whom Wilde later described as 'harsh', 'stupid' and 'lacking in imagination', with 'the eyes of a ferret, the body of an ape, and the soul of a rat'. There was no meeting of minds. Wilde objected to the slopping out, the poor diet, the imprisonment of children within the gaol and the strict enforcement of silence. He told André Gide, after he had been released, that he had been at Reading for some six weeks when 'I heard someone murmur, "Oscar Wilde, I pity you because you must be suffering more than we"', to which Wilde reports that he had replied: 'No, my friend, we are all suffering equally.' A day or two later, both prisoners were brought before Isaacson and punished for having dared to speak to each other.[22]

Wilde did get on well with a warder called Tom Martin, on whose behalf he wrote to the *Daily Chronicle* on 28 May 1897 after Martin had been dismissed from the service for giving some of the children in the gaol biscuits. There were again concerns about Wilde's physical and mental health – indeed, he petitioned the Home Office for his immediate release on the grounds of his imminent insanity – and a committee of five was sent to Reading, which duly pronounced him fit and healthy. However, there were some concessions: in July 1896 Wilde was allowed pen and ink and access to more books, as well as being excused the treadmill. Above all, Wilde's life improved with the transfer – ironically on promotion – of Isaacson to Lewes Prison, and his replacement by the far more sympathetic Major J. O. Nelson. Wilde, with no little hyperbole, would later describe Nelson as 'the most Christlike man I ever met',[23] given that he had allowed Wilde access to more books, and to retain what he had written – a facility that led to the production of De Profundis.

It was also in July that Trooper Charles Thomas Wooldridge of the Royal Horse Guards was executed, and it is this execution that is the centrepiece of 'The Ballad of Reading Gaol'. Wooldridge, a rather jealous and temperamental man, had brutally murdered his wife Laura with a cut-throat razor, although this aspect of the story has tended to be forgotten. Wilde also takes some poetic licence with several details within the ballad. For example, the Royal Horse Guards wore bluish-green coats, not the 'scarlet' of Wilde's opening line, and we are not certain where Laura met her death, although, for the benefit of the rhyme, Wilde has her die in her 'bed'. Even so, what Wilde recounts within the ballad is the process of execution – with all its quirks and oddities – within the state's prisons.

Executions at Reading were carried out on the sixth Tuesday after a sentence of death had been imposed. Executions took place at eight in the morning in the 'Photographic House', which was situated in the court-yard between C and D Wings, prior to a new, purpose-built 'Execution Centre' being built in D Wing in 1900. The day before the execution was scheduled to take place, the hangman would arrive at the prison. His time would be spent observing the prisoner so as to better assess the length of rope that he would have to use from a guide called a 'Table of Drops'. If, for example, a prisoner weighed 140 lb (63.5 kg), a length of rope of 7 feet 2 in. (2.18 m) would be required, whereas if the prisoner weighed 20 lb (9 kg) more, a length of 6 feet 3 in. (1.91 m) would be sufficient.[24] The executioner would also test the gallows equipment and make any adjustments that he deemed necessary.

On the day of the execution, the executioner would pinion the prisoner by applying leather straps to the arms and wrists, and the execution party, which would include the governor, the under-sheriff of the county, the chaplain and the medical officer, as well as the executioner and the condemned prisoner, would walk to the gallows. A white hood would be placed over the condemned prisoner's head, then the rope around his neck. This would be adjusted to the left side of the jaw so as to force the head to twist and turn, which would result in the neck being broken. After the rope had been fastened around the neck, the condemned prisoner's legs would be pinioned, and then the executioner would pull the lever which would open the trapdoors on which the prisoner had been standing. Executioners would boast of how quickly they could complete this process.[25] After the execution had been completed, there would be a formal inquest to confirm that the death had been lawful, and then the dead prisoner would be buried within the prison in an unmarked plot in unconsecrated ground. There would also be a burial service, but the whole process would be finished by noon of the day of execution.

Verses in the Chapter

I have chosen only six of Wilde's 109 verses to illustrate several of the themes which have been described in the chapter about the separate system, and about the private rituals of an execution day within a prison. I want to use these verses to allow the voices of prisoners in the late Victorian period to tell how they experienced the grinding relentlessness of the gaol. Clearly this is not a particularly scientific sample, given the fact that they were written by someone as celebrated as Wilde and the occasion that they commemorate. However, they do in their own small way allow us to peer beneath the official rhetoric about prison and how its routines were organized and, above all, lived through.

From the first section of the ballad, when Wilde is still introducing Wooldridge to the reader, both as a person and as a condemned man, the following verse is particularly revealing:

> He does not sit with silent men
> Who watch him night and day;
> Who watch him when he tries to weep,
> And when he tries to pray;
> Who watch him lest himself should rob
> The prison of its prey.

In this verse Wilde is describing the practice that when someone was under sentence of death, they would be accompanied at all times by two warders whose job it was to prevent the prisoner committing suicide. These warders would sleep in the condemned cell with the prisoner, but their role was not to befriend or offer support to the prisoner at any time, even when he tried to weep or pray. Wilde loved paradox, and here he is deliberately drawing attention to the fact that it was the state – and only the state – who had the power to take Wooldridge's life, and so if he committed suicide, the prison would be robbed 'of its prey'. Of course, he uses 'prey' and 'pray' to make very different points.

We next encounter Wooldridge six weeks later:

> Six weeks the guardsman walked the yard,
> In the suit of shabby grey:
> His cricket cap was on his head,
> And his step was light and gay,
> But I never saw a man who looked
> So wistfully at the day.

After being sentenced, appeals for a reprieve were made to the home secretary. What is of interest here is the uniform that Wooldridge is wearing: his 'suit of shabby grey' and the 'cricket cap' on his head. This was not a cricket cap at all, but a 'Scottish cap', which kept the identities of prisoners hidden from each other. It is interesting that Wilde describes the uniform as 'shabby'. Perhaps he was also remembering his own very public discomfort when he was transferred to Reading Gaol and had to wait on the railway station platform in his prison uniform, a memory that he found 'grotesque'. Here Wooldridge is 'walking the yard' – taking exercise within the prison – but looking 'wistfully' at the day. By all accounts, Wooldridge seemed to accept his fate, a reality that was also in marked contrast to Wilde.

In the third section of the ballad Wilde provides some further details about the routines of the gaol:

> We tore the tarry rope to shreds
> With blunt and bleeding nails;
> We rubbed the doors, and scrubbed the floors,
> And cleaned the shining rails:
> And, rank by rank, we soaped the plank,
> And clattered with the pails.

This verse describes what passed as work within the gaol, and in particular oakum picking. Wilde's fingers had bled when he had picked oakum, and he was lucky to have been eventually employed as the schoolmaster's orderly within the gaol. This passage also feels very current given the continuing emphasis on cleaning within our prisons. Even today, parties of prisoners scrub floors and clean rails rather than being trained for work that might actually help them to find a job after they have been released.

In the fourth verse that I have chosen, Wilde describes his uniform and the separate and silent system. We need to appreciate how important having to wear a uniform must have been to a prisoner, as it robbed them of their former identity, as would their mandatory haircuts and being given a prison number. These were all relatively new developments. And, in doing all of this, a new identity was forged for the prisoner as belonging to the state:

> Like ape or clown, in monstrous garb
> With crooked arrows starred,
> Silently we went round and round
> The slippery asphalte yard;
> Silently we went round and round,
> And no man spoke a word.

The 'crooked arrows' that Wilde is referring to are the black arrows that were stamped on prisoners' uniforms, indicating that they were the property of the Crown. Wilde's negativity about the uniforms can be gleaned from the fact that he sees them as being worn by an 'ape' or a 'clown'; the first is less than human, the second a figure of fun. Again he draws attention to exercise within the prison's yard – with the prisoners going 'round and round' – and the silence as they did so. This inability to 'speak a word' was yet another 'pain of confinement' that had to be endured, and marked out the prisoner as different to other human beings.

The penultimate verse that I have chosen is one of the most quoted of all those within the ballad. It generalizes Wilde's view about being a prisoner beyond what is happening to him within Reading Gaol, or in relation to the execution of Wooldridge. As a short but sustained piece of writing about what it means to be incarcerated, this is an extraordinarily powerful polemic which is still capable of generating a reaction.[26]

> This too I know and wise it were
> If each could know the same
> That every prison that men build
> Is built with bricks of shame,
> And bound with bars lest Christ should see
> How men their brothers maim.

Wilde touches on the fact that prison is hidden from public view; the 'bricks of shame', after all, are to prevent Christ from witnessing what is taking place within the walls of the prison. It is Wilde who knows, because he has been a prisoner and therefore seen for himself what happens when people are locked up. His plea is that everyone should 'know the same' about the reality of imprisonment.

The final verse I shall discuss is taken from the sixth and final section of the poem and returns to several themes which Wilde had already employed within the ballad. In particular it returns to the idea of men 'killing the thing that they love' – which in Wilde's case may have been a direct reference to his sense of betrayal by Bosie, as much as it was about Wooldridge killing his wife.

> In Reading gaol by Reading town
> There is a pit of shame
> And in it lies a wretched man
> Eaten by teeth of flame,
> In a burning winding-sheet he lies,
> And his grave has got no name.

Wooldridge was buried in an unmarked grave on unconsecrated ground – a 'pit of shame' – the final ignominy that the state was able to heap upon him.[27]

Wilde would eventually move to France on his release from Reading Gaol, but he wrote twice to the Daily Chronicle about his time in prison. He wrote first to support the warder Tom Martin, and then again on 28 May 1898 to support the Prison Bill, which would very quickly become the Prison Act of 1898. This Act incorporated almost all of the recommendations made by the Gladstone Committee, and in effect swept away the preceding twenty years of penal practice by abolishing hard labour, allowing prisoners to speak and introducing remission for good behaviour. Of course, it is also clear that the bureaucratization that the Prisons Act

of 1877 had introduced was intensified by the Act of 1898. One consequence of that intensification was that sources of information about what
happened inside prisons became the preserve of penal officials, with
their technical knowledge and scientific expertise. The voices of prisoners, on the other hand, all but disappeared. Sadly, the reforms of the
Prison Act of 1898 came too late for Wilde, who was to die only three and
a half years after his release in 1900, at the age of 46.

FOUR

Decarceration and the Interwar Years

The mood and temper of the public in regard to the treatment of crime
and criminals is one of the most unfailing tests of the civilisation of any
country. A calm and dispassionate recognition of the rights of the accused
against the state, and even of convicted criminals against the state, a
constant heart-searching by all charged with a duty of punishment, a desire
and eagerness to rehabilitate in the world of industry all those who have
paid their dues in the hard coinage of punishment, tireless efforts towards
the discovery of curative and regenerating processes, and an unfaltering
faith that there is a treasure, if you can only find it, in the heart of every man
– these are the symbols which in the treatment of crime and criminals mark
and measure the stored-up strength of a nation, and are the sign and proof
of the living virtue in it.

Winston Churchill, speech to the House of Commons, 20 July 1910

Churchill's speech has bequeathed to the topic of prisons and
imprisonment one of its most often quoted aphorisms.[1] As a
former prisoner himself during the Boer War, Churchill explicitly
linked civilization with what takes place behind the prison's walls and
is done there to prisoners in society's name. Wilde would have approved.
And, since the pioneering work of Norbert Elias, sociologists, historians
and increasingly criminologists have also become keen to discuss the
ways in which a society that punishes reveals, or at least is believed to
reveal, how 'civilized' that society might be at that point in its social
development.[2] 'Civilized' here can be taken more broadly to mean that
no punishment would be arbitrary or indefinite; neither would it involve
floggings, public executions or vigilante action. Rather, it would be
characterized by the state's monopolistic control over all forms of punishment, which would not be aimed at physically inflicting pain on
the offender, but instead at encouraging his rehabilitation and reform.
In a civilized society, punishment is technical, precise and in the hands
of experts.

However, as Zygmunt Bauman has pointed out, 'civilized' Germans were quite adept at using their bureaucratic state rationalism and scientific expertise to eliminate 6 million Jews in the Holocaust, and the Norwegian criminologist Nils Christie has similarly argued that the growth of mass imprisonment – or 'hyper-incarceration' – is a 'natural outgrowth of our type of society, not an exception to it'.[3] It is also interesting to note that the 'constant heart-searching', as Churchill would say, about the abuse of Iraqi prisoners of war by American servicemen at Abu Ghraib prison has not seen any fundamental questioning of penal conditions in the USA, where 'supermaximum facilities', solitary confinement, huge prison numbers, spiralling costs and of course the death penalty characterize domestic policy about 'treatment of crime and criminals'. As is so often the case, punishment and civilization make very strange bedfellows.[4]

Two unusual phenomena dominate what follows. First, I seek to understand one of the world's longest sustained periods of decarceration in penal history, which took place in England and Wales between 1908 and the outbreak of the Second World War, and was partly prompted and promoted by the views that Churchill expressed. Second, I use a case study of an incarcerated child-killer to examine how prisons operated at this time. In doing so, I peer beneath the surface of the various tensions operating within our prisons between the wars. This case study has also been chosen because it introduces Wales and a specific Welsh offender directly into our discussion for the first time.

The remarkable decarceration of England and Wales has been written about before,[5] but the decline in the prison population of England and Wales between 1908 and 1939 from 22,029 to 11,086 – or, in terms of the numbers of prisoners per 100,000 of the general population, from 63 to 30 – is a truly extraordinary period in our penal history and one that deserves greater scrutiny. In effect, our prison numbers halved, and as a result around twenty prisons had to close down, despite the fact that the crime rate in this period actually increased by around 160 per cent.[6] By 1938 our prison population was among the smallest in Europe, and the reduction of our prison numbers was attracting the attention of American criminologists such as Edwin Sutherland, who wrote – almost in disbelief – that 'prisons are being demolished and sold in England because the supply of prisoners is not large enough to fill them'.[7] At the outbreak of the Second World War the prison system of England and Wales consisted of 22 prisons and seven borstals (institution designed on a public-school model to house young people) with a total capacity of 19,600.

Reading Gaol, for example, the subject of Oscar Wilde's ballad, desperately searched for a role – any role – after hostilities with Germany ended in 1918, especially since the few offenders who were being imprisoned by the local courts were being sent to HMP Oxford. In January 1920 the gaol reinvented itself as the county's secure food store and locked up tinned salmon instead of prisoners. It also operated as an army surplus clothing store in 1925 and then in 1936 as a driving test centre. With war approaching once more, it was used as an army recruiting office. However, even as late as 1938 all the cells of the prison were still empty, and one local councillor who visited the empty buildings thought that 'the only practical thing seems to be to raze it to the ground, and utilize the site for a building more in keeping with our social needs.'[8] War would change all of this.

The same process of decarceration was also present in Scotland, although it was more of a continuation of policies from an earlier era rather than marking a departure in public policy. Even so, Scotland reduced its overall prison population from 2,749 people in 1899 to 1,639 in 1928, and the Prison Commission of Scotland, which had taken over 57 prisons when it was brought into being in 1877, had only twelve left by the time it was disbanded in 1929.

Explaining Decarceration

So how can this phenomenon be explained? We need to consider three issues. First, for decarceration to have taken place to this extent there has to have been a great deal of scepticism about what prison and imprisonment could do, and that scepticism must have been shared by a wide range of people who were able to exercise influence over the political process. Second, there had to be a credible, practical alternative to incarceration and, finally, prisons and prison staff – some of whom occupied powerful roles within the Prison Commission – responded to this changing sensibility, both prompting and actively supporting the drop in prison numbers.

In relation to the first of these three points, one of the realities that characterizes this historical period is that several politicians and key social groups became absolutely convinced that prison was a corrupting and counterproductive experience. In short, one of our three 'audiences' – the public – turned against prisons and imprisonment.

The most obvious example to give is Winston Churchill himself, who as home secretary between February 1910 and October 1911 set about reducing the use of imprisonment, especially for those who had hitherto been sentenced to very short sentences, or who were fine defaulters. He noted, for example, that in 1910 some two-thirds of sentenced prisoners had received sentences of two weeks or less, and he described this as 'a terrible and purposeless waste of public money and human character'. So while 95,686 fine defaulters were received into prison in 1908, by 1938 this number had dropped to 7,936. And, as we have seen, in July 1910 Churchill specifically linked civilization with what happened within a country's prisons. Without doubt he helped to create the climate for change that would allow George V, on his accession to the throne in May 1910, to introduce remission for any convicted prisoners who still had more than a month to serve of their prison sentence, for example. Just why Churchill was so against prison is a matter of conjecture, but perhaps we can trace his antipathy back to his own experience as a prisoner of war during the Boer War, and it is worth noting that those politicians who themselves have had direct experiences of incarceration – such as Nelson Mandela in South Africa and Václav Havel in Czechoslovakia[9] – are usually the most ardent penal reformers when they come to power.

Churchill's scepticism was mirrored in this period by other influential groups and commentators who created the right 'mood music' for decarceration to take place. Wilde and 'The Ballad of Reading Gaol' played a part here, but we should also note the contribution of two other influential groups of prisoners. Just prior to the First World War, the incarceration of suffragettes and their experiences of prison, and thereafter the imprisonment of conscientious objectors (COs), created two powerful groups of people who were prepared to campaign for changes in relation to imprisonment. The literate middle class are always unusual inhabitants of prisons, and their ability to describe what had happened to them while imprisoned – in effect, to make public what had been private – allowed ideas about the need for reform to spread more widely. Stephen Hobhouse and Fenner Brockway, for example, two conscientious objectors who had been imprisoned, concluded in their book about prisons, *English Prisons Today: Being the Report of the Prison System Enquiry Committee* (1922), that

> Our prison system, whilst it sometimes makes good prisoners, does almost nothing to make good citizens. It fails to restore the weak will or to encourage initiative; it reduces energy by the harshness of its routine and adds depression to the depressed

... and the more the system costs the country, the more highly it is organised, the more monumental must that failure be.[10]

The Prison System Enquiry Committee had been set up in 1919 by the Labour Party's research department, but broke its formal connection to Labour two years later. In the same year that Hobhouse and Brockway's indictment of prisons was published, so too was Sidney and Beatrice Webb's *English Prisons Under Local Government*, which concluded that 'the most practical of all prison reforms is to keep people out of prison altogether.'[11] A year earlier, the Howard Association and the Penal Reform League amalgamated to became the Howard League for Penal Reform – the oldest penal reform organization in the world.

In Scotland, nearly half of the country's male population between the ages of eighteen and 45 were in uniform by 1916, although anti-war protestors such as James McDougall, Tom Bell, John Maclean and John MacCallum, the former captain of the Scottish rugby team, attracted most of the headlines and the government's resultant anxiety.[12] Part of this anxiety seems to have stemmed from the fact that these protestors that were being locked up were of a very different class. David Kirkwood, for example, a native of Parkhead, an eastern suburb of Glasgow, recalled that in all his life his father had 'never earned as much as thirty shillings a week', although Kirkwood himself would later become a magistrate, an MP and the first Baron Kirkwood. In his autobiography, Kirkwood describes his anti-war agitations in Glasgow – which became dubbed 'Red Clydeside' – as a shop steward at Parkhead Forge, which was owned by William Beardmore & Co. Kirkwood was especially antagonistic towards the Munitions Act of 1915, which prevented the resignation of munitions workers without the factory owner's consent, and which Kirkwood described as amounting to 'slavery'. When the Munitions Minister – Lloyd George – came to Glasgow in 1916, it fell to Kirkwood to introduce the Minister before an assembled group of workers. Kirkwood remembers that he said:

> We regard you with suspicion because the Munitions Act with which your name is associated has the taint of slavery about it, and you will find that we, as Scotsmen, resent that. If you desire to get the best of us, you must treat us with justice and respect.[13]

Kirkwood – and others like him – were seen as harming the war effort, and so on 25 March 1916, at three o'clock in the morning, armed police came to his house with a warrant to arrest him under the Defence of the Realm Act. Kirkwood was first taken to Central Police Station in Glasgow and then 'deported' to Edinburgh, where he was not allowed to venture beyond 5 miles of the city centre. This fate also awaited others who had been arrested with Kirkwood, including James Messer, another shop steward, Sam Shields, 'a decent hard-working, home-loving Bridgeton engineer, Robert Wainwright, a young man of high character and much respected as a workman and as a man.'[14]

Kirkwood was separated from his wife and children, and the whole experience made him 'think of Russia'. However, he had his family come to stay with him in Edinburgh, and quite quickly other shop stewards and 'revolutionary workers' started to visit Kirkwood in the capital too. This again made the authorities uneasy. Kirkwood addressed the Labour Party Conference in Manchester in January 1917, but instead of returning to Edinburgh he once again went back to Glasgow, where he was again arrested and thereafter imprisoned in Edinburgh Castle. He recalled that:

> My new habitation was a vault far below the ground, into which the only light entered from a small grated window high up near the roof. Above my vault were the guards' quarters, occupied by German and Austrian officer-prisoners.[15]

Kirkwood was kept in solitary confinement for fourteen days, and he remembered his 'filthy bed', the food 'that gied me a scunner' – in other words, he didn't like it – and the guard who pointed to his loaded revolver and declared that he would rather shoot Kirkwood than a German. He also remembered that solitary confinement had brought him close to 'breaking point', although he was again deported and eventually allowed back to Glasgow because of his wife's illness. In all Kirkwood was deported for some fourteen months, and although he would not take up the cause of penal reform as a parliamentarian, it is interesting to note that the foreword to his book is written by Winston Churchill. In this Churchill hardly comes across as Kirkwood's best friend, and describes him and his ilk as 'radically minded wage-earners' who are characterized by their

> sturdy independence, their mood of political revolt, their strong suspicion that they are being 'got at' and put upon, their super-developed sense of injustice, their hatred of snobbery and affectation, their readiness to use their rights as citizens to the full,

their innate conviction that one man is as good as another, or better – these traits show themselves on every page.[16]

From the records which survive, John Maclean seems to have suffered much more than any other CO. Sentenced to three years' hard labour, he served his sentence first at Calton Jail in Edinburgh and then at Peterhead. He was released from Peterhead in July 1917, but was again in the prison the following year. Maclean went on hunger strike, and so the prison authorities tried to have him certified as insane.[17] Maclean's wife Agnes complained that her husband had to 'resist the forcible feeding by mouth tube, but two warders held him down, and these men never left him thereafter, night or day, till he was forced to give in'. One of his friends noted that after his release Maclean's thoughts were

now disconnected, his speech was irresponsible, his mind from solitary confinement was absolutely self-centred. In a word prison life had done its work on a delicately-balanced psychology, and our unfortunate comrade was now a mental wreck.[18]

Suffragettes were members of a votes-for-women campaign that, while having its roots in the early Victorian period, started to garner support and public attention with the formation of the Women's Social and Political Union in 1903. At their inaugural meeting those women attending decided that extreme measures of civil disobedience would be one of the tactics they would employ to promote their campaign; they soon began smashing windows, chaining themselves to railings and committing acts of arson. One member, Emily Davison, died after throwing herself in front of the King's horse at the Derby in 1913. This militancy, which today we might call 'direct action', resulted in large numbers of suffragettes being imprisoned in Holloway, including Christabel Pankhurst, Annie Kennedy and Marion Wallace Dunlop. It was Dunlop who first reacted to her imprisonment by going on hunger strike – a response soon adopted by other suffragettes – and the prison authorities in turn countered by force-feeding them. All this ensured that prison conditions and the treatment of prisoners remained a subject of public interest, debate and controversy.

The second necessary precondition for decarceration to take place at this time was the development of a credible alternative to incarceration, and it is during this period that probation was introduced. The

Probation Service can trace its roots from 1876 and the Church of England Temperance Society aimed at saving the working class from the evils of alcohol, and by 1907 the Government had passed its first Probation Act so as to give probation a statutory footing. In short, imprisonment was no longer seen as the only policy option when it came to responding to offenders, and this allowed the dominance of incarceration to be challenged.

Third, the Home Office, prisons and prison staff responded to these changing social and policy developments. They were not the passive recipients of change, but rather both prompted and responded to it. Their response is perhaps best symbolized by the Gladstone Committee and the Prison Act of 1898, which has previously been discussed, both of which completely redefined the purpose of imprisonment. The former, for example, concluded that

> We think that the system should be made more elastic, more capable of being adopted to the special cases of individual prisoners; that prison discipline and treatment should be more effectively designed to maintain, stimulate, or awaken the higher susceptibilities of prisoners, to develop their moral instincts, to train them in orderly and industrial habits, and whenever possible to turn them out of prison better men and women, both physically and morally than when they came in.

These challenges were admirably taken up in prisons and by prison staff, most obviously through the development of the borstal regime for young offenders, which was modelled on the English public school; for example, it had housemasters in charge rather than governors.[19] It was named after the first institution of its kind, which was located in the village of Borstal in Kent. The borstal – which housed young people up to the age of twenty-one – was viewed as such a success that it would not be replaced as a form of punishment until the 1980s. Apart from the developments of borstals, it is also during this period that psychiatrists, psychologists and educationalists were introduced into prison regimes. There is therefore an understandable tendency to think of all of this as 'progress'.

But how did all of this work in practice? What tensions existed beneath the surface of the prisons of the interwar years, and how did prison officials and administrators – and prisoners themselves – respond to the opportunities that undoubtedly exist when numbers are cut, and prisons start to empty? Let us consider how to answer these questions by looking at a case study of one young prisoner called Harold Jones, who was sent to prison in 1921 and only released when Britain was at war in 1940.

A Child-killer Goes to Prison

Harold Jones was a fifteen-year-old shop assistant in Abertillery, Monmouthshire, when he committed two separate, sexually sadistic murders of young girls in 1921. If he had been slightly older, he would have been executed. Given the nature of his offences, he was not sent to a borstal, instead being detained at His Majesty's Pleasure, during which time two prison commissioners – Dr W. Norwood East and Alexander Paterson – formally reported on Jones on a regular basis and made notes of his progress on his file kept by the Prison Commission. In this respect Jones was unusual – perhaps because of the nature of his offences and the age at which he committed them – for Norwood East and Paterson were both central figures in how the prison service evolved in the interwar period, although each came from a different tradition. Norwood East, for example, emphasized his scientific and clinical expertise, while Paterson was known for his efficient, calculating humanitarianism.

Norwood East had served on the 1932 Departmental Committee on Persistent Offenders and, with Dr W. De Burgh Hubert, wrote *The Psychological Treatment of Crime*.[20] He had joined the Prison Medical Service in 1899 and published extensively on criminal behaviour and the criminal justice system. His first publication, in 1901, discussed physical and moral insensibility; another paper in 1913 was concerned with attempted suicide. In 1920 he wrote on mental disorder and crime and in 1927 produced the first introductory text on the application of forensic psychiatry in criminal courts. Two of his other major publications were on the medical aspects of crime and on society and the criminal.[21] He was knighted in 1947 for his services to the study of criminal psychology and he particularly influenced the passages in the Criminal Justice Act of 1948 concerning mentally disordered offenders.

Paterson had made his name as an inspirational volunteer at a boy's club in Bermondsey, London, prior to the First World War, and subsequently wrote about his experiences in *Across the Bridges; or, Life by the South London River-side*, which was published in 1911. As a prison commissioner between 1922 and 1946, he was considered to be the dominant influence on penal policy to the extent that this period became known as 'the Paterson era'.[22] Indeed, Harold Scott, chair of the Prison Commission between 1932 and 1938, viewed Paterson as one of the most remarkable men that he had encountered, considering him as transforming imprisonment not only in England but throughout the world.[23] He was seen almost as a saint, and his reputation remains high even today. Paterson too was knighted in 1947. His obituary in *The Times* of 10 November 1947 was titled 'Faith in Human Nature', and as one historian has commented:

> It is very much in that vein that Paterson has been immortalised both within and outside of the prison service. To a large extent that has also been the case in popular and academic histories that have considered Paterson and his role in shaping penal reform during the early decades of the twentieth century.[24]

So both Paterson and Norwood East were senior civil servants responsible for running the prison system during the interwar years, and had been imbued with the optimistic view of the time that suggested that prison could change an offender's behaviour. The drop in prison numbers also provided an opportunity to encourage experimentation and increase flexibility within the prison estate. For a variety of reasons, Paterson in particular wanted to take advantage of this opportunity; his ultimate objective was to have prisoners experience 'ordinary standards of citizenship by promoting personal responsibility'.[25] More famously, he suggested that 'men come to prison as a punishment, not for punishment'.[26] In the main these views held sway with politicians and civil servants, with one historian observing that 'the majority of members [of parliament] supported the policies of the commissioners during the 1920s.'[27] Jones would become the recipient of their attention.

However, it is also important to note that even though 29 of the country's 56 prisons had closed, the Prison Service had largely still to deal with Victorian buildings which had been designed in a different era and with a different purpose in mind. Very few new prisons were built during this period. This caused resentment among both prison staff and prisoners.[28] That all was not well in the Prison Service during this interwar period is dramatically demonstrated in the Dartmoor 'mutiny' of January 1932, when prisoners rioted and took control of the prison for almost two hours. Alison Brown has suggested that the mutiny was partly caused as a consequence of grievances that had no outlet and which in some cases developed into retribution against those seen as responsible. There is no evidence to suggest that this was a kind of appeal extending outside of the prison. Rage, frustration and hatred were vehemently expressed during the riot but so too were confusion, excitement and even elation.[29]

A new prison governor had been appointed at HMP Dartmoor – Stanley Norton-Roberts – who, against the seeming prevailing ethos of the time, had introduced a harsher regime with less flexibility, curtailing both education classes and trust.[30] New economic constraints introduced in 1931 had also meant that prison officers who left the prison were not replaced, so that there were fewer staff available to supervise prisoners. Furthermore, a decline in demand for prison-produced products meant that sewing mailbags became the primary occupation. The disturbance was not due to overcrowding, since there were only 442 inmates in a prison that had 935 cells.

The mutiny at Dartmoor generated a great deal of public attention about some aspects of the work of the Prison Service, but this publicity rarely captured the pressures that existed beneath the surface of the penal system of the interwar years, especially the tensions between prison governors and civil servants concerning how prisons should be managed. A glimpse of these can be gleaned from a more critical source about the interwar years: the autobiography of Lt Col. Charles Rich, a prison governor who published his memoirs in 1932, and who was consistently and vehemently critical of civil servants, whom he saw as 'idealists' intent on 'destroying' the prison service. There is no doubt that one of his major targets was Paterson, although he is not named.

However, what all of this suggests is that penal policy in the interwar years might be a fruitful territory to investigate, even if it has been largely unexplored by historians. By looking at the specific case of Harold Jones we can begin to see how various governors, civil servants and doctors came to view Jones and assess his suitability for release. In this way we begin to see how the penal system actually worked and how different personalities – from varying backgrounds – could leave their stamp on that system. The differing views of Paterson and Norwood East about Jones and whether or not he should be released came to a head when considering his suitability for return to the community. Jones was eventually released on licence from HMP Wandsworth on 7 December 1941, after having served twenty years. His time inside therefore straddled the careers of both Paterson and Norwood East, which is why this rather odd young man is so very interesting.

The local historian Neil Milkins provides substantial detail on Jones's early life and offences which allows us to build up a picture of Jones as a boy living in Abertillery.[31] Milkins also speculates on Jones's life post-release, suggesting that he may have been responsible for the murder of the Swansea eleven-year-old Muriel Drinkwater in 1946 and the Cardiff six-year-old Carol Stephens in 1959, along with the so-called 'Jack the Stripper' serial killings between 1959 and 1963 in London. This is territory which I do not explore here, but it is clearly of interest. It is possible to build up a reasonably accurate picture of Jones and his prison career as files about him are contained in the central Prison Commission file stored at the Public Record Office at Kew, which was only released under the Freedom of Information Act in 2007.[32]

It should also be noted that in addition to committing these two murders and denying at court during his first trial that he had killed Freda Burnell, Jones had directed Freda to a storage shed and then arrived minutes later to sexually assault and kill her; joined in the police search to find Freda when her family reported her missing; calmly informed the police that he had served Freda early in the morning in the shop where he worked as an assistant; and carefully removed Freda's body from the storage shed, laying it in a nearby lane where it was found early the next day.

After taking the life of Florence Little, Jones was able not only to inform her mother, who was looking for her daughter after she failed to return home, that she had left his house some time previously, but also to enquire after her son, who was ill at that time. Again Jones assisted the police with their search. When Florence's body was found in the loft of his house, he informed his father that he was not responsible.

Jones was described by the counsel for the Crown as callous, with a heart of stone, 'devoid of pity, sympathy and compassion'.[33] A newspaper report of the trial noted his rapid changes of temperament and how he laughed when his mother wept after his initial acquittal.[34]

Norwood East, in a report that he wrote about Jones in November 1923, considered Jones's sexual development and noted that Jones fantasized about girls 'certainly during masturbation' and that 'all his desires seem to have been associated with girls considerably junior in age'. During his consensual sexual relationship with the daughter of his employers,

Jones had asked her to spit in his mouth. Norwood East came to the view that if Jones were willing to engage in 'prolonged mental analysis', this might reveal a connection between spitting and Jones's sexual experience. Norwood East also considered that 'both murders were due to sadism', and that 'the sex impulse [in Jones] has developed in an irregular manner'; specifically, that 'the manifestation of power over a woman, normal in the sexual act has in him developed to an abnormal extent'. As a result 'the highest [sexual] gratification' comes when 'accompanied by cruelty'. Norwood East was particularly certain that 'the spitting should be regarded as a sadistic manifestation'.

Ten years later, Norwood East commented that he had no reason to alter his opinion on Jones that his release would involve a risk to the public, though when he had served twenty years it might be that such risk could be acceptable. In 1936 Norwood East was more cautious, writing in the Prison Commissioners' file that he would view Jones's release with very grave anxiety and that he would not be surprised if he was convicted of another sex murder after release.

In contrast, Paterson was a continual advocate for Jones. For example, he commented on the Prison Commissioners' file in 1929 that Jones was a 'wholesome influence among the other young adults', even though in 1927 it had been alleged by an ex-Maidstone prisoner that Jones had entered into a sexual relationship with another prisoner. Paterson also considered in his report of 1940 that Jones was 'as normal now as most fellows of his age', while in 1941 he was even more effusive, recording that 'it has fallen to me to be the only person to be in regular contact with [Jones] since three months after his conviction.' This statement can at best be seen as an exaggeration and at worst as simply untrue. Jones was visited regularly by his parents and other family and friends throughout his sentence and their various successful requests for financial assistance to visit their son are documented within his files. He also received a number of visits from other prison officials and served the majority of his sentence at HMP Maidstone (eighteen years, from January 1923 to July 1941).

As for sadism, Paterson further suggests that there had been no indications of this during his twenty years of imprisonment and that Paterson had 'watched his growth with deep interest, and marvelled at his patience'. At times, apparently without question or prompting, Paterson had experienced Jones speaking of his crimes, punishment and future openly and sensibly, never 'lying or sniffling'. Paterson thought that the war would give Jones his opportunity, so that as 'Harry Jones' he could be specially enlisted in the Royal Engineers, where he would give good service and should, someday, 'be the father of happy children'.

Dissenting Voices

Major Benjamin Grew, the governor of Maidstone, and after the war of HMP Wormwood Scrubs, did not share Paterson's optimism and, like Norwood East, was more guarded in his assessment of Jones. In a report from 1936 Grew stated that

> Jones works very well. He is intelligent and very alert. I have had many talks with him and am convinced that his crime causes him no worry. He is callous but would be the last to admit it. Sad as it may seem I can see no hopeful prospects for Jones in the future. I have watched him carefully in association with other prisoners and come to the conclusion that my opinion of him concurs with that of the Chaplain.

This disagreement related to one prisoner, but there is also contemporary evidence to suggest that there were more fundamental tensions between Paterson and his peers, and his senior staff. The most vociferous of these was Lt Col. Charles Rich, a former governor of HMP Liverpool, who had seen active service in the Boer War and the First World War and who published his autobiography – *Recollections of a Prison Governor* – in 1932, after his retirement. In this he acknowledged that while prison reform had been a 'crying necessity' 30 years previously, 'these days we are wasting much sentiment upon wholly undeserving objects'.[35] Rich believed that 'our Prison Service is – or perhaps I should say, was – the best in the world, but unpractical idealists have messed it up', and that prisons had become the 'idealizations of unpractical visionaries'.[36] He added that

> things might have been different if the Prison Department possessed a few more members who could boast of a little more practical experience of governing large prisons. There is not at present a single Commissioner who has governed a prison . . . it is all very well to go deeply into the reformative side, but the disciplinary side, too, is all-important.[37]

Rich suggested that these 'unpractical' idealists and visionaries, who had no experience of governing prisons, had come to prominence after the retirement of Sir Evelyn Ruggles-Brise, the chair of the Prison Commission in 1921. Paterson had become a commissioner in 1922.

Rich does not name Paterson within his autobiography, but in order to ensure that no one could be mistaken as to the object of his censure, he describes a story of how all the 'soft, sloppy, "sob-stuff" has crept in and is slowly but surely ruining the chances of effecting reformation not only among borstal boys but among criminals and offenders in general'. He recounts how young men were being recruited into the prison service from universities and had invariably prepared themselves for this work by volunteering in boy's clubs, or at summer camps that catered for offenders. Rich recounted how at one summer camp

> one young man, who habitually walked about in a rather tight and scanty bathing-suit as his sole covering, was far too familiar with the lads to my way of thinking . . . possibly his views coincided with those of the high official, who was by this time more or less running the Prison Service, or at all events appeared to be.[38]

To make it clear who his target was, Rich recounted how one new prison governor that he had worked with – a 'sterling good fellow' – had had to go through a 'terrible ordeal' at a boy's club 'somewhere in Bermondsey, if my recollection serves me' before joining the prison service. As Rich described it, the governor had tried to find his host at the boy's club and 'he presently descried him, however, crawling about on his hands and knees with small urchins swarming all over him'.[39]

In *Across the Bridges* Paterson had described for his readers that across the river from the Strand 'there lies a quarter of London where it is not possible to find a good tailor or a big hotel', and that 'on these streets poverty has set its seal, and its many problems have sunk their tangled roots deep into the life of a people.'[40] Given these circumstances, Paterson suggested that 'it is probable that by the age of twenty his character will have set, tendencies have hardened into qualities, and the manner of the man will be determined',[41] which also helps to bring some focus on why Paterson was so concerned with developing the Borstal system. In a later passage Paterson was at pains to remind his readers that 'the boy is only a beginner, and stands at the most critical stage of his life.'[42] Above all, he believed that 'crime and the recruiting sergeant draw upon much the same class in South London ... for the army will make a man of him, if he serves long enough, but prison may dash all his hopes.'[43]

Even so, Paterson did have his supporters. Lilian Barker, the governor of Aylesbury, took the view that, as far as borstal was concerned, there had been too many governors prepared to administer repressive regimes; they had used the strait-jacket as a punishment far too regularly, for example. Consequently she created 'a place of creative hobbies, open air activity in the grounds ... [as she] shared Paterson's faith in the value of constant activity and the absorption of morality from staff and the group'.[44]

Penal Policy Tensions

As I have begun to reveal, during the interwar years there were various tensions bubbling beneath the surface of the day-to-day operation of the penal system. Sometimes these were those that are inherent between those who claim operational experience of managing prisons and those who do not. These tensions were made all the more acute by attempting to impose the recommendations of London-based prison commissioners, who lacked those practical experiences but nonetheless attempted to impose these views on to those who were running prisons up and down the country.

However, there were other tensions too, and these were of a much more fundamental basis. Put simply, there seems to have been a philosophical disagreement about the direction in which the Prison Service was travelling. On the one hand there were those like Paterson, who were interested in how prison could contribute to the reform of the individual, especially those who had offended while they were still young men; as Rich unfairly puts it, the 'soft, sloppy, sob-stuff'. On the other hand, Rich, who was likely to have been even more condemnatory given that he had retired and therefore did not feel constrained by Home Office protocol, probably represented the views of many of his peers, who had to run prisons based on this type of philosophical reasoning but still had years of service ahead of them. In this light we should question why Rich didn't name Paterson in his autobiography. Was this at the insistence of his publisher, or did Rich believe that by lambasting a serving prison commissioner he might simply cause trouble for his friends – including the 'sterling good fellow' – who were still acting as prison governors?

This particular question about whether prison could reform the individual also characterized the relationship between those who came from a medical and/or psychological background and those who had other professional expertise. In other words, there was a tension not only about whether prison could reform the individual, but also concerning how to effect that reform. This tension was not one-dimensional. Norwood East, for example, may have been impressed by psychoanalysis, and optimistic about what psychotherapy could achieve: it could have been a philosophical means of countering contemporary eugenicist enthusiasts. Nevertheless, throughout his career Norwood East sought to 'counter the barrage of deterministic thought from the pens of recent converts to psychoanalysis. Given his official position and his deference to the law he could do nothing other than to espouse free will.'[45]

So Norwood East's optimism about psychotherapy had limits and in his analysis of Jones we begin to see what these limits were. For example, he believed that psychoanalysis 'with its present uncertainties . . . would probably be doomed to failure', especially as Jones had showed no remorse for his crimes, or expressed any real wish to change or, as East puts it, 'no apparent desire for any alteration in his condition'. Indeed we would now term Jones a 'high risk' offender. East goes as far as to suggest that providing Jones with psychoanalysis might simply provide 'a false sense of security' – a security which could only be tested 'by the enormously hazardous experiment of releasing the prisoner'. As a result, East wanted Jones to be employed with the aim of making him 'a skilful tradesman'; Jones was to be encouraged to 'stimulate his efforts and arouse in him some ambition' and to that end 'carpentry and particularly cabinet making appear particularly suitable'. If that were not possible, East thought that Jones should be given mechanical or engineering work.

Paterson, on the other hand, believed that his own individualized – and perhaps idiosyncratic – humanitarian approach towards Jones had proved more beneficial. As the editor of his papers has described it, Paterson had 'faith in the ultimate value of the most apparently worthless individual, and was possessed of a greater power of evoking the best from the worst than is given to most men'.[46] And, while acknowledging that he was a 'layman' on the subject, Paterson also went to great lengths to normalize Jones's sadism and, echoing views that he had expressed in *Across the Bridges*, believed that the army would 'make a man of him'. He did not have the same doubts as Norwood East that Jones could be successfully reintegrated back into the community.

Assessment of Paterson's Assessments

What are we to make of Harold Jones, and how he came to be viewed by the various prison governors, prison commissioners and doctors that encountered him? How should we interpret the fact that he was eventually released in 1941 without ever undergoing any rigorous assessment of, or treatment for, his offending behaviour? Nor had he expressed any explanation or even regret for his crimes. However, we should remember that Britain was at war and that Jones had served twenty years, which was the prevailing tariff of that time for those under the age of sixteen who had murdered. So, at this time, there would have to have been good reasons for keeping Jones in prison for longer. And if someone would not talk in detail about their offence, then greater focus was placed on their prison behaviour and their attitude towards those in authority. In both these areas Jones clearly came across as an 'ideal prisoner'. Finally, the expectation would also have been that Jones would serve in the armed forces (though there is no verification that this actually occurred). It was argued that Jones would benefit from the structure of army life and being given the opportunity to prove himself, as well as serving his country.

However, what we also know is that despite twenty years being the prevailing tariff and the norm for this period for those under sixteen convicted of murder, and even considering that structured risk assessments are only now a critical component when indeterminate sentence prisoners are considered for release on licence by the parole board, there was a notable number of influential people throughout the 1930s who considered Jones to be a significant risk to the public and potentially a dangerous repeat offender.

Yet Jones, in his applications for release in 1940 and 1941, had an influential advocate in Paterson, who had also strongly supported him throughout his sentence. Even though Paterson acknowledged his lack of medical or psychological training, he nevertheless attempted to explain away Jones's offending behaviour by likening it to the actions of public schoolboys. It seems fair to conclude that Paterson – even allowing for our growing and more recent understanding of the behaviour of sexual sadists – went too far in his reports. He should have been able to deduce, especially from institutional reports that had been written about Jones and from the accounts of his trial which were on the official file, that Jones was cold and calculating, and that his offences were extremely violent. He should also have been able to note Jones's lies to the police and the sexual nature of his offences, and to have been able to make some assessment of why Jones had become involved in the searches for his two victims. Finally it also seems clear that Paterson failed to consider Jones's lack of empathy for his victims and the actual pain that he had inflicted on the girls, their families and the community in which he lived.

It is of little comfort that Paterson, in his comment that Jones 'has throughout that long period been under close and constant supervision, but neither in manner, speech or habit has anything been disclosed', gave us an indication of how sexual sadists – whether from the 1920s and '30s, or more recently – behave while in custody. In short, sexual sadists will conceal their true feelings and, given the nature of their personalities and backgrounds, do not display conduct disorders during periods of imprisonment. As a consequence it is accepted that this makes assessment of such offenders difficult, especially if those making the assessment are imbued with an implicit belief in the goodness of human nature, the possibility of change without treatment or even the need to explore and discuss what promoted the offending behaviour. While this was the case for Paterson, it was not so for Norwood East, nor for some interwar prison governors.

Cavalier not Saint

Paterson was cavalier in his advocacy for the release of Jones. Put simply, his was an over-optimistic assessment of Jones, given that there was no evidence of change or reduction in his risk factors. We now know that a failure to see evidence of these changes would make it difficult for someone like Jones to be released under our current penal arrangements, but even allowing for historical differences in relation to the state of knowledge about sexual sadists, Paterson's view seems remarkably charitable. Indeed, others at that time would also contend that Paterson was over-optimistic in his whole approach to penal reform, and in how he considered that prisons should be managed. Of course, his defenders would argue that this was not the case and that what he did was to begin the process of humanizing the official approach to imprisonment, although concerning Jones and in his advocacy for his release, it is hard to escape the conclusion that for Paterson the ends justified his means.

What does all of this tell us more broadly about the work of the penal system during the interwar years? In thinking about Jones and his eventual release from prison, we begin to see something of the reality that all prisoners at all times have to encounter: that the power to fundamentally affect every aspect of your life is in the hands of others. Prisoners are told when to get up and when to go to bed, what sort of work they should do and with whom they should associate. Their behaviour is watched and assessed on a regular basis, and reports are written about them which can alter the course of their institutional life and sometimes whether they will be released. Some prison officials will make decisions that might seem perverse and unfair or, at other times, generous – even kind – but no matter what the outcome, what happens to that prisoner and shapes his future is determined by someone else.

Perhaps the oddest thing about the decisions related to Jones is that so many of the officials actually knew who he was and had at one time met him. In some senses he became a lightning rod for two different but equally powerful views about whether prisoners could change their behaviour, and what would make them do so. Prisoners today, reading about Harold Jones, would no doubt shake their heads in disbelief that so many senior prison staff had actually spoken to the prisoner about whom they had to take a view as to his suitability – or otherwise – for release. This was the real benefit of falling prison numbers: there was the time and space to get to know who was being locked up and how they were progressing during their sentence.

Falling prison numbers were not to last. Even so, we should not get carried away and imagine that being a prisoner during the interwar period had any fewer 'pains of confinement' for the prisoner, or that prison officials – whether influenced by Paterson or Norwood East – were suddenly blessed with criminological insight that had been denied to their predecessors.

FIVE

From World War to World Cup, 1945–1966

What a miserable failure, then, has been that
of the so-called prison reformers.
Rupert Croft-Cooke, *The Verdict of You All* (1955)

H
istories of prisons and criminal justice policy in the period following the Second World War largely concentrate on government
White Papers and Criminal Justice Acts. The Criminal Justice Act
of 1948, for example, the first major piece of legislation about criminal
justice after the war, abolished penal servitude, whipping and hard labour;
the Prison Rules – introduced for the first time in 1949 – suggested that
prison existed to help prisoners lead a 'good and useful life'; the Prison
Act of 1952 laid the foundations of our current arrangements within
prisons; the much-lauded White Paper *Penal Practice in a Changing
Society* of 1959, which attempted to bring the penal system into line with
post-war social circumstances, would heavily influence the Criminal
Justice Act of 1961; and HMP Grendon, still the only prison in Europe to
operate wholly as a therapeutic community, opened in 1962. In short, these
various initiatives have led to the period often being seen as an era of
reform, welfare and rehabilitation. Indeed, the criminologist Andrew
Rutherford uses the title of a Dickens novel to characterize this period
in our penal history as 'Great Expectations', and therefore at odds with
what was to happen in the 1970s, which he sees as 'Bleak House'.[1]

Yet this was not how these so-called changes were viewed on the
ground by prisoners experiencing them. Rupert Croft-Cooke, who had
been imprisoned in 1953 for gross indecency, argued that we should
ignore the 'lofty sentiments' and 'high minded claims of Government
White Papers about prisons', which he saw as being characterized as the
product of 'cold cynicism'.[2] He quotes one prisoner that he encountered
at HMP Wormwood Scrubs complaining: '"It's all in the Criminal Justice
Act of 1948", he used to say, smiling. "They can't do these things. Wait till
I'm released. I'll get 'em."'[3] So too Peter Wildeblood, who like Croft-Cooke

had fallen foul of the laws against homosexuality and had to serve time at HMP Wormwood Scrubs, remembered going to the House of Lords on his release to listen to Lord Mancroft, under-secretary of state at the Home Office between 1954 and 1957, who defended the current state of the penal system on behalf of the government. Wildeblood likened Mancroft to a 'car salesman', although

> His purpose this evening, was not to sell their Lordships a Jaguar or a Rolls Royce; it was to sell them an account of prison admin- istration so grossly ill-informed that I could scarcely prevent myself unscrewing the nearest brass gargoyle and throwing it at his brilliantined head.[4]

So we should be careful to balance our understanding of those devel- opments that took place after the war, and so too should we remember that it was in this period that 'English exceptionalism' took hold; in other words, when the penal policies of England and Wales (and to a lesser extent Scotland) started to move away from those of mainland Europe. This is perhaps best symbolized by the failure of Paterson's 'Howard Houses' to survive the war; instead, in their place, the Criminal Justice Act of 1948 introduced Detention Centres. These new institutions for young people below the age of 21 were designed, according to the Labour home secre- tary James Chuter Ede, because there was a 'type of offender to whom it appears necessary to give a short but sharp reminder that he is getting into ways that will inevitably land him in disaster'.[5] These were the origins of the 'short, sharp, shock' of Margaret Thatcher's Conservative government in the 1980s – a time which saw a different approach being adopted by the French government of François Mitterrand, which launched a programme of social investment aimed specifically at the young people who had rioted throughout the summer of 1981. The French wanted to be seen to be valu- ing their children, rather than inventing new ways to punish them within institutions. Is it too fanciful to imagine that while mainland Europe wanted to make sense of and come to terms with having lived under the jackboot of Nazi occupation – and therefore saw a common bond with those whom it imprisoned – Britain, which had had to stand defiantly and alone, had much less sympathy with those who committed crime and therefore had no hesitation in locking them up? Perhaps we can still see this 'English exceptionalism' more recently in, for example, the astonished public reaction here to the maximum sentence available in Norway – 21 years –

a penalty which was imposed on the Christian fundamentalist terrorist Anders Breivik, who murdered 77 people in 2011.[6]

This chapter considers the post-war period from the perspective of three prisoners in the 1950s who have left accounts of their time at one London prison – HMP Wormwood Scrubs. It compares their recollections and experiences with those of the governor of the prison – Major Benjamin Grew – whom we have previously encountered in his dealings with Harold Jones, and who published his autobiography in 1958. These autobiographies allow us to build up a picture of our post-war penal system, which would see the prison population increase from under 10,000 in 1940 to just under 40,000 by 1970; the number of prisons increase from 40 in 1946 to 73 by 1960; and the number of prison officers increase at more than twice the rate of the increase in the prison population between 1950 and 1980 – an expansionary trend that differs markedly from what happened in Europe.[7] However, I am interested in how prison was experienced as much as I am concerned with what these numbers might tell us about the formal policy rationale that was claimed for the prison system and how this might have been accepted – even championed – by the state. I want to know how staff and prisoners got on; what the food was like; whether there was work and education; and if going to prison actually helped offenders to lead a 'good and useful life'? Was this really an era of reform, or were the same old continuities of punishment still at the forefront of what prison was really like and experienced?

However, before discussing the post-war period, let us consider what prison was like during the war and at the height of the Blitz. Governor Grew, for example, in his autobiography, simply titled *Prison Governor*, offers us an unique insight of wartime life in prison for those who were not pardoned by the state and had to complete their sentences inside, or who were conscientious objectors, and of the staff who had to administer and manage the penal system at this most difficult of times.

Wandsworth and the Blitz

Grew provides us with a number of interesting anecdotes about the organization of prisons during the war, and for example, advises that at the outbreak of hostilities in September 1939 he had he received a 'coded telegram' advising him that any prisoner serving less than three months had to be pardoned immediately.[8] At this time he had been serving as governor of HMP Durham and, as he puts, 'Durham Prison has never been a happier place', since just under 200 men were immediately discharged. However, their places in Durham were taken by prisoners serving long sentences at HMPs Liverpool and Manchester – described by Grew as 'danger zones' – and their evacuation to what was seen as a safer place to serve their sentence caused Grew and his staff problems. For example, he noted that many prisoners wanted to use the opportunity of their evacuation to play 'childish larks', and that 'the worst elements among them were openly violent.'

In any event, Grew was not to stay at HMP Durham for much longer, as he was soon to be posted to HMP Wandsworth in London. Seemingly in preparing him for this transfer, Alexander Paterson – who would see out the war with the rest of the Prison Commission in Oxford – had rather oddly suggested to him that 'London will be either the safest place in the country, or the most hellish.' Events soon proved that it was hellish, and Grew himself wondered 'how the prisoners would react, for Wandsworth contained some of London's toughest criminals'. For Grew, it was made all the more problematic because 'the prison staff had been weakened by the call-up, and we were left with the older or less fit younger officers to cope with extra work under the most trying circumstances.' Indeed, Wandsworth was to become the first prison in England to be hit by bombs, and Grew leaves us the following extraordinary account.

As soon as the sirens sounded we followed our normal procedure of evacuating prisoners from some of the workshops to the more substantial parts of the halls which offered pretty solid defence against air attack. One hundred or more men were employed on sewing machines in the basement of A hall, for instance, and they had instructions to take cover in the empty cells only if bombs began to fall. I had just arrived in A Hall to see if all was well when our observers on the roof sent down their warning: 'three enemy planes have been detached from the main foundation and are flying in our direction.'

I immediately gave the order: 'Disperse. Disperse.' There was no panic, for the men had practiced the procedure so many times; they got up from their benches and in an orderly manner hurried for cover to the cells allotted to them.

Hardly had the last man reached his place before there was the whine of bombs winging their way down and then the gigantic roar of explosions which made the earth boil with their rumble.

While the dispersion order was being carried out the blast carried me along some yards, brickwork and masonry crashed down, and there was much choking dust; it was a relief to find that I was still whole. Around me was chaos.

Thankfully no one was seriously injured in this explosion, although Grew noted that it was not so much daylight raids on the prison that caused distress; 'with the coming of night bombing and the blitz, fear and a certain amount of hysteria were only to be expected.' At night, during the Blitz, prisoners remained locked in their cells – except those who acted as fire-watchers – and Grew suggests that many thought that they were being left to 'die like rats in a trap', despite his assurances to him that their thick cell walls provided 'first-class air-raid shelters'.

As Grew's account above suggests, some prisoners also acted as observers and as fire-watchers during an attack, and seemingly this was a position that was eagerly sought after, for it allowed them to get out of their cells at night. This suggests that Grew's assurances about their cells being 'first-class air-raid shelters' fell on deaf ears, although he continued to refuse to unlock their cells, or to consider allowing prisoners to share a cell. His only concession to the understandable fear that many prisoners must have had was to 'talk as loudly and as cheerfully as possible' on his rounds. It is also clear from what he writes that regular drills took place within the prison to prepare for an attack and that the prison was regularly subjected to blackouts. Reflecting on how he had managed the prison during the Blitz, Grew maintains in his autobiography that he was pleased that he had 'stood firm'. No doubt it was this type of personal resolution that resulted in him being awarded a Defence Medal at the end of the war, but his certainty about his decisions would not win him too many friends among the prisoners he would encounter at HMP Wormwood Scrubs.

HMP Wormwood Scrubs: Some Prisoners Speak Out

HMP Wormwood Scrubs was built entirely by convict labour between 1875 and 1891, on 20 acres of scrubland in West London that had been purchased in 1874. Despite the relatively isolated location which its name suggests, there were at the time local objections to the building of the jail.[9] Edmund du Cane, the first chair of the Prison Commission – in whose honour the road where the prison is located is named – designed the prison. At the time it was a 'new model design' consisting of four individual cell blocks (named A, B, C and D) containing a total of 1,380 cells. The prison's impressive chapel was completed in 1892; it is sometimes known as 'the little Cathedral'. Around 200 prisoners from Millbank Prison worked on the construction during the day and lived in huts at night. The prisoners were not paid for their labour, as Grew notes with some relish, other than 'an extra pint of cocoa a day, and for that they had to work on Sundays too!'[10] The entrance to the prison – which has now been listed – has plaques dedicated to the penal reformers John Howard and Elizabeth Fry, and during the war, after the prisoners had been evacuated to HMP Wandsworth, the prison housed MI5.

Grew spent eleven years as governor at HMP Wormwood Scrubs, where he was first posted in February 1945. He suggested that he was pleased at this posting because the prison had both a 'more hopeful approach to penal problems, and [a] feeling of cloistered serenity'.[11] During his time as governor there were nearly 73,000 receptions into the prison, including three who wrote about their time at the jail: Peter Wildeblood, Peter Baker and Rupert Croft-Cooke.

Autobiographies of serving or former prisoners are a staple of the 'true crime' genre and as such can trace their origins back to the picaresque novels of the eighteenth century, the exemplary confessions contained within the Newgate Calendar and even execution broadsheet pamphlets, which were distributed on 'hanging days'.[12] They often reflect the authors' views about prison based on their previous experiences outside of the jail. In other words, accounts of time spent in prison by former MPs are always going to be different from those who write about their time inside as if it was merely a professional hazard. Criminologists sometimes refer to these autobiographical categories as the accounts of 'cons' and 'straights'.[13] A 'con' is someone who had a criminal lifestyle prior to entering jail, while a 'straight' account is written by those authors who never dreamed that one day they would end up inside. By and large, 'straights' want to express their surprise about who and what they find in prison, while 'cons' want to demonstrate how their expectations of jail – and those who do the jailing – are merely continuations of the reality of their lives, which up to the point of their incarceration have been dominated by other authority figures, many of whom were less than helpful or even corrupt.

Despite the popularity of prisoner autobiographies, these sources are rarely included in any evaluation of imprisonment, and there remains

Wormwood Scrubs, London, prisoners and guards at the turn of the 19th and 20th centuries, and exterior view, 1960.

Wormwood Scrubs, 1960.

an official scepticism about the veracity of what these books describe. Their stories of violence, corruption, poor staff–prisoner relations, trafficking, suicide and self-harm are seen as partial and incomplete, selected to suit the commercially driven dictates of the publishing industry and then skilfully edited into an 'artful enterprise'. In short, prisoner autobiographies are usually seen as untrustworthy.

However, both 'cons' and 'straights' challenge the official picture of prison, which has often been carefully constructed for wider public consumption, presenting what happens inside as rational, clear, consistent and in the public interest. Often nothing could be further from the truth, and prisoner autobiographies create an alternative way of seeing and understanding the reality of how prison is experienced by those who are being imprisoned. Of course, we have to consume their contents with care, as we would with other sources, but given that all three of our prisoners were imprisoned at roughly the same time, within the same institution, we can perhaps give their observations greater weight, especially if what they describe is consistent and corroborated within their different accounts.

All three of our prisoners are 'straights', although there is an irony in using this description for Rupert Croft-Cooke, who was imprisoned for nine months in 1953, and for Peter Wildeblood, who got an eighteen-month sentence in 1954. Both were highly educated, literate, professional, middle-class men who were imprisoned for being gay at a time when homosexuality was still against the law. Peter Baker was MP for South Norfolk at the time of his imprisonment in 1954 for fraud, and served for the longest period of the three. He was imprisoned not only at HMP Wormwood Scrubs, but also at HMP Leyhill. He published his account of his time inside in 1961.[14] So we cannot claim that Baker, Wildeblood or Croft-Cooke were typical of the prison population at the time – auto-biographies by 'cons' are still relatively rare[15] – but they do offer us a way of getting on to the landings of HMP Wormwood Scrubs and determining whether the claims that were being made for the prison specifically, and imprisonment more generally, were fair or, at best, partial.

Three broad areas are touched upon in each autobiography: the routine of and regime within HMP Wormwood Scrubs; relationships between staff and prisoners, including their views on Governor Grew; and the authors' opinions about imprisonment more generally. The first of these areas encompasses a variety of issues and observations about different aspects of life in the jail from food, education and exercise to 'slopping out', and how tobacco, and sometimes sex, acted as an informal currency. For example, Baker thought that the food in the prison in 1954 was 'not fit for pigs to eat', and Croft-Cooke commented that it was 'totally uneatable'. So bad was his diet that Baker lost 3 stone (19 kg) in the first six months

The entrance to Wormwood Scrubs in 2013.

of his sentence. He also thought that exercise at the prison was worse than that which he had experienced in a German prisoner-of-war camp, which had been 'less formalized than the deadening sordid uniformity of exercise at Wormwood Scrubs in 1954'. Baker described how prisoners taking exercise became a 'grey crocodile of men which encircled the exercise yard ... the grey-clad men, in twos, who marched stolidly around made up a weird mime of the retreat from Moscow'. Given their recent wartime experiences it is perhaps unsurprising that all three authors often used military metaphors, and Wildeblood thought that HMP Wormwood Scrubs was run 'as a kind of caricature of military life'.

Baker described how he 'learned ... that tobacco ruled the prison world. It was both wealth and power.' As such tobacco became 'the only universal medium of exchange, and its possession enabled the owner to demand almost any service from his fellow prisoners.' According to Baker, these services included

> All sorts of homosexual practices, with a standard scale of rates, and there were, I understand, at least three prisoners charging customers half an ounce a time for a gammarouche. This was one of the few facts reliably reported to me that I did not put to practical test.

Croft-Cooke provides a measure of corroboration when he assures his readers that the 'only thing that shocked me at Wormwood Scrubs was to hear men of all ages openly boasting of their habits of masturbation'. As Baker put it, 'to pretend that no homosexuality, no masturbation and no emotive release could be found in a long-term prison would be hypocritical.'

All three men described the process of 'slopping out' – a practice that was not to end until the 1990s – whereby prisoners were required to empty the contents of their chamber pots, which were kept in their cells for use overnight, into a central sluice in the morning. Baker describes this most vividly:

> I righted my chamber-pot, put back its lid and went out to get rid of what remained of its contents. The recess was in the middle of the landing, only two cells from mine. The queue of prisoners waiting to use it reached almost to my cell-door. The smell from it was heavy and all-pervading. As I approached the

recess itself, it was almost overpowering . . . The recess itself was a large cavity between the cells, in which were a lavatory and a large sink. Over the sink was a tap, and at the bottom of it was a large gulleyed wastepipe through which all excreta had eventually to flow. The stench, as pot after pot was emptied of its contents from the night into this rugged whirlpool of plumbing made me retch. When it was my time to empty and clean mine, the sink was already stagnant, as the outflow was stopped up. I held my breath as I took my turn and turned thankfully back to my cell.

This process was clearly bad at the best of times, but when the 'rugged whirlpool of plumbing' broke down for any reason it became that much worse. If this happened prisoners had no place to deposit their excreta and resorted to throwing the contents of their chamber pots out of their windows into the exercise yard below. In more modern penal parlance, this is known as a 'shit parcel'.

As Baker describes in the passage quoted above, he had to 'right' his chamber pot because he claimed that an officer had deliberately kicked it on entering his cell. This small incident is indicative of the general issue of the sometimes fraught relationship between staff and prisoners, and each of the three authors had something to say about this. Wildeblood, for example, thought that it was 'impossible to speak freely' to anyone in authority at the prison and that 'the word of a prisoner is never accepted against that of an officer'; and Croft-Cooke believed that 'the prisoner has no remedy against the tyrannical or malicious screw. No appeal to higher authority will help him for no Governor will believe his word against that of an officer.' Nor did they believe that it was possible to appeal outside of the prison to the Home Office, and Baker described the process of petitioning as 'largely a delusion'. All three prisoners had wanted access to notepaper and books, but this proved to be virtually impossible and resulted in Baker writing 'surreptitiously in corners and under blankets at night, and the notebooks I used – forty-six of them – had to be smuggled in and smuggled out again as I filled them up'. Clearly what was happening inside our prisons was at this time being kept hidden from public view both by the deliberate policy of internal rules and regulations and more illegitimately.

Baker, for example, also recounts a very revealing personal anecdote about contacting people outside of the prison. After his conviction he had to write to the Speaker of the House of Commons resigning his seat, which he did on 2 December 1954. Several days later, he was called into the governor's office. Major Grew explained that the Speaker had been expecting a letter, but that this had not arrived. Baker assured the governor that he had indeed written such a letter, but on hearing this Major Grew coughed, and then said, 'Yes. But – er – some little accident must have prevented or delayed its delivery, so I suggest that you send another copy. I'll authorize a further special letter for the purpose.' Still not quite understanding what had happened to his letter, Baker left the governor's office and was then taken to the office of the censor, who advised him that while letters to MPs were recorded as being posted, 'We then tear them up . . . we destroy them. You'd be surprised at the amount of trouble it saves.'

This control over communication with those outside of the prison inevitably allowed practices to develop within the prison that were unsatisfactory. Baker, for example, was concerned with staff brutality towards prisoners, and described how difficult younger prisoners were often subjected to a 'severe and scientific beating up'. He suggested that staff at HMP Wormwood Scrubs 'were experts in giving severe beatings-up without leaving undue traces and breaking any bones', but concluded that 'you cannot apply two codes of justice, two punishments to the same case. You cannot use both the law of the land and the law of the jungle. This is unfortunately what is happening today.' This would not be the last time in the prison's history that staff at the jail would be accused of unlawfully using violence against prisoners.

Did Major Grew's cough indicate that he knew exactly what had happened to Baker's letter to the Speaker, but that he was prepared to turn a blind eye to what had taken place? All three prisoners were less than enthusiastic about Major Grew. Croft-Cooke, while he recognized that Grew was 'a man of breeding', maintained that he had 'not sufficient knowledge of what went on in his prison'. This conclusion rather lets Grew off the hook, which neither Wildeblood nor Baker were prepared to do. Baker described Grew's 'mania for security' and thus compared his tenure at HMP Wormwood Scrubs to 'the Dark Ages'. Wildeblood goes further, and while noting in passing that Major Grew had never visited prisoners in their cells, he concluded that it was Grew's leadership that was at fault and that he should 'not escape criticism . . . it is generally accepted that the Scrubs, of which he had been in charge for many years, is the worst prison to which first offenders can be sent.' Wildeblood went further and maintained that there did not seem to me to be the slightest attempt by the authorities to discover, understand or grapple with the problems presented by the 1,000 individuals in their charge; the men were simply herded together like sheep for whatever period the judges had been pleased to allot to them.

Here Wildeblood is not just attacking the circumstances that he found in HMP Wormwood Scrubs, but commenting more generally about the nature of imprisonment. Far from helping prisoners to lead a 'good and useful life' – the new purpose for imprisonment – Wildeblood suggested that 'men do change in prison, but seldom for the better'. In his view 'no attempt was made to fit [prisoners] for life "outside". The work they did in the shops was monotonous and almost useless to the point of view of a future career.' Wildeblood concluded that prison was characterized by 'boredom, squalor, the sheer nagging hopelessness of it all'. Croft-Cooke thought that 'in prison a man ceases to live, in anything but the organic sense. He merely waits, lets time pass over him, remains supine and spiritually comatose until enough months or years have passed by.' So, too, Baker thought that there was a 'constant pressure' exercised over prisoners by those in authority: '"play along with us," is their attitude, "and we will make things easy for you. Make a nuisance of yourself, and you'll be sorry".' Croft-Cooke agreed and suggested that 'a prisoner who just rubs along without asking questions and without sticking his neck out is ideal. It's a very easy thing to do.'

Baker seems to have stuck his neck out on many occasions and as a result was regularly in trouble. He suggests that as a consequence there had developed 'a strange duel between me and Governor Grew', who started to infer that Baker was suffering from hallucinations and that he had a 'neurotic condition'. On the other hand, Baker believed that what he had encountered inside allowed him to conclude more generally that 'as the days, the months and the years wore on I was to learn of the pointlessness, the weariness and the monotony of a seven-year sentence . . . I was to learn of the wicked waste of time and opportunity.'

All of this suggests that far from prison helping those that it increasingly locked up to lead a 'good and useful life', there were continuities of pain and punishment that could be dated back to the Victorian era, if not to the Dark Ages. Indeed Baker offers an interesting example of these continuities when he describes being moved from HMP Wormwood Scrubs with another prisoner to the open prison HMP Leyhill, which involved him catching a train from Paddington Station. The passage is worth quoting in full.

> We were, of course, both dressed in our civilian clothes, and, because we were destined for an open prison, were not hand-cuffed. Nevertheless, our burly and uniformed escort, grouped menacingly around us, made it quite clear to the world that we were apprehended felons. In addition, I was carrying all my prison property in a pillow-case which the authorities had generously provided. Although, therefore, we tried to assume the normally sanguine attitude of seasoned travellers as we crossed the dias to the platform, I was personally very conscious that I must cut a furtive and fugitive figure to the wide free world beyond our encircling guards. Then, just as we had reached the middle of the vast platformage and were like children in the frightening farthest-from-all-sides centre of a play-pen, a rasping voice sounded right across the station.
>
> 'That's Baker.'
>
> I could not believe my ears. It was two years since my case, and eighteen months since all the major hurly-burly of publicity had died down. Yet this hideous voice of recognition – it was cer-tainly not the voice of a friend – sounded certain, immediate and irrefutable.
>
> I glanced unhappily in its direction. Her two male compan-ions were following her arm, and most of the travellers around us had stopped to look at us.
>
> 'Yes' she repeated her corncrake's cry, 'that's Baker. You know, the man who swindled all those banks. The forger fellow.'
>
> I could only just hear her companions' reply.
>
> 'You mean the politician, Peter Baker?'
>
> She laughed.
>
> 'Politician?' she bellowed. 'He wasn't fit to govern the Gorbals.'

All of this is reminiscent of Wilde's description of what had happened to him at Clapham Junction station in the 1890s. Unlike Baker, Wilde had been in prison clothes and had been handcuffed, but Wilde's sug-gestion that he had felt like a 'grotesque object' which had allowed the 'jeering mob' that had surrounded him to laugh at him echoes the experi-ence of Baker 60 years later at Paddington Station. Baker – just like Wilde

– remained a 'furtive and fugitive figure' to members of the public; an object of fun and ridicule that was in sharp contrast to how he had previously been viewed. It is also interesting that both Baker and Wilde immediately lost weight on being sent to prison; neither was complimentary about the work that they were expected to perform; they were equally scathing about the more general purpose of imprisonment; and they were less than impressed by some of the governors and staff that they met and who had power over them. All of this suggests that not much had changed in 60 years, and that Croft-Cooke's lament – 'what a miserable failure, then, has been that of the so-called prison reformers' – might not be too far from the truth.

The Governor's Revenge

Major Grew did not take all of this very public criticism lying down. In his own autobiography, published in 1958 – thus before the publication of Baker's book, although it is clear from what is contained in *Prison Governor* that Grew knew what some of its contents were likely to be – he tried to put the record straight, as he saw it, complaining that the 'severe and vindictive criticism' of an 'articulate few' (he specifically recounts a story related to Baker, but does not name the former MP) could 'be most annoying'. Indeed, Grew suggested that 'There were occasions when I thought nostalgically of service in other Government departments where servants of the public were not as liable to be in the public eye.'[16]

This secrecy is exactly what Grew would have preferred and, if we are to believe Baker, he actively encouraged it, although he hardly needed to have worried. By this time Section 7 of the Prison Act 1952 had invested formal legal authority and administrative status in the governor of every prison, no matter what some annoyingly articulate prisoners might have thought.[17] This Act was in fact a consolidation measure, given that the legal basis of the governor can be traced back to 1839 when the Act for the Better Ordering of Prisons provided that if the persons authorized by law to appoint the gaoler or keeper of any prison 'shall appoint such Keeper by the style of Governor such Governor shall have all the Powers and Duties of the Gaoler or Keeper of that prison; and all Enactments made with regard to the Gaoler or Keeper shall apply to the Governor so appointed.'[18] As one historian has suggested:

The title 'Governor' was associated with the rise in social standing of the occupation; many authorities introduced the term in
an attempt to improve the dignity of the office. It would have
been unthinkable, for example, to sully the sense of moral mis-
sion and social prestige of Millbank or Gloucester Penitentiaries
by giving their chief officials the title of 'gaoler' or even 'keeper'.
'Governor' was evocative of deputizing duties on behalf of higher
authority; an image reminiscent of colonial administration.[19]

Ironically the Act of 1952 goes into much greater detail in defining the
role and authority of the chaplain than the governor, although the Wynn-
Parry Report of 1958 summarized the latter's role as follows:

The Governor is responsible to the [Secretary of State] for everything that goes on inside his establishment. The principal aspects
of his work are the maintenance of security, good order and
discipline; the leadership of those sections of his staff more
closely concerned with the training of the inmates, and the direction of their efforts to this end; the co-ordination of the various
departments within the establishment; the development of useful activity in work, education and recreation; co-operation with
outside bodies such as the education authority and with voluntary agencies and workers; and responsibility, as sub-accounting
officer, for the proper use of public money and property.[20]

In practice it was up to each individual governor how they should interpret
these various duties and how they should go about leading both staff and
prisoners. It is no easy task to create the right ethos and shape the regime
within a prison, and nor should we forget that governors exercise great
power over prisoners on behalf of the state. As one current prison govern-
or has put it, 'prisoners can be segregated, transferred, confined to their cells,
strip-searched, refused physical contact with their families, sentenced to
"additional days" and released temporarily by the governor.'[21] With all of
this in mind, we can turn to Grew's autobiography to see how he decided
to turn this theory into practice as the most senior governor in the prison
service at the time of his retirement in 1956. What type of philosophy had
he used to guide his actions? Where did he find his inspiration?

Grew had joined the Prison Service in 1923 after leaving the army
because of ill health. The army had been very important to him, and if

he hadn't become unwell there seems little doubt that he would have remained within the military. That was not to be, and he was recruited directly by Alexander Paterson – they were both members of the same London club. His first ever posting was as deputy governor at Borstal in Kent. He was later to become governor at HMPs Dartmoor, Shrewsbury, Durham, Maidstone and Wandsworth before eventually serving at HMP Wormwood Scrubs. His approach was characterized by the culture of the army that he had left behind, and his fundamental personal philosophy was 'discipline, I believe, is a fundamental law of nature. We cannot exist as a community without it.' While recognizing that some might find him 'old fashioned', he nonetheless believed that the 'short, sharp smack inflicted after fair warning' was not only just but 'kindest in the long run'. So he supported capital and corporal punishment because, as he put it, 'birching lowers the culprit's dignity and humbles his vanity.' As for capital punishment, he participated in his first execution as governor at HMP Durham, admitting that he was not philosophically worried about overseeing the execution because he believed that this type of punishment was just. He was, however, 'uncertain about its possible effect on myself'. In other words, he wanted to retain control over his emotions; to maintain personal discipline at all times.

Perhaps the most revealing passages in his autobiography relate to slopping out, which also provides us with a way of comparing Grew's approach to imprisonment and his views of prisoners with what had been described by the three men who had been imprisoned by him. After all, they each – from their different vantage points – accepted that this practice did take place. Grew complained that

> Prison sanitation is still at the mercy of unco-operative prisoners, for the many blockings of the pipes that occur are, in my experience, due not so much to the faults of plumbing or to negligence on the part of the staff, but quite simply to the unpleasant habit of a few prisoners who deliberately block the lavatories with old hair-brushes, tins and other articles, solely for the purpose of causing inconvenience.

Thus Grew did not imagine that 'new prisons with modern plumbing' would improve the 'wretchedness of slopping out', as he was convinced that 'some psychopathic types' would block the plumbing there and that 'blocked pipes and smells would still remain a part of prison life'. Indeed, he thought that slopping out could be done 'hygienically', and did not believe that 'the method of having a water closet in each cell [would] offer a lasting cure'.

So, for Grew, the problems related to slopping out were the fault and responsibility of 'psychopaths' who blocked the drains. He does not consider that this process in itself – at the best of times – was degrading for both the staff and especially for the prisoners. This was a process which had made Baker 'retch'. There may well have been prisoners who deliberately blocked the drains, but Grew dwells on this possibility rather than considering other, more civilized processes which might have seen prisoners being given access to toilets in the cells – sometimes known as 'integral sanitation'. In fact, he did not think that this was a solution at all: 'it is up to the prisoners themselves.'

In short, Grew's prison philosophy was all about discipline for the staff, himself and especially for the prisoners, who were all to be held individually responsible for their actions. Of course, if you can hold someone personally responsible for their actions, it is much easier to birch or to hang them. If we add to this the complaints that Wildeblood, Croft-Cooke and Baker all made that the word of a prisoner was never accepted over that of a member of staff, then perhaps we can begin to glimpse the reality of Wildeblood's conclusion that the prison was run as a 'kind of caricature of the military life', and for Baker remained in the 'Dark Ages'. For them prison was part of civil society and as such, especially for men such as Wildeblood and Croft-Cooke, old attitudes, ideas and cultures had to be challenged.

Three Escapes

In some ways the spat between Grew and his three former prisoners might be seen as a storm in a penal teacup. After all, their disagreements hardly penetrated public consciousness and they were certainly not enough to cause anyone to fundamentally reconsider the purpose of imprisonment. Inside prisons, governors supported their staff and, by and large, the staff supported their governors, united in the face of criticism from prisoners below. Prisons and the people who managed them were largely indifferent to public opinion, especially as they were able to keep much of what happened inside secret. What is more, the Home Office and its politicians and civil servants seemed to have confidence in the Prison Service's abilities to manage what happened inside, to the extent that one criminologist has described how the penal establishment became in the 1950s a 'unified, exclusive, bureaucratic organization in which the state itself had confidence'.[22] All of this was aided by the abolition of the Prison Commission in 1963, which meant that the management of prisons became a responsibility of the Prison Department within the Home Office. Prisons were largely uncontroversial and their operation non-political and, because they were remote from public view, the Prison Service could basically do as it pleased. The public had been almost totally excluded. This was all about to change and once again HMP Wormwood Scrubs was at the heart of the story.

George Blake pleaded guilty at the Old Bailey on 3 May 1961 to five counts under Section 1 of the Official Secrets Act of 1911, and was sentenced to a total of 42 years' imprisonment – at the time, the longest non-life sentence imposed on any prisoner. On sentencing Blake the Lord Chief Justice stated that 'your case is one of the worst that can be envisaged in times of peace', and later in dismissing his appeal against sentence, the Court of Appeal argued that the severity of the sentence was justified by a 'threefold purpose. It was intended to be punitive, it was designed and calculated to deter others, and it was meant to be a safeguard to this country.'[23]

Blake had worked for the Special Operations Executive and MI6 during the Second World War. After hostilities had ended, he had been posted to Korea, where he was tasked with setting up a network of agents. He was captured by the North Koreans and imprisoned for three years. It was during his imprisonment that he was 'turned' into a Communist, and on his return to Britain he started to leak information about British and American operations to the KGB. He was exposed as a double agent in 1961 by the Polish defector Michael Goleniewski. Blake was said to have betrayed as many as 400 agents, many of whom died as a result.[24] He was initially on remand at HMP Brixton before being transferred to HMP Wormwood Scrubs.

Two years later, on 8 August 1963, the 'Great Train Robbery' took place when a Glasgow–London mail train was stopped near Cheddington, Buckinghamshire, after the robbers – led by Bruce Reynolds – had tampered with the signals. Fifteen men wearing ski masks and helmets then boarded the train, struck the train driver – Jack Mills – over the head and grabbed 120 bags of money, which contained £2.6 million in used bank notes. It is estimated that today their haul would be worth about £40 million.[25] The gang, which included Charles Wilson and Ronald

Biggs, then took cover in a hideout in Leatherslade Farm, which was some 20 miles from where they had held up the train. The police launched a manhunt, but the gang fled from the farm before the police arrived. Nonetheless, they left a great deal of incriminating evidence and nine days after the robbery Wilson was the first to be arrested and charged. By January 1964 the police had gathered enough evidence to bring charges against twelve of the gang at Aylesbury Crown Court. Three months later, eleven of the twelve received sentences of between twenty and 30 years' imprisonment, while the twelfth – solicitor John Wheater, who had obtained the farm as a hideout – was given a sentence of three years. In passing sentence, Mr Justice Edmund Davies focused attention on the violence used against Mr Mills and commented, 'let us clear out of the way any romantic notions of daredevilry. This is nothing less than a sordid crime of violence inspired by vast greed.' Wilson was sent to HMP Winson Green in Birmingham and Biggs to HMP Wandsworth to begin their 30-year sentences.

By the time that England had won the World Cup on 30 July 1966, only Blake remained in prison. Wilson had escaped from HMP Winson Green on 12 August 1964 and Biggs from HMP Wandsworth on 8 July 1965. Wilson's escape, coming only four months after receiving his sentence, was particularly unusual. Prison security works on having secure layers through which a prisoner would have to pass before being able to exit into the outside world. The more secure the prison, the more layers there will be in place. Prisons are not organized so as to prevent someone breaking into the prison and then taking the prisoner out with them, which was what happened in Wilson's case. An unknown number of his accomplices scaled the prison's walls and, while the night patrol officer was in the prison kitchen getting porridge ready for breakfast, his colleague was knocked down, bound and gagged. Wilson's accomplices were able to locate him in the prison because he had been placed on the escape list, which meant that he had to leave his clothes on a chair outside his cell at night. Even more worryingly, his accomplices were able to move freely within the prison, since they had keys. These keys were not carried by the night patrol officers, which therefore indicated that there had been internal collusion with Wilson's accomplices and that there had been what is known as a 'key compromise'. It was later established that a copy had been taken of the prison's master key. As one former prison governor has put it, 'It was clearly an inside job.'[26]

After Wilson's escape, three prison officers stood guard outside Biggs's cell at night, and so seriously did the prison take the possibility that he might escape that Biggs complained to his MP about the security conditions under which he was serving his sentence. There were some 50 prisoners on the escape list in the prison at this time and they took their exercise on the yard in two groups, always at the same time, either in the morning or in the afternoon. The exercise yard could be viewed from nearby residential accommodation. Biggs managed to escape after a gang parked a furniture van alongside the perimeter wall and then threw two ladders into the exercise yard. The four officers supervising the exercise period raised the alarm, but other prisoners prevented them from stopping Biggs and four others climbing the ladders and scaling the wall. His escape was completed in about two minutes. Biggs first fled to Australia and then to Brazil, but he voluntarily returned to England in 2001 and was eventually given compassionate release in August 2009 – the day before his eightieth birthday.

The 'Great Train Robbery' had created a great deal of public and media interest, and therefore the escapes of two of the principal protagonists of the gang from prison brought the media spotlight back on to jails and how they were being managed. Prisons became an object of ridicule, and Rutherford notes that 'one television news programme displayed a scorecard of escapes each evening.'[27] This was nothing compared to the furore that greeted the escape of Blake.

Blake escaped from HMP Wormwood Scrubs on Saturday, 22 October 1966. He used a rusty iron bar to break a first-floor window at the end of the cell block, climbed out on to the roof of a small porch which covered the cell block entrance, and then dropped to the ground. The prison wall was only about 20 yards away. In an obviously choreographed move, a rope ladder was then thrown over the wall, which Blake used to make his escape. As he landed on the other side of the wall, he broke his left wrist and had to be helped into the car that had been driven by his accomplices – an alcoholic Irishman and two middle-class Campaign for Nuclear Disarmament (CND) activists, who had all been prisoners with Blake in HMP Wormwood Scrubs. In other words, it wasn't members of the KGB who were behind the plot to help Blake escape, even if he was eventually smuggled out of England and into Russia just before Christmas 1966 after having been hidden in various safe houses in and around London. As of 2007 Blake was still living in Moscow on a KGB pension and was awarded the Order of Friendship on the occasion of his 85th birthday by Vladimir Putin.

The political impact of Blake's escape was immediate, and produced something akin to panic in the Home Office. The retirement of the then governor of HMP Wormwood Scrubs was brought forward and Roy Jenkins – the home secretary – attempted to placate the political storm that was brewing by appointing Lord Mountbatten of Burma to conduct an enquiry into prison security. Mountbatten started work almost immediately, but there was yet another escape before his report could be concluded – Frank Mitchell, the 'mad axeman', absconded from a farm-working group from HMP Dartmoor in December 1966.[28] Nonetheless, it is this report that introduced the security categorizations that remain in operation within our prisons even today, and which have become the most important internal procedure used by the Prison Service.

The era of Major Grew, which had relied on the secrecy and remoteness of prisons from public scrutiny, had come to an end. Prisons and what happened inside them had, through these escapes, once again become visible to the public – and to politicians – so that their operation and management were viewed as legitimate issues to be discussed within public policy. There were other developments too: in particular, the often cosy and supportive relationship between the governor and his staff began to deteriorate as prison officers began to exert their industrial relations powers and their own working culture to shape what they saw as the right way to run a jail. So these three escapes, as important as they were in themselves, also acted as a platform on which more widespread penal issues could come to the fore. These issues were related not just to security and control, but to the broader culture of imprisonment.

SIX

Custody, Security, Order and Control, 1967–1991

Custody refers to containment of prisoners within the prison perimeter, and ... security is the arrangement by which this is achieved. If we assume that order refers to the absence of disruption, then control is the means by which staff can achieve order.

Sir Richard Tilt, former Director of the Prison Service, 1995

How were security and order achieved within our prisons in the period following the recommendations made by Lord Mountbatten? And, given this renewed focus on security, how are we to understand the escapes from HMP Whitemoor in 1994 and from HMP Parkhurst in 1995, nearly three decades after Mountbatten's recommendations were supposed to have been implemented? This breach of the chapter's walls by these dates seems justified because, in many ways, the reactions to the escapes from Whitemoor and Parkhurst were echoes of the problems that Mountbatten had had to deal with, even if by the mid-1990s prisons had changed considerably from those of the 1960s. However, as Sir Richard Tilt's description at the start of the chapter indicates, custody, security, order and control are not easy terms to unravel and are often used interchangeably. I use 'order' here as Tilt describes it, to mean the absence of disruption – which is achieved through control – and 'security' as those practical, procedural and physical measures which prevent escapes and help to keep prisoners in custody.[1]

Two different lenses allow us to consider all of these issues, as well as analysing the inevitable official reports, inquiries and formal investigations which took place during this period. First, I will contrast two different ways of achieving order which were developed during this period. As such, there are case studies of HMP Gartree and of the Special Unit at HMP Barlinnie in Glasgow. The former received its first prisoners in April 1966 and became part of the 'dispersal estate' in 1969, while the latter, which opened in 1973, adopted a very different approach to managing long-term, sometimes difficult and potentially violent prisoners.

The second lens through which to view this broad period is through the autobiographies of prison officers. When Major Grew retired from HMP Wormwood Scrubs the Prison Service effectively spoke with one voice; it was an unified, bureaucratic and hierarchical organization in which the state had a great deal of confidence, and from which the public were largely excluded. It was also largely non-politicized. By the end of the 1970s – and certainly by the end of the period captured within this chapter – prisons were seen as sites of disorder and disruption and what happened within them often as shameful or 'scandalous', for one reason or another. Public reaction to the Special Unit at HMP Barlinnie is perhaps one of the best places to view this process and might also have been the first modern prison to experience this phenomenon. Nor did the Prison Service speak any longer with one voice, largely because prison officers increasingly used their industrial relations powers to emphasize their own particular prison skills. More often than not, these were related to the security functions that Mountbatten had asked them to exercise. In effect, they became during this period one of the three audiences to which prison has to make itself legitimate. And, as the period under discussion wore on, one home secretary after another became increasingly keen to use prison and imprisonment as a means of displaying ideological differences from their political opponents.

Security Categorizations

One of the most extraordinary continuities about prisons and imprisonment over the last fifty years has been the persistence of the security classifications that were outlined by Lord Mountbatten. His *Report of the Inquiry into Prison Escapes and Security* recommended that prisoners should be assessed according to the lowest level of security believed to be necessary to hold them in custody, and he suggested that all prisoners (apart from women and young offenders) should be placed in one of four categories according to the level of dangerousness that they would present to the public if they were able to escape.[2] Despite all of the changes and improvements to internal and external security since 1966, these security classifications have endured and have become 'perhaps the most important internal procedure that the prison service has.'[3]

Security Classifications of Prisoners

CATEGORY A Prisoners who must in no circumstances be allowed to get out, either because of security considerations affecting spies, or because their violent behaviour is such that members of the public or the police would be in danger of their lives if they were to get out.

CATEGORY B Prisoners for whom the very high expenditure on the most modern escape barriers may not be justified, but who ought to be kept in secure conditions.

CATEGORY C Prisoners who lack the resource and will to make escape attempts, [but] have not the stability to be kept in conditions where there is no barrier to escape.

CATEGORY D Prisoners who can reasonably be entrusted to serve their sentences in open conditions.

Adapted from Mountbatten Report, 1966

Why have these security classifications survived for so long, especially given the changes that prisons have gone through since their first introduction? What are we to make of the confusion of objectives and principles at the heart of these classifications which are very loosely defined, so that Categories A and B are concerned with the seriousness of what would happen if a prisoner did escape, while Categories C and D are more related to the likelihood of escape happening? All four classifications allow for subjective decision-making and this might in turn allow the classification decision to be influenced by factors other than security. For example, a member of staff might alter a prisoner's security level so as to establish a greater amount of control over that prisoner, or perhaps use security classifications to ease overcrowding.

Ironically these sorts of issues have been less debated than the fact that Mountbatten had recommended that all Category A prisoners should be housed in a single maximum security prison to be built on the Isle of Wight – which he named 'Vectis' – and which he thought would hold about 120 prisoners. He also imagined that, in due course, another maximum security prison might be necessary. This idea found immediate favour among the Prison Officers Association (POA) members, who were perhaps also responding to Mountbatten's naval and operational background, which might not have been too dissimilar to their own. The Home Office, however, was less convinced and so commissioned a further inquiry from the Advisory Council on the Penal System, chaired by Sir

Leon Radzinowicz. This council was largely made up of academics, and recommended that Category A prisoners should be dispersed – hence the name the 'dispersal system' – among the general population of a number of high-security prisons.[4] Much to Mountbatten's annoyance, Radzinowicz's advice found favour, and so we had first the dispersal system before moving to 'the high security estate' to hold Category A prisoners.[5] By 1970 there were five dispersal prisons and ten years later there were seven.

The relative merits of dispersal and concentration are almost a perennial discussion point in the history of our prisons, but here we might simply like to consider whether the policy of dispersal did indeed lead to good order and security; in other words, whether it resulted in an absence of disruption, achieved through having good control within these dispersal prisons, and whether the number of escapes was reduced, demonstrating the security of these prisons.

There were indeed sharp reductions in the number of escapes following the Mountbatten recommendations, although these did slowly rise again throughout the 1980s and early '90s, culminating in the escapes of nine prisoners from HMPs Whitemoor and Parkhurst, after which numbers again started to fall. However, while it might be possible to argue that the range of security measures that Mountbatten had introduced – from dog patrols to CCTV cameras and emergency control rooms – did have a temporary effect on the numbers able to escape from prison, there is a very different story to tell about the dispersal policy's impact on control. There were riots at two new dispersal prisons in 1972 – HMPs Gartree and Albany – at HMP Hull in 1976 and in D Wing, the dispersal wing of HMP Wormwood Scrubs, in August 1979. At the latter riot control was only re-established through the use of specially trained officers – known as the MUFTI (Minimum Use of Force Tactical Intervention) squad – which had been formed in response to the riots at Hull. Initial reports suggested that no prisoners had been injured when the MUFTI squad regained control of D Wing, and it was not until the end of September, when the governor finally submitted a written report to the Home Office, that the true figure of 53 injured prisoners was revealed. The official inquiry into the riot at D Wing suggested that there were

indications that members of the POA committee played a more intrusive role in the operational decision-making process than is appropriate, whereas some members of the management team,

133

notably the Deputy Governor, the duty Medical Officer and the Assistant Governor in charge of D Wing, were either not involved at all or were inadequately consulted and briefed.[6]

This conclusion has uncanny echoes of the observations of a previous generation of prisoners at HMP Wormwood Scrubs, such as Croft-Cooke criticizing Major Grew for not having 'sufficient knowledge of what went on in his prison' and Peter Wildeblood criticizing the same governor for never visiting prisoners in their cells. To understand these issues more fully, let us consider the development of one dispersal prison over this period: HMP Gartree.

Years of Incessant Trouble

HMP Gartree's only biographer notes that the prison 'very much reflected national developments in the Prison Service',[7] and this was especially the case for the prison's first twenty years of existence. Built near Market Harborough in Leicestershire, the prison officially opened on 1 April 1966, although plans to build it had first been considered some six years earlier. At a public meeting to consider this proposal in 1960, only 30 local people bothered to attend, which perhaps suggests how uncontroversial prisons were as far as the public were concerned. Clearly prisons were not yet sites of disruption and disrepute. How quickly this was to change can be gleaned from the fact that plans to build a second prison on the site in 1969 – which was to be called HMP Mill Mound – unleashed a 'storm of protest in the local community'.[8]

The name 'Gartree' is believed to be derived from the Scandinavian word *geirtree*, which means 'spear-shaped tree'. When the prison opened it was able to accommodate 450 prisoners. It was of a typical 1960s design and therefore not dissimilar to other prisons built and opened in the period at Blundeston (1963), Stoke Heath (1964), Albany (1967) and Coldingley (1969). The buildings were meant to facilitate 'treatment and training' and thus reflected architecturally a very different official intention to those prisons built during the Victorian era. However, these design principles seem to have been at the heart of most of the problems that HMP Gartree had to face.

The prison had four identical, four-storey, T-shaped blocks, unimaginatively called A, B, C and D wings. Each wing had 100 cells and there was also a small segregation unit. A and D Wings and B and C Wings were connected by a corridor and the prison was formed by the connection of these two corridors by a linked central block corridor which housed the education department, a communal dining hall and two chapels. There was some early, rather fanciful talk that a swimming pool was also going to be built, although this never materialized. The first prisoners to be received into the prison arrived on 5 April 1966 and the prison's first governor – who had been in post since 1965 – was Bernard Chilvers. Ominously, by the time that Lord Mountbatten visited the prison in November 1966, there had already been an escape attempt, which had resulted in a full search of the prison.

By the end of 1966, when the prison had been opened for eight months, Gartree had had an average prison roll of 112 prisoners, but nonetheless still recorded 223 offences against prison discipline, which suggests that there was an absence of control even with this very small number of prisoners. Fourteen of these offences were for violence and assault, the most serious offences which a prisoner could be charged with. Perhaps all of this was why Mr Chilvers was quietly removed from his duties in August 1967 and replaced by a new governor, Murdo Macleod. Despite these difficult beginnings, either Mountbatten, or perhaps some of the prison officials who had accompanied him, must have been sufficiently impressed by what they had seen to decide that Gartree was suitable as a 'dispersal' prison and could accommodate Category A prisoners. It received the first of these on 10 July 1969.

However, from this point on in HMP Gartree's history, let us consider the prison and its role in the dispersal system and beyond until 1991 in three different ways. The first of these is how the prison went about trying to establish control over its charges and the second, how prisoners responded to these attempts. This latter consideration clearly will introduce issues related to escapes, riots and other acts of prison indiscipline. Finally, we need to consider how prison officers began to assert their authority during the post-Mountbatten period and how, in doing so, they began to articulate a very different view from their governors and Home Office officials about what the experience of prison should be all about. Increasingly the POA became more than happy to exert their industrial relations powers so as to translate their vision of prison into reality.

Whether as a result of design and architectural flaws, or perhaps the relative inexperience of some of the staff employed at the new prison, there was never a sense that control had been established inside the jail after it was opened. As we have seen, this was a problem which pre-dated the arrival of Category A prisoners. A revolver had been found in the jail in May 1968 and there had also been a number of escape attempts. Some of these difficulties may have been the result of the prisoners eating in association; they were obviously more difficult to control as a group. In addition, some prisoners had discovered that the prison's walls were only one brick thick and that they could therefore very quickly kick, gouge or knock holes in the exterior walls of their cells. Developing control within the jail was not aided by the high turnover of staff. It was especially difficult to retain catering officers, which again suggests that food was central to some of the early tensions within the prison. There was also an almost yearly change of governor: in the first five years of the prison's history there were four governors.

Prisoners seem to have challenged staff in almost every way imaginable. There were food and work refusals; a workshop was flooded; a number of staff were assaulted; there was a roof-top protest and a number of escape attempts. Clearly the most difficult issue for staff to have to deal with is when prisoners decide to act in concert with one another to protest and challenge those supposedly running the jail. In the early 1970s, throughout the prison system more generally and at HMP Gartree specifically, this type of protest was seen to be the work of PROP – an organization aimed at the preservation and the rights of prisoners. Whether or not this was actually the case – PROP perhaps loomed larger in the minds of prison officers than in reality on the landings – all of these acts of indiscipline were to culminate in the events of 1972, which has been dubbed a 'year of incessant trouble' and the 'worst year ever experienced in prison history'.[9] There was, for example, a sit-down protest on the exercise yard at HMP Brixton in April and over the next five months 130 demonstrations took place in over 40 institutions. In August PROP called for a national strike and there was a riot at HMP Albany.[10]

At HMP Gartree on 26 November 1972 the prison experienced one of the worst riots in penal history. At around teatime a group of thirteen prisoners forcibly exited A Wing and headed for the prison's fence. They used cutting equipment that had been smuggled into the prison to cut through two fences and then attempted to scale the prison's walls. They were unable to do this and so ran to the north side of the prison, where there was a wooden gate which was easier to scale. Prison staff had by this time been alerted to the danger and three dog handlers challenged the prisoners who were attempting to get out of the jail. There was then what Callan describes as a 'violent confrontation', which left twelve prison officers and five prisoners with injuries.[11]

Most of what had happened had been witnessed by other prisoners – many of whom had been eating in the dining halls – and rumours of prison officer 'brutality' seem to have spread very quickly throughout the jail. A riot ensued, with prisoners destroying the dining halls where they had been eating. They then erected barricades to prevent staff entering C and B Wings. Significant damage was done to most of the fixtures and fittings of these wings and C Wing was still barricaded on the Monday after the riot. The governor recorded that there was 'confusion and chaos' everywhere.[12] The cost of the riot was put at £150,000 and eventually seventeen prisoners were convicted of gross personal violence to a prison officer and ten were found guilty of trying to escape. Even so, staff refused to go on duty on 1 December 1972, only eventually doing so on receiving the promise that there would be a review of staffing levels.

As bad as all this was, six years later the prisoners rioted again after rumours that a prisoner had been ill-treated in the prison's hospital on 5 October. Even after three prisoners had been allowed to go to the hospital to check on the well-being of their colleague, this did not quell the rumours of ill-treatment, and A and D Wings rioted. The disturbance moved to B Wing and only C Wing remained calm. The metal gate to A Wing had been wired to the mains electrical supply to prevent staff from entering, and there were various efforts made to get on to the prison's roof. The rioting continued all night, but control was re-established the following day and some 136 prisoners were transferred to other jails. Two wings of the prison were so badly destroyed that they could not be reoccupied. Lord Harris, Minister for State with special responsibilities for prisons, visited the jail soon after and stated that he was in 'a mild state of shock' about what had happened and what he could observe.[13]

All of these events allowed the POA to campaign for changes in how the prison should be run. This campaign usually centred on issues to do with staffing numbers and, in particular, how many staff were needed to be on duty within the prison before prisoners could be unlocked from their cells. This issue is obviously linked to money, as most of a prison's budget is spent on staffing costs. Running a prison with more staff than is actually needed is costly to the public purse. Indeed, governors, especially now that budgets have been devolved to the local level, recognize that there are limits to how much money they can spend and so there is a constant tension between how many staff the POA think are needed to unlock the prison and how many the governor might want or, more recently, can afford to deploy. In turn the POA is able to argue that the safety of their members has to take precedence over budgets and that if the governor cannot guarantee greater staffing numbers, prisoners will have to be locked in their cells for longer periods of the day. Keeping prisoners locked up obviously alters the regime within the prison and fundamentally challenges what imprisonment is meant to be achieving. It also – to put it mildly – annoys the prisoners, some of whom might have to spend up to 23 hours of each day locked in their cells. This might be of little concern to some prison officers, and there is a prison aphorism that captures this outlook – 'happiness is door-shaped'.

Here we have in essence the classic managerial prison-power stand-off. Who wins depends on a range of local and national circumstances that can sometimes work in favour of prisoners or, more usually, in favour of prison officers, whose ability to win in these situations is aided by the fact that unlike prison governors, who are regularly moved to different prisons on promotion, they tend to stay in the same prison for significantly longer periods of time.

Added to this state of affairs was another issue which kept the tension high between prison officers and prison governors of various ranks. In the absence of actual bodies of additional staff to deploy, the governor could agree to allow existing staff to work overtime. Most did, and they could earn significant sums of money by doing so. It was not uncommon – in fact it was the norm – for prison officers to be earning at least double the amount of money that was being paid to the governor, his deputy or assistant governors.[14] The May Committee, set up in 1979 after a long period of deteriorating industrial relations, found that over a quarter of prison officers were working more than 60 hours of overtime a week, although the subsequent May Report is probably best remembered for recommending the establishment of the Prison Inspectorate, which was established by statute in 1982.[15] This state of affairs continued until the Fresh Start initiative of 1987, which ended overtime payments to prison officers (by significantly increasing their basic salary) and also unified the Prison Service's rank structure by amalgamating the roles of chief officer and assistant governor, and creating the new ranks – depending on seniority – of governor 4 and governor 5.

As a result of the riot of 1972 Gartree housed only 285 prisoners and a programme of 'cell-strengthening' was initiated. A new segregation block was also constructed at the cost of £400,000. However, quite quickly it was decided that Gartree should remain as part of the dispersal system and so a 'Manpower Control Team' recommended that the prison should have an extra 90 prison officers to bolster this role. This number of extra officers is in fact exactly the total number of officers who run the prison today[16] – although the prison no longer houses Category A prisoners – and this gives a small indication that, no matter the costs involved, there were those who were determined to keep the prison within the dispersal estate, and who thus had to accommodate the power of the POA to influence staffing levels and other factors related to the internal running of the jail.

After the 1978 riot, for example, the POA at HMP Gartree insisted that fifteen prisoners had to be transferred out of the jail, including ten Category A prisoners, whom they deemed to have been ringleaders. The POA also demanded a 'controlled unlock' of the prison, which meant that only a certain number of prisoners would be allowed out of their cells at any given time; reached an agreement with the governor that the prison's roll would not exceed 140 prisoners; and determined that the two empty wings of the jail would not be filled until secondary access routes had been installed. At this time there were 241 prison officers of various ranks, sometimes called the 'uniformed staff' (governors do not wear uniforms but civilian clothes[17]), for a prison population of 155. Even so, prisoners were still locked in their cells for up to fifteen hours per day and evening classes in the Education Department were restricted to one evening per week. The number of hours prisoners worked during the week was only 21 on average and the cost of keeping a prisoner at HMP Gartree in 1980 was estimated at £1,000 per week.[18]

As the prison gradually accepted more prisoners during the 1980s, partly prompted by developments taken by two governors – Richard Tilt (quoted at the start of the chapter) and Phil Wheatley, each of whom would eventually become Director General of HM Prison Service – two other incidents are worthy of note. First, in November 1983, Michael Hickey, who had been convicted of the murder of a newspaper boy called Carl Bridgewater in 1979, climbed on to the roof of B Wing to proclaim his innocence and began what was to become the longest rooftop protest in prison history. He was eventually to come down from the roof on 21 February 1984 after having protested for 90 days, having clearly been helped by other prisoners at the jail who supported him in his campaign. Hickey's conviction for murder was eventually overturned in 1997 by the Court of Appeal and he was awarded £990,000 compensation for all the years that he had been wrongly imprisoned. This award was eventually cut by 25 per cent to account for the fact that Hickey had received 'board and lodgings' from the prison service during the time that he had been locked up.[19]

The second incident of note relates to an escape and was so significant that it 'perhaps unfairly defines the place and occupies the memories of many individuals'.[20] Part of the reason that this escape is so infamous and significant is that it not only involved two Category A prisoners – John Kendall and Sydney Draper – but also a helicopter, which landed on the prison's sportsfield on 10 December 1987 and was used by Kendall and Draper to effect their escape. The helicopter was on the sportsfield for only 23 seconds and it subsequently landed on the Valley Way Industrial Estate, close to Market Harborough railway station. Draper and Kendall then hijacked a van and drove to the village of Dingley, where they stole another car and continued to Corby, at which point they split up. Kendall was recaptured after 51 days of being on the run but Draper remained at large for over a year. The codename for a helicopter escape is 'Operation Rogue Elephant', but seemingly this was unknown to the communications staff at RAF West Drayton who, when informed of what was happening, are reported to have asked not only 'what's a rogue elephant?' but also 'where's Gartree?'[21]

Gartree was to leave the dispersal system in April 1992 and become a Category B Training Prison and a main lifer centre. The prison now houses only life-sentenced prisoners and with a prison population of nearly 700 is one of the largest prisons in Europe holding this type of prisoner.

These issues at HMP Gartree bring into view the many and varied problems of attempting to manage the long-term prison population. They also allow us to observe the workings of the dispersal system at close quarters and see how the balance of power within a jail is often in a constant state of flux between governors, prison officers and prisoners. The public, except when there was a major incident of some kind at the prison, were still largely excluded from prisons, although an appeal to what was seen as what the public wanted would begin to characterize how decisions would increasingly be made in later years. However, were there other ways of attempting to manage long-term prisoners who were seen to be difficult and potentially dangerous?

Barlinnie and its Special Unit

Scotland too had its problems with the long-term prison population in the 1970s and adopted a similar policy to England and Wales of dispersing its most troublesome prisoners, especially to prisons in the Highlands, such as HMPs Peterhead and Inverness. There was a rooftop protest at Peterhead in 1972 and a riot at Inverness in the same year. The latter prison was particularly infamous at this time given its use of so-called 'cages' between 1966 and 1972, in which the most recalcitrant prisoners were kept in solitary confinement for up to a year at a time. One unnamed prisoner would later describe what it was like to be 'caged':

> The caged area is approximately 9 ft by 6 ft. The only moveable objects besides the human body are a small plastic chamber pot – lidless, a woolen blanket and a book that is issued each week. Human contact is made three times a day when the 'screws' enter to search the body of the prisoner. His mouth, armpits, anus and the soles of his feet are searched each time even though he could not have left the cell between searches. This humiliation and degradation takes place daily. There is no communication between the 'screws' and the prisoner. He is alone and at the complete mercy of the 'screws' who take full advantage of his helplessness. Brutality and abuse of human rights is rife.[22]

However, this type of control did little to thwart the efforts of a number of prisoners who during this period continued to riot, attack staff or engage in 'dirty protests' – a euphemism for covering themselves and their cells in excrement.

As a result the Special Unit at HMP Barlinnie in Glasgow was set up following the *Report of the Scottish Office Working Party on the Treatment of Certain Long-term Prisoners and Potentially Violent Prisoners* of 1972, which saw units of this kind as far better at being able to manage this type of prisoner. The choice of Barlinnie to house the Special Unit (BSU) may have been taken so as to distance the BSU both physically and metaphorically from prisons in the Highlands, but it was still nonetheless an odd choice of location. HMP Barlinnie is one of the world's most iconic and infamous jails, and originally opened in 1892. By 1896 it had five 'Halls' (as wings are known in Scotland), but it was 'almost from the moment it opened, overcrowded'.[23] To this day the prison is rarely out of the news and was the location of a particularly notorious riot in 1987. Ironically, rioting by prisoners usually prompts positive public relations for the prison service, since it is often seen as confirming a stereotype that prisoners get what they deserve and that nothing can be done to change their behaviour. Prisoners are viewed as dangerous and predatory and so some interpret behaviour of this kind as an indication that not only should these prisoners be locked up, but the keys to their cells should also be metaphorically thrown away.

The BSU attempted to deal with violent and potentially violent prisoners in a completely different way from isolating them in solitary confinement and using officially sanctioned violence by staff to control their behaviour. Instead, it offered them art and education classes and encouraged prisoners to write – and they soon started to produce their own newspaper called The Key; they were allowed to wear their own clothes; there were few limits placed on who could visit the unit; and each week one prisoner was allowed to go shopping in Glasgow accompanied by a prison officer. Quite quickly the BSU evolved into a self-styled therapeutic community in which there was freedom, responsibility and choice given to prisoners within the confines of the unit itself. Any prisoner who broke these very generous rules was put into the 'hot seat' – instead of being segregated – and while he was there other prisoners and staff would criticize the behaviour that had led to this problem. A number of prisoners found this approach so encouraging that they would later go on to write autobiographies of their time in Scottish jails and explain how the BSU had changed their lives for the better.[24]

The BSU was the inspiration of Ken Murray, a Scottish prison officer, and Ian Stephen, who worked for the Scottish Prison Service (SPS) as a forensic psychologist. The unit was staffed by prison officers – thus demonstrating that in the right environment prison staff could undertake more complex and difficult tasks than simply locking prisoners up – and was partly modelled on the therapeutic communities at HMP Grendon. Grendon's regime emphasizes communalism, responsibility and democratic principles, which are displayed in a variety of community meetings where issues are discussed and voted upon by prisoners and staff.[25] On Tuesdays at the BSU, the unit's governor, staff and prisoners gathered under an elected chairman – who could be a prisoner – to discuss any issue relevant to the unit's functioning. There were more informal meetings on a Friday and special meetings could be called to cope with problems that had suddenly arisen. The aim of these meetings was to teach prisoners social responsibilities and ways to overcome problems without resorting to violence.

There was no formal work on the BSU but it had a particular strength: developing any latent artistic talent that the prisoners might have had. Jimmy Boyle, for example, once dubbed 'Scotland's most violent prisoner', became an excellent sculptor and the use of art to transform the outlook of formerly violent and difficult prisoners can be seen in the changes to prisoners such as Hugh Collins, Larry Winters, Bob Brodie and Tom Galloway. However, some members of the public either found all of this unconvincing – even in the face of very good evidence that art was changing the outlook of these prisoners – or simply could not support it. It was almost as if they did not want prisoners – 'hard men' like Boyle – to be able to change; it made them somehow uncomfortable. Jeffrey, for example, cites Ron Ferguson – a chaplain who had worked on the unit – as stating that he had discovered 'powerful people who wanted [Boyle] to fail, in order to prove their own theories that the likes of Boyle couldn't change'. There is some indication that these powerful people included senior clerics, who wanted Boyle to reoffend as his 'redemption wasn't according to church formulae'. Ferguson concluded that 'somehow a changed, articulate Boyle was more of a threat than one who lived like a caged animal'.[26]

What was true for clerics was also true for other members of the public who might want prisoners to change their behaviour, but not if this was done within a regime that was seen to be 'soft' or 'easy'. Stories of BSU prisoners going to art galleries, wearing their own clothes, cooking their own meals and making shopping trips to Glasgow were rarely off the front pages of some Scottish newspapers and in doing so created a scandal. What that scandal seems to indicate was that the public did not want prisoners to experience conditions inside that were better than they might have experienced on the outside and which might still be being experienced by those who had not committed violent crimes. A changed prisoner was all well and good, so this reasoning seems to go, but not if he or she was seen to be benefiting from his or her crimes and if the punishment amounted to better treatment than law-abiding taxpayers might be able to afford, should they wish to purchase these opportunities for themselves, or for members of their family.

Such is the tightrope walked by the penal reformer, although ultimately not by the SPS, which closed the BSU 'in the face of relentless public criticism' in 1994 – the same year that the Inverness 'cages' were also abolished.[27] As Jeffrey puts it, the BSU was 'so successful they shut it down', although thankfully – despite still being described as a 'penal experiment' – HMP Grendon continues to prosper. But what did the basic grade prison officer make of all of these issues?

The Prison Officer Autobiography

The obvious market for books describing prison conditions by serving or former prisoners has not been replicated in the case of prison officers offering us their views on prison life. In common with the historic academic neglect of prison staff more generally, there is a comparative dearth of prison officials who have put pen to paper and that small number who have done so have tended to be of a senior rank.[28] But what does it mean to be a prison officer, patrolling the landings on a day-to-day basis? Could the nature and experience of imprisonment be shaped by small, seemingly banal decisions, routines and relationships between the basic grade officer and the prisoner? After all, as the criminologists Alison Liebling and David Price have put it, prison officers play a 'peacekeeping' function in our jails, which they feel has allowed them to become the 'human face of the Prison Service'. As such 'the role of the prison officer is arguably the most important in the prison.'[29]

Of late there has been a growing academic interest in prison officers that has uncovered a working culture that sees itself as part of an unvalued, unappreciated occupational group.[30] Prison officers' understanding is that they are regarded by the public as unintelligent, insensitive and sometimes brutal, and 'that their work is perceived as entailing no more than the containment of society's deviants and misfits'.[31] However, we should also note a recent warning from Professor Joe Sim that this interest can amount to 'an uncritical, political and popular view that prison officers are victimised by an implacable prisoner enemy on the landings intent on violent retribution towards them'.[32]

What appears to be missing are accounts provided by prison officers themselves who, in comparison to their charges, have been loath to put pen to paper. But recently, and for no apparent reason – just like buses – along came Jim Dawkins's *The Loose Screw* (2005), Robert Douglas's *At Her Majesty's Pleasure* (2007), Ronnie Thompson's *Screwed: The Truth About Life as Prison Officer* (2008), and Tony Levy's *A Turnkey or Not?: My 25 Years as a Prison Officer in Her Majesty's Prisons* (2011). Taken as a group, these four autobiographies (one of which – *Screwed* – was written under a pseudonym by a serving prison officer) cumulatively cover the period between 1962 and 2008, with Douglas describing his work at HMPs Winson Green and Durham; Dawkins at HMPs Wandsworth, Wormwood Scrubs and Belmarsh; Thompson (who has since left the Prison Service to pursue a writing career) at a prison he names 'HMP Romwell'; and Levy at HMPs Pentonville, Woodhill and Grendon.

While I will consider these four autobiographies as a whole, it is also important to note their differences from each other – especially differences in their intended audience. Thompson is clearly writing for a 'lads' mag' readership, with his stories of clubbing, drinking and acts of random violence. Indeed, his book opens by name-checking a number of bands, such as Oasis, Arctic Monkeys and the Kaiser Chiefs, and he is at pains throughout to point out that he is a 'normal bloke, with normal values'. Dawkins, on the other hand, uses his book almost as a confessional and ends his introduction with the observation that writing a book was 'not bad for a "drunken, tattooed, penniless wanker", eh dad?!!' His autobiography also includes a foreword written by the serving prisoner Charles Bronson, who also appears on the front cover, neatly subverting the tradition of the genre of prisoner autobiographies to have such a foreword written by an academic or senior criminal justice official. Unsurprisingly, Dawkins's book can also be read as a polemic that argues that Bronson should be released from jail. Douglas, the most polished of the four writers, uses his time as a prison officer to bring the trilogy of his life history up to date. At Her Majesty's Pleasure is the third of Douglas's books, which trace his life from growing up in Glasgow after the Second World War in Night Song of the Last Tram: A Glasgow Childhood; its sequel, detailing his time in National Service, is called Somewhere to Lay My Head. This trilogy can be read within the tradition of 'misery memoirs'. Finally, Levy uses his book 'to share with the reader the more personal experiences I've had in the hope that they will entertain, rather than describe incidents that have probably been portrayed more dramatically and in greater detail by more accomplished authors'.[33]

Leaving these differences to one side, what do these four autobiographies tell us about the skills and qualities that it takes to be a good prison officer, about life in jail more broadly and the relationship between prison staff and prisoners more specifically? What do they tell us about power, punishment and how these might be practised by the some 25,000 prison officers, senior officers and principal officers who work in our penal system and who have become one of the audiences that prison must now satisfy to be seen as legitimate?

The first point to note is an absence. Douglas joined the Prison Service in 1962 and resigned in 1977; Dawkins served between 1992 and 1999; Thompson for approximately seven years from 2000 (he is deliberately imprecise about some details); and Levy between 1983 and his retirement in 2008. Thus only Levy was working as a prison officer in the 1980s when, as we have seen, there were major changes introduced into the management of prisons through the series of reforms known as Fresh Start. This was an important time for the management of the service when, for example, the old ranks of chief officer and assistant governor were unified and the practice of directly recruiting assistant governors was abolished in favour of an accelerated promotion scheme. Thus Douglas worked in the old system of governors and chiefs, Dawkins and Thompson in the new, unified rank structure and Levy under both systems.

It is therefore interesting to speculate why Douglas only once mentions a governor in his autobiography – on p. 201, when Lionel Steinhausen, the governor of HMP Durham in the early 1970s, reportedly tells Douglas that he will 'leave it to you' to deal with a troublesome prisoner in the prison's segregation unit. Perhaps this is another reflection of the fact that during this period, prison staff still spoke with one voice. On the other hand, governors appear on almost every page in the autobiographies of Dawkins and Thompson – who describes governors as having 'permanent PMT: indecisive, moody and always fucking wrong'.[34] Dawkins lets us know that 'I detested those high-flying Governors that I would come across in my Prison Service days who gained promotion [not] on merit but by kissing the right arse.'[35] Levy's book too is filled with stories of his disagreements with various prison governors, over a number of different issues, during the 25 years he served as an officer of different rank.

We should also note that these autobiographies all describe local prisons – specifically HMPs Winson Green, Durham, Wandsworth, Woodhill, Belmarsh and Wormwood Scrubs – even if the authors also performed duties in other jails during their period of service for one reason or another. From the descriptions that Thompson provides, 'HMP Romwell' would also appear to be a busy London local, and in all likelihood he is describing HMP Pentonville. (Levy did end his career at HMP Grendon but he does not tell us anything in his autobiography about therapy.) Thus we have a partial view of the Prison Service contained within these accounts given that they do not describe training prisons, open prisons, young offender institutions or the female prison estate.

Nor does Douglas describe the training that he received prior to joining HMP Winson Green in 1962, even if Dawkins, Thompson and Levy provide accounts of their days at prison service colleges in Newbold Revel, Aberford Road and Wakefield and at the officer training school at HMP Leyhill respectively. All seem to have used their training courses to have got drunk as often as possible, with Thompson in particular observing, 'this wasn't training, it was worse than fucking Ibiza'; Dawkins, too, characterized his training as 'nine weeks of constant parties'.[36]

These omissions notwithstanding, the four books do provide us with a view of prison from the perspective of a prison officer from the days when capital punishment was still practised – Douglas attended the execution of Russell Pascoe at HMP Bristol in 1963 – to almost the present day. What do they reveal about the working culture of prison staff? Perhaps it is best to look at what we can learn about prisons through the lens of the prison officer by considering this in two ways: first, the effect of prison officers on prison life – and specifically the effect of prison officers on the lives of prisoners – and second, the impact that prison has on prison officers.

The Effect of the Prison Officer

The most consistent issue in the autobiographies concerning the impact of prison officers, which three of the four books deal with, is the violence that is central to the working lives of the basic-grade patrolling prison officer; violence which would have been dismissed as exaggeration had it been recounted by a prisoner. This is no small matter, for, as one criminologist has maintained, 'a key part of the everyday working life of the prison officer is witnessing the physical manifestation of the suffering of others.'[37] And while each of the authors wants to claim that he was especially fair, professional and good at his job, and not at all from the 'old school' that would beat up prisoners, all of their books document slaps, punches, kicks and worse meted out by staff, witnessed by the authors, and used as a way of maintaining control.

The distance that Douglas, Dawkins and Thompson want to create between themselves and their more 'bully-boy' colleagues (as described by Dawkins) is somewhat spoiled when each documents their own participation in routine forms of violence. For example, Thompson, who revels in his self-proclaimed ability at C&R,[38] states that if he needs to give a prisoner 'a slap, so be it', and then describes how with one prisoner he 'grabbed the little bastard by the throat and began throwing him around his cell'; Dawkins describes snapping at a prisoner, 'pick[ing] up a pool cue and a plastic dustbin lid and charg[ing] at him like a knight on a joust', knocking him out 'sparko'; and Douglas recalls a prisoner called Jack McKue whom he 'punch[ed] once, full force, in the solar plexus . . . [he was] out cold. Jeez! I did enjoy that.'[39]

Thompson and Douglas in particular describe routine violence meted out against prisoners. The latter recalls a prisoner called Wilshaw, for example, who had had something passed to him on a visit but refused to give the contraband over to staff. Douglas maintains that while the prisoner was being held down by staff he continued to 'struggle violently' and attempted to get to his feet. A prison officer called Jimmy Green appeared.

> [He] leans forward, places a hand on the shoulders of the two officers who are holding Wilshaw's arms, and pushes both men apart. This leaves a space above the con. Without a word, this slight, sixty-year-old man takes a little leap into the air, tucks his legs up behind him and drops, knees first, onto Wilshaw's upper back. There is a distinct crack, and a scream from Wilshaw, as one of his shoulder-blades is fractured.[40]

This anecdote is told by Douglas almost with humour, and certainly in admiration for the actions of his colleague.

How are prison officers able to deny the human suffering which they witness, or indeed mete out, when performing their duties? Here we might want to employ the idea that there are three 'states of denial': literal denial; interpretative denial; and implicatory denial.[41] Refusing to validate that there had been human rights abuses against prisoners whilst they had been serving their sentence would be literal denial; interpretative denial would involve normalizing violence as a 'necessary evil', or the product of overcrowding and so forth; and, following Sykes and Matza's 'techniques of neutralisation',[42] implicatory denial implies that for various reasons nothing can be done. In other words, there will be a denial of responsibility (it is not the fault of the person witnessing the suffering); a denial of injury (he wasn't really hurt, or experienced limited harm); a denial of victim ('they got what they deserved'); a condemnation of the condemners – the person claiming to have been hurt is a hypocrite, or a liar; and an appeal to higher loyalties, so that the harm that has been done is seen to serve a greater purpose, or that we should be worried by the suffering of another, more innocent or vulnerable group.

None of the autobiographies considered here deals in literal denial. Indeed they are all, for different reasons, keen to stress that violence in prison is commonplace. Douglas, for example, in the first few pages of his autobiography, advises his readers that 'to lift a hand to an officer entitles a con to a mandatory good hiding. It's an unwritten law.' Thompson also suggests that 'it is obvious that as a screw you will have to fight with the cons', and, moreover, that there are four types of 'screws': 'the officer'; 'the con with keys', 'Mr No' and 'the screw'. He claims that he fell into the last category, and as such his working approach was to view the prison as a battleground between 'us and them'; a screw knows 'what's going on', and could 'distinguish between the shit rules and the good ones'. A screw wanted to 'police these criminals, putting some law and order in their lives', and therefore 'if need be, a screw will go into a prisoner's cell to give him a personal lesson, so he knows exactly what the score is . . . a bit of man-to-man can sort it out [through] a scrap in the cell.' Dawkins claims that staff 'incited' acts of violence; after witnessing a young prisoner being beaten up by two staff members and having his nose broken, 'over the next few years I would witness many incidents such as this one.'[43]

Thompson and Douglas use a combination of interpretative and implicatory denial to explain the violence that they witnessed, or engaged in. Thompson, in particular – the 'normal bloke, with normal values' – sees the violence that goes hand-in-glove with being a prison officer as part of his broader attempt to deter crime. As he puts it, 'I think that it is just too easy for the career criminal. These regimes are no deterrent to stop people re-offending. It if were harder perhaps people wouldn't come back.' And as far as overcrowding is concerned, 'build more fucking prisons you thick cunts'.[44] This 'common sense' approach to dealing with prisoners is both a way of normalizing his own violence and the violence that he witnesses and of justifying that violence by harnessing it to the cause of reducing crime. Douglas, on the other hand, constantly reminds his readers that the staff with whom he worked had all served in the armed forces during the Second World War, and that many sported combat medals (including the prison officer called Jimmy Green who broke Wilshaw's shoulder blade). By inference, their violence in prison is also viewed as a means by which the state survives and prospers. Indeed Douglas, who unquestioningly participated in the most extreme form of violence that the state can perpetrate against a citizen – execution – describes how Harry Allen and his assistant executioner carried out their duties, with Allen leaving a cigarette to burn in an ashtray. 'It's just over three minutes since they left. The cigarette Allen placed in the ashtray still burns.'[45] What Douglas wants the reader to take from this passage is not the horror of state-sanctioned execution, but rather the routine, speed and precision of the process of execution, with the implication that this all adds up to humanity.

Dawkins, on the other hand, seems to have resigned from the Prison Service because of the violence that he witnessed being perpetrated by staff against prisoners. He writes that 'for many prison officers, to "roll around the floor" with an inmate is all they come to work for.' Dawkins's autobiography is also a passionate plea to have Charles Bronson released from prison and so Dawkins claims that Bronson has been 'bullied' by other prison officers whom he labels as 'insecure little pricks' who have 'lied and exaggerated to cover up their own violent and unprofessional conduct to create the ultimate prison monster'. This is obviously a very partial reading of the circumstances that Bronson finds himself in and so, for example, taking a librarian hostage at HMP Woodhill is merely dismissed in half a line that Bronson 'was let down badly by his old solicitor'.[46]

These techniques of denial are perhaps strongest when the authors describe their dealings with sex offenders. Dawkins, for example, suggests that he did not want to treat sex offenders as people, and states that he 'never wanted to work on the nonces' wing . . . listen[ing] to these creatures describe in great detail their crimes and blame their actions on their parents or upbringing made me feel sick to the pit of my stomach.' Thompson is even more condemnatory and claims that 'the crime that we know is not sentenced correctly is paedophilia. The punishments are pathetic.' He further suggests that there are 'many outside agencies whose job it is to keep an eye on paedophiles and make sure they are not mistreated. And all of that is funded by us, the taxpayers', although he does not name any of these outside agencies. The link between denying the humanity of sex offenders and the corresponding institutional violence that they face is also rather neatly provided by Thompson, who describes escorting a paedophile to the Visits Room. Seemingly the prisoner kept talking about his offending, and Thompson 'couldn't take anymore. I punched the cunt so hard. I ripped into him with everything. I was screaming for him to shut his filthy mouth as I was battering him.' He then explains that he was able to have this assault covered up. This attack was clearly intended to literally silence the prisoner, which in turn was related to his broader complaint that prisoners generally and sex offenders specifically were being sentenced too leniently.[47]

The Effect on Prison Officers

As Thompson's description of his feelings leading up to his assault on a paedophile testifies, prison work can have an effect on prison officers. Indeed, there has been academic interest in the stress that prison officers face as part of their working lives, but here we might wish to consider why Douglas, Dawkins and Thompson chose to become prison officers, especially when we know that all three would eventually resign from the Prison Service. Only Levy saw the Prison Service as a career and achieved promotion to a more senior rank before retiring from his job. On the other hand, neither Douglas, Dawkins nor Thompson had the motivation of pursuing a career in the prison service. Douglas joined because 'not only do I need the money, but a house comes with it [the job]'; Dawkins had left the army and became a prison officer because he too needed the money. He also advises that 'it was not a job I would have considered under normal circumstances, but I was in a pretty desperate situation at the time'. Thompson, who reveals that he would have preferred to have become a fireman or a police officer, states that 'it paid the mortgage, looked after the family and gave me beer tokens.'[48]

In other words, their motivations were simply pragmatic. None of them viewed their work as a profession in which they might want to progress through the acquisition of skills. Indeed, their attitude to their training is indicative of this approach, and the only skill that they mention as having been of use in their work was learning C&R techniques. Here we might also note the Howard League for Penal Reform's call that prison officers should be educated to degree level in order to better manage prisons and reduce reoffending rates, and that their vision of the twenty-first-century prison officer is one who can be compared to a social worker, nurse or teacher.[49] However, as far as Thompson, Dawkins and Douglas are concerned, it should come as no surprise that when their pragmatic needs could be serviced in other ways, these three prison officers chose to resign.

Prior to leaving, Thompson and Dawkins both describe how they drank to excess, sometimes turning up to duty still under the influence of what they had consumed the night before (which makes their claims of professionalism difficult to accept). Thompson goes so far as to call the Officer's Club 'the dark side'. However, it is also clear that drinking large quantities of alcohol was part of the lifestyle of Thompson and Dawkins prior to becoming prison officers and it is therefore difficult to assert that they drank to excess because of stress brought about as a result of the pressures of the job. Indeed, Dawkins describes how he had drunk so much while on his training course that in his drunken state he thought that he had killed another prison officer. While at HMP Belmarsh he also admits to smuggling brandy into the prison, which he then gave to prisoners: 'I had to laugh later in the day when they were all staggering around half pissed and the other members of staff were going mad trying to find out where the hooch was stashed, a secret that I also kept to myself.' Douglas and to a lesser extent Dawkins describe extramarital sexual liaisons, and all three had difficulties in their relationships. As Douglas puts it, 'Nancy knows I'm at it. But she can't do anything about it.' He even advises that a fellow prison officer explained how the process of maintaining extra marital relations worked: 'meet at the club once or twice a week. Have a couple of drinks, a few dances, then head off in the car to some quiet parking place for a session.' Douglas and Dawkins were divorced and Thompson describes arguing with his wife – 'I was pushing her away. I was wrecking everything in my life. I was letting the Prison Service ruin me.'[50] Thompson's refusal to accept his own part in how his life was being wrecked is in marked contrast to how he considers those prisoners in his charge completely responsible for the course of their own lives. Most of them, he alleges, just needed more severe punishment to act as a deterrent; then 'these sods wouldn't play up as much'.

Every autobiography is a product of selection and memory, and this should be borne in mind when assessing the veracity of these three particular works. However, Levy's autobiography offers a contrast to the experiences and memories of Dawkins, Douglas and Thompson, since his career can be viewed as successful – he was promoted – and lasted for significantly longer than the careers of the others. (Levy served for 25 years, while Douglas worked in prisons for fifteen years, and Dawkins and Thompson for approximately seven years each.) How does Levy's account of what life was like patrolling the landings differ from that of Douglas, Dawkins and Thompson? Does he agree with the latter that

the truth of what it is like working as a screw [is a] fucking headache. The pressures, duties, life-wrecking conditions, corruption, danger – none of this is known to the public, but all of it makes up a day in the life of a prison officer.[51]

Levy deliberately does not dwell on any violent encounters that he might have experienced during his career and seems to have written his autobiography so as to make sense of a working life devoted to locking others up in a cell. He does not so much want to question why he became a prison officer as he wants to account for and explain the value of the role. One clue to this is in the question posed as the title of his book, A Turnkey or Not? Levy does not want to be thought of as someone who simply contained other people, but as someone who had personal values and work skills which could be used to set an example to others. Ultimately he became disillusioned with the Prison Service through his belief that, because of political interference and financial cuts, 'there was no longer any substance to what we were doing, and no one really seemed to care what we were achieving or if we were reaching our goals.'[52] In this respect his autobiography would confirm a number of academic findings which suggest that prison officers feel unappreciated.

However, there are many problems with what Levy recounts. In particular, for all Levy's criticisms of recent financial cutbacks and how this might have created disillusionment among staff, he suggests that the best years of his career came at HMP Pentoville in the early 1980s, before Fresh Start. So the very personal experiences that Levy wants to share with his readers happened at a time when prison officers were almost all concerned with 'Spanish practices', as he describes them, and being an 'overtime bandit'. These 'Spanish practices' included, for example, being one of three prison officers charged with producing a prisoner at Dover Magistrate's Court, with two of the prison officers dropping off the prisoner and then taking the ferry to France for the rest of the day on a 'booze cruise'; staff feigning injury so as to be able to go on holiday on full pay; and uncovering other staff who drank in the Officer's Club from ten in the morning and then slept it off in handily placed portakabins while they should have been on duty.[53] No doubt this all helped to keep staff morale high, but it weakens Levy's questioning of staff cuts and greater financial scrutiny. It also goes some way to confirming what had been described by Dawkins, Douglas and Thompson.

No doubt all four autobiographies were highly selective and interpretative. Dawkins wants to justify his resignation and also use his experiences to help the campaign of Charles Bronson, whom he views as having been unfavourably treated. Thompson, on the other hand, wants to reinforce an image of himself as doing a dangerous, thankless job dealing with 'fucked up junkies', corrupt management and 'cons . . . that aren't afraid to cut your face off', and revealing a world that has been hidden from public view.[54] As a consequence, Thompson's account does not dwell on the routines and boredom of being a prison officer but rather on those incidents that best portray his views about life inside and his part in that life. Douglas is somewhat different and produces what we might call an 'orthodox' autobiography, in that his is a celebration of his life – his tale of overcoming adversity. Levy's viewpoint is different again: he is keen to explain that he was not a 'turnkey' and that he had had something to offer that was positive and worthwhile. However, he would have made this case much more persuasively if he had reflected more deeply on his time at HMP Pentonville.

The fact that each book was aimed at a different readership, but that violence remained central to the stories that three of these autobiographies recount, is significant. While Thompson claims that he was a 'good screw . . . good at getting the job done efficiently', Dawkins wants to put some distance between the violence that he witnesses staff engaging in and how he performed his duties. Douglas, too, wants to present himself as professional, 'firm but fair', but violence seeps through these claims of individual professionalism and almost every page documents incidents of prisoners being slapped, punched and kicked, leaving the reader with little choice other than to accept that violence and pain are part of the everyday currency of prisons. Should this conclusion be dismissed as merely a byproduct of the publishing and commercial imperative to sell autobiographies about prisons? Or should we instead conclude that three accounts provided by prison officers about their work seem to confirm what prisoners have been describing for years?

Finally, we should note what these autobiographies reveal about the culture of prison staff – one of the key audiences to which prison has to represent itself as legitimate. A close reading of these autobiographies would suggest that prison officers do indeed articulate a view about prison which would be different from the views of Home Office or now Ministry of Justice officials, prison governors and the prisoners themselves. Indeed, Dawkins, Douglas, Levy and Thompson are distrustful of people within these positions of authority and repeatedly describe circumstances in which their view of what should be done was in marked contrast to that of those who were managerially responsible for running the prison in which they worked. But what did this view amount to? While it is difficult to be precise, most of their thoughts about prisoners and imprisonment seem to have been centred on making it a tougher and more unpleasant experience. In other words, they believed that prison should be much more painful and retributive and that prison officers should be given much greater freedoms to make that vision a reality. These autobiographies were characterized by absences and, albeit to a lesser extent with Levy (who after all worked at HMP Grendon), what is missing from what is described is the idea that prison could change its charges for the better. Violence permeated the landings where Dawkins, Douglas and Thompson worked, rather than 'treatment and training', rehabilitation or, indeed, hope. In that respect, their vision is depressing and dispiriting.

Before ending this chapter about custody, security, order and control I will describe two further sets of escapes, even if they breach the chapter's boundary of 1991. My intention here is not to investigate the political fallout from these escapes, which I will cover in the next chapter, but rather to simply consider the mechanics of these escapes and what they might reveal about security and custody. I will also consider one other major disturbance: the riot at HMP Strangeways in 1990.

HMPs Whitemoor and Parkhurst

After the escapes of Draper and Kendall in their helicopter from HMP Gartree, Category A was subdivided into three groups. Category A prisoners were to be assessed as either 'standard', 'high' or 'exceptional risk'. Those in the last category had to be held in small special security units (SSUs) located in several of the country's dispersal prisons. The SSUs were in effect 'secure prisons within secure prisons' – or at least were supposed to be.[55] One such SSU existed at HMP Whitemoor, located just north of March in Cambridgeshire, and was opened in 1991. The opening paragraph of the subsequent Woodcock Enquiry provides both a flavour of life in Whitemoor's SSU and what happened on one Friday night in September 1994.

It was 8.10 on Friday, 9th September 1994, when the concentration of the prison officers in the Special Security Unit (SSU) at Whitemoor Prison was disrupted by a telephone call announcing that several of their charges were in the process of escaping over the prison wall. Until that time, 4 of the 7 officers on duty had

155

been playing a game of Scrabble; a fifth was reading whilst the remaining two were busying themselves in the control room. All were no doubt looking forward to the impending end to their evening shift, at 8.45 p.m. It had been, until then, a normal, quiet shift in the ssu.[56]

The escapees that this rather racy official account alludes to included five members of the Provisional Irish Republican Army (PIRA) and a sixth prisoner who had been involved in a previous prison escape. They were armed with two pistols and, in attempting to prevent their escape, one prison officer was shot. After breaching the prison's walls, two of the escapees managed to avoid recapture for several hours, and were only subsequently apprehended through the use of Essex Police's helicopter, which had been deployed because it had a thermal imaging capacity. A few weeks later, during the Cambridgeshire Constabulary's investigation into the shooting, a pound of Semtex explosive, short fuses and three detonators were found in the ssu, concealed in the false bottom of a prisoner's artist's paintbox. Unsurprisingly, the Woodcock Enquiry found a great deal of evidence of lax security, ineffective searching routines, a number of poor practices which prison officers had been 'conditioned' into accepting and an extraordinary catalogue of unearned privileges that prisoners within the ssu were allowed at taxpayers' expense – such as free telephone calls – which were alleged to have been used to 'appease' the prisoners. The public reacted much as the Scots had done on being informed about the Barlinnie Special Unit, although no information was given as to who actually won the game of Scrabble.

Some four months later – on 3 January 1995 (only two days after the serial killer Fred West hanged himself at HMP Birmingham – Winson Green) – three Category A prisoners escaped from HMP Parkhurst on the Isle of Wight by slipping out of the sports hall during an evening exercise period. Then,

> with master key made in the workshops at the prison, they make their way the length of the sportsfield and open a deserted training workshop. They spend a short while assembling the constituent parts of a ladder – also made in the prison – and take with them wire cutters, a step ladder and a pair of pliers. They also have with them a gun, the parts of which were also made in the workshops. They scamper back the length of the football field, somehow evading

the sight of the many CCTV cameras dotted all over the prison and the dog patrols circling the perimeter fence, and cut through the wire mesh of this first barrier. There is no alarm, no noise save the snap of the wire cutters.[57]

The three escapees then placed their ladder against the second and outer wall and descended the other side using hose pipe and some electrical cable. They were at large on the Isle of Wight for four days, having failed to steal a light aircraft with which they had hoped to flee to the mainland.

The political fallout from these events is discussed in the next chapter, but here we should simply consider what we have learned about prison security since Blake made his escape from HMP Wormwood Scrubs in 1966. Had Mountbatten's security classifications helped to make our prisons more secure? The straightforward answer to that question is yes, despite the persistence of high-profile escapes. Consider, for example, that all Blake needed to do to get out of prison in 1966 was kick a rather rusty bar and then climb the prison's wall using a ladder which he had strengthened with knitting needles. He also managed to flee the country. The escapees from both Whitemoor and Parkhurst needed a great deal more kit to execute their plans – a master key, guns, ammunition, pliers, wire cutters, hammers, screwdrivers, money, hose pipe, a metal clamping device, a torch, electrical cable and so forth – and they were all caught very quickly. Clearly prisons are much more secure than they were. We might question whether every prison needs to be as security conscious as the high-security estate, although it is also evident that since the Woodcock and Learmont reports most escapes no longer involve prisoners breaching the prison's walls but occur when they are being moved out of the prison, such as when they are produced at court or attend hospital. Of course there remains what a number of commentators have described as a 'conceptual confusion' about these security classifications, as they are often wrongly seen as being about control as well as security, which should remind us about Tilt's definitions used at the start of the chapter. More secure prisons are not necessarily better controlled prisons and it is to control – or at least the loss of it – that we now finally turn.

There's Going to Be a Riot!

On April Fool's Day in 1990 prisoners rioted at HMP Strangeways in Manchester. They were to remain in charge of the prison for 25 days. The riot started in the prison's chapel and resulted in violent attacks against prison staff and prisoners who had committed sexual offences. Some newspapers incorrectly claimed that a number of these sex offenders had been killed. Even so, 147 staff were injured, as were 48 prisoners, one of whom did eventually die of his injuries. The riot spread quickly throughout the prison because keys were taken from two of the officers who had been on duty in the chapel. Day after day, the country's newspapers were filled with pictures of prisoners holding court on the roof of the jail. Most of the prison's infrastructure was destroyed and staff – and, by implication, more senior prison officials and politicians too – appeared powerless, disorganized and incapable of regaining control. Rioting was not only confined to HMP Strangeways but spread to HMPs Bristol and Cardiff, two overcrowded local prisons, HMP Dartmoor and HMYOIs Glen Parva and Pucklechurch, as well as to a number of other prisons. The damage done to HMP Strangeways – which at the time of the riot was severely overcrowded and holding 1,647 inmates – was estimated at £60 million.

An independent public inquiry was established under the chairmanship of Lord Justice Woolf to look into the causes of the riots. His report *Prison Disturbances, April 1990* was published in 1991.[58] The first half of the report considered what had caused the riots and the second half – co-written with Judge Stephen Tumim, at the time Chief Inspector of Prisons – provided an overview of prison conditions and made twelve key recommendations and 204 specific proposals. The inquiry concluded that while there had been specific reasons for the riots in different jails, a content analysis of the letters that Lord Woolf had received from prisoners suggested six reasons which were common to every prison that experienced problems. These were physical conditions, in particular the fact that 'slopping out' resulted in poor sanitation; overcrowding; prisoners being locked in their cells for long periods of the day – in other words being 'banged up' with no access to exercise or association; the quality of the food; the attitudes of staff towards the prisoners; and, finally, what was described by Woolf and Tumim as an absence of 'justice'. All of this resulted in 'copycat' action which saw bored and hostile prisoners respond to what was happening at HMP Strangeways by rioting within their own prisons.

We should not ignore this finding that staff attitudes towards prisoners were seen by the prisoners themselves as a contributory factor in causing the riots. After all, as the analysis of the four prison-officer autobiographies suggested, prison officers do indeed shape the culture of what

Exterior wall and tower of Strangeways Prison, Manchester, in 1990, and gatehouse, 1960.

Prisoners on the roof of the prison during the riot of 1990, watched by staff in C&R uniforms.

happens on the landings of our jails, for good or for ill. HMP Strangeways was at the time known as a prison which had been built on unchecked prison officer power, 'underpinned by a militarized hierarchy of masculinity and sustained violent interventions' into the lives of prisoners.[59] The prison was widely acknowledged to have a strong 'canteen culture' which celebrated hard drinking and an associated, authoritarian 'ethic of hard men doing a hard job' which involved them physically confronting prisoners.[60] There is much here that we can recognize from the writings of Thompson, Dawkins, Douglas and Levy. As John Bowden, an ex-prisoner, has commented:

> Prisoners had shown that even one of the most brutal gaols in England, a true bastion of screw power and authority, could be reduced to a burning wreck if and when prisoners decided that enough was enough.[61]

This much more critical analysis was not pursued by Woolf, who in his twelve recommendations concentrated on more pragmatic issues related to closer cooperation between different parts of the criminal justice system; more visible leadership within the prison service by a director general who was to be in charge on a day-to-day basis; and improved standards of justice within prisons, which would involve new grievance procedures for prisoners, relieving the lay Boards of Visitors of their adjudicatory role and providing final access to an independent ombudsman. He also recommended that politicians – at the time of his report, the home secretary was Kenneth Baker – should make a public recommendation that 'slopping out' should end by early 1996. Woolf seemed to create a much more optimistic view about prisons and he – or at least the riots – also helped to contribute towards significantly reducing the willingness of magistrates and judges to send people to prison at this time. As a result the prison population fell.[62] In the end Baker was replaced in April 1992 by Kenneth Clarke, who remained in the post for a year until he himself was replaced in May 1993 by Michael Howard. Nonetheless, for a few brief months, there seemed to be more general and public acceptance that prisons could not continue to be run as they had been and that things had to change. That acceptance was to be short-lived.

SEVEN

Politicians, the Public and Privatization, 1992–2010

Let us be clear. Prison works. It ensures that we are protected from
murderers, muggers and rapists – and it makes many who are
tempted to commit crime think twice.

Home Secretary Michael Howard in a speech at
the Conservative Party Conference, October 1993

O n the afternoon of 12 February 1993, in Bootle, Liverpool, two ten-
year-old boys called Robert Thompson and Jon Venables, who were
truanting from school, abducted two-year-old James Bulger from the
Strand Shopping Centre while his mother was being served in a butcher's
shop. The abduction was captured on the shopping centre's CCTV system
and the images of James being led away to his death quickly became iconic.
After his abduction, Venables and Thompson took James on a walk of two
and a half miles through the town, battering him along the way. They were
passed by at least 38 witnesses, none of whom intervened effectively to
save James. As darkness fell, Venables and Thompson finally brought James
to a railway line where they brutally kicked him to death and hammered
him with bricks and an iron bar before leaving his partially stripped body
on the tracks. His body was later further mutilated by a train.[1]

Venables and Thompson were arrested on 18 February, and first
appeared in South Sefton Magistrates Court on 22 February, outside of
which an angry mob had gathered. They were finally sentenced to be
detained at Her Majesty's Pleasure in November 1993 and their tariff was
set at eight years. This was later increased to ten years, although Michael
Howard – partly responding to a public campaign in The Sun newspaper
– increased this further to fifteen years in 1994. Eventually, after various
appeals to the European Court of Human Rights, this was reduced by
Lord Justice Woolf to eight years, the original tariff, and Venables and
Thompson were subsequently released in 2001, although Venables has
since been re-imprisoned for breaching a number of conditions of his
release licence, and released once again.

162

These simple – if horrifying – details of the case hardly captures how central the murder of James Bulger is to the recent history of criminal justice of this country. It was the tipping point in penal sensibilities which saw prison regimes toughen and custodial sentences lengthen and prompted the numbers of children and adults being sent to prison to increase dramatically. This murder was the trigger for the massive number of people that we are currently imprisoning and, even in its immediate wake, created the ground for mandatory minimum sentences, Anti-Social Behaviour Orders (ASBOS), personal responsibilization and moral condemnation. Even Michael Howard's 'Prison Works' speech, quoted at the start of this chapter, came after James's death – not before – and so one can assume that what started the growth in prison numbers was the murder of this small child rather than the right-wing ideology of the then home secretary.

I will return to the use that politicians made of James's death later in the chapter, but here it is important to reinforce how the murder of this two-year-old boy by two other children sparked a debate about a range of social and moral issues, including single mothers; 'home alone children'; bad parenting; 'video nasties'; and violent video games. It shaped the Criminal Justice and Public Order Act of 1994, which lowered, for example, the age at which a child could receive an indeterminate sentence and created the Secure Training Order, which allowed twelve- to fourteen-year-old juvenile offenders to be locked up in newly created and privately run Secure Training Centres. In short, this tragic and horrifying crime changed the context in which crime and punishment was debated, as had the 'garrotting panic' of the 1860s, and brought the public back to the forefront of thinking about prison and what should happen inside our jails. That situation continues to this day.

How do the public – one of our three key audiences – view prison and prisoners and what circumstances led to the (re)introduction of prisons being run for profit? In relation to this latter issue I will compare HMP The Wolds with HMP Woodhill – the former the first privately run prison in Britain, and the latter opened in Milton Keynes in July 1992, and at the time seen as the public sector's response to The Wolds. But what about the public? How might we understand what they think about prisons and what happens inside our jails, given that very few people ever actually enter a prison? How should we define what is meant when we use the term 'the public'? Is this the 'general public', or specialist commentators about prisons, such as charities or NGOs who know more about prisons and prison conditions than the average man or woman on the street? And what about politicians, who are also part of 'the public'? How do they 'use' issues related to prisons to make political points and how keen are they to actually intervene in the day-to-day running of our jails? I will suggest that it is the 'general public' and their views about prisons and prisoners that we should be concerned with, and that politicians and others do not necessarily represent the general public's views accurately.

In relation to the issue of politicians interfering in the running and operation of our prisons I will again turn to the events that unfolded after the escapes from HMPs Whitemoor and Parkhurst. More generally, in an effort to overcome some of the difficulties related to knowing what the general public might actually think about prisons and prisoners, I will consider how the media present issues about prisons to their readers and viewers. After all, dramatic presentations about prisoners and what happens inside our prisons will have an impact on how people view prisons and those who are held there. Popular TV programmes and films, such as Bad Girls (1999–2006) and Porridge (1974–7), can be used as a crude device to infer what finds favour with the general public and in turn how TV programmes and films about prisons might be used to generate penal reform. However, given how central the murder of James Bulger is to creating the context to what is going to be described, let us return to the political reaction that took place in its aftermath.

A Re-consensus of Left and Right

The murder of James Bulger served to create (some might argue, recreate) a political consensus between New Labour and the Conservatives around the idea that each was the party of 'law and order' – a consensus which largely continues. Crucial here was the fact that a young politician called Tony Blair, at that time the shadow home secretary, had been influenced by a recent visit to the USA where he had come under the spell of Bill Clinton: a Democratic president who had supported the use of the death penalty.[2] In short, Blair was not prepared to be outflanked by the right as far as 'law and order' was concerned. So in January 1993, in the month prior to James's murder, Blair argued on ITV's The World This Weekend that New Labour would be 'tough on crime, and tough on the causes of crime'. Following the murder, he argued that 'children should be taught the

'Happiness is door-shaped': a prison wing after 'bang up'.

value of what is right and what is wrong'. More broadly, he told a Labour Party audience in Wellingborough that

> The news bulletins of the last week have been like hammer blows struck against the sleeping conscience of the country . . . a solution to this disintegration doesn't simply lie in legislation. It must come from the rediscovery of a sense of direction as a country . . . not just as individuals but as a community . . . we cannot exist in a moral vacuum. If we do not learn and then teach the value of what is right and what is wrong, then the result is simply moral chaos that engulfs us all.[3]

Not to be outdone, the prime minister, John Major, argued in the *Daily Mail* on 21 February 1993, that 'I would like the public to have a crusade against crime and change from being forgiving of crime to being considerate of the victim. Society needs to condemn a little more and understand a little less.' It was in this context that Michael Howard delighted the Conservative Party Conference by reminding his audience that 'prison works'.

So, as these soundbites of political sloganeering – which more broadly might be described as 'populist punitiveness' – suggest, James Bulger's murder became the battleground of a political culture which was oppositional and confrontational, even if both main parties were in fact largely saying the same things and appealing to similar popular emotions. The description 'popular emotions' has been carefully chosen. For it was the political reaction to James's murder which signalled, quite deliberately, that politicians would increasingly pay attention to what they saw as the emotional dynamics of the general public. In another sphere this has been called 'emotional governance'.[4]

One way of viewing how James's murder fed into particularly British political, popular and media cultures and was variously used by them is to compare his murder with that of five-year-old Silje Redergard, who was killed in October 1994 in Trondheim, Norway. Silje was murdered by three six-year-old boys who had her strip and then took it in turns to hit and beat her with stones and sticks before finally stamping on her body. They left her unconscious in the snow; she would later die of hypothermia. None of the three boys were punished; there was no outpouring of anger or outrage from the families involved, no cries for vigilante justice and no political manoeuvring by any politician to politicize the incident. Rather, it was treated as a tragic event – a terrible aberration – rather than an incident which was iconic of broader political or moral anxieties. As a result there were no policy developments related to this incident in Norway; their prison population remained unaltered; and a few days afterwards the three boys returned to their schools.[5]

Neither Blair – who of course would never become home secretary – nor Howard sought to reflect on the different reactions that Silje's murder created in Norway to that which had taken place in Britain and both would become increasingly happy to intervene in the affairs of criminal justice policy more generally and prisons specifically.[6] This was shown rather dramatically in the events that took place after the escapes from HMPs Whitemoor and Parkhurst.

A Tale of Two Home Secretaries

Michael Howard's 'prison works' mantra was clearly going to be put under a great deal of pressure in the wake of the escapes from Whitemoor and Parkhurst. After the first set of escapes he was, according to one civil servant, 'running about like a headless chicken, apparently making policy on the basis of whatever was in that afternoon's *Evening Standard* editorial'.[7] The escapes from HMP Parkhurst compounded his embarrassment. John

Marriott was at the time the governor of the prison and Philippa Drew, who was the director of the prison service area that included H M P Parkhurst, was sent by Derek Lewis, the first private sector incumbent of the post of Director General of the Prison Service, to tell Marriott that he was to be moved to a job at Prison Service Headquarters in London. Drew explained that

> Marriott was very upset and angry when I gave him the bad news.
> But I said that the Home Secretary was going to make clear in
> his statement to parliament that this was an administrative move
> and not to be seen as a punishment. And that Marriott would have
> time to clear his desk and say his goodbyes. I made various phone
> calls from the Isle of Wight to London to agree the wording of the
> statement. When the final text was read over to me I went ape, and
> Marriott went absolutely spare. Howard was determined that the
> move should be made that same day. It would not have made a
> halfpenny worth of difference which day he went but this was a
> sign of Howard's petty-minded punitiveness. It was an example
> of a small-minded, nasty man I am afraid.[8]

Worse was to come, as recounted in Derek Lewis's autobiography *Hidden Agendas: Politics, Law and Disorder*. Lewis went to the House of Commons, where Howard had to make a statement about the escapes. In this statement Lewis heard Howard claim for the first time that he was only responsible for penal policy, while operational matters were the responsibility of the director general. However, the removal of a governor from his post was clearly an operational matter and therefore this could not be seen as a decision taken by the home secretary. Nor, Lewis noted, were the newspapers being briefed that Marriott was being moved, or even suspended. Rather, they were reporting that he was being sacked. As Lewis puts it 'it was an outrageous misrepresentation which had staff in the prison service up in arms.'[9]

Lewis's and Drew's recollections about this matter simply cannot be reconciled with what Howard claimed. Even so, Lewis was sacked a few months later. Howard got something of a comeuppance when he was interviewed on *Newsnight*, the B B C's flagship news programme, in May 1997, in the wake of the Conservatives' defeat at the general election. *Newsnight*'s pugnacious anchor Jeremy Paxman asked Howard on twelve separate occasions if the former home secretary had 'threatened to overrule'

Derek Lewis, who did not want Marriott suspended or sacked. On twelve separate occasions Howard offered an evasive answer, although he tried to stick to the line that he was simply responsible for penal policy. This interview was widely seen as being responsible for Howard's political career stalling, although he would not be the last home secretary who intervened – or threatened to intervene – in the day-to-day management of Britain's prisons. Sadly, John Marriott died in June 1998 and his obituary in *The Independent* noted that he had been a 'successful, imaginative, creative Prison Governor' during his time at HMP Parkhurst between 1990 and 1995, during which period there had been 'neither significant disorder nor serious assault'.[10]

The home secretary who replaced Howard was Jack Straw. He too was prepared to intervene in the running of prisons, although about some very different matters – of all things, so-called prison 'parties' and the arts in prison. In September 2008 *The Sun* newspaper carried a story under the headline 'Monsters' Ball', clearly incensed by a Halloween party that was seemingly being planned at HMP Holloway. The newspaper criticized the fact that 'women killers [are to] enjoy a sickening knees-up.'[11] It was obvious that the story had been leaked from staff working in the prison – who presumably were also 'sickened' that their charges were to be allowed a 'knees-up' – and Straw, detecting public (or at least *The Sun*'s) disapproval of the proposal, intervened to ensure that the Halloween party was cancelled.

However, Straw did not stop there. Through Prison Service Instruction 50 (PSI 50), introduced in January 2009, he forbade prisons to run any 'recreational, social or educational activity' unless it met 'the public acceptability test'. This was in part Straw's more general response to the news that HMP Whitemoor had been running comedy classes – through an organization called The Comedy School – for prisoners, which had again been reported on in *The Sun*.

The difficulty relating to this for those working in the arts within prisons more generally is that if comedy is unacceptable, what about opera, drama, radio, sculpture, music or dance? Might not the general public also object to there being writers or artists in residence within our prisons, teaching inmates to write or to paint? Perhaps the general public would also object to prisoners getting access to computers, or to Open University courses? Perhaps also to hot meals? The arts have played a long and honourable role in helping prisoners to change their behaviour, as I have discussed in relation to the Barlinnie Special Unit, which a range of recent research can also demonstrate.[12] Even the Comedy School had been working in prisons since 1998. Erwin James, a former prisoner who now works as a journalist for *The Guardian*, for example, remembered that when he was being held at HMP Long Lartin he had attended a concert by the singer-songwriter John Martyn:

> He gave the performance of a lifetime. For two hours, in a place where hope was the rarest commodity, he lifted hearts and humanized souls like nothing I had experienced. [It] reminded us that we were members of the human race.[13]

Would the general public really want to deny prisoners this type of experience? Might they actually want to encourage activities within our prisons that helped prisoners to change their behaviour?

On coming to power in 2010, Crispin Blunt, the new minister for prisons under the coalition government, spoke out against PSI 50 and called it a 'deleterious, damaging and daft instruction' in a speech hosted by Nacro.[14] He said that the ban had been 'typical of the last administration's flakiness under pressure' and that Straw had 'over-reacted'. Blunt made it clear that PSI 50 was to be rescinded. Two days after his speech – in the wake of a barrage of hostile, tabloid headlines and stories – Blunt's proposal was disowned by the government and the 'public acceptability test' remains in place.[15]

Publicly Acceptable?

How should we assess what the general public actually thinks about prisons and prisoners? Are their views always as popularly punitive as some of our politicians seem to think and in the way that is usually implied when crime and prison stories get reported on in our tabloid media? Through opinion polling, it would seem that while the British public may indeed be more punitive in their attitudes towards sentencing than our European neighbours (but less punitive than the Americans), they do not have closed minds. They are found to be in favour of offenders being asked to give compensation to their victims, or sentenced to a community punishment or a restorative justice initiative, and, more generally, of alternatives to custody.

A survey conducted in 2011, for example, found that while the general public talk tough in response to opinion polls about sentencing, when asked to consider specific criminal cases and the individual offenders involved, far from having knee-jerk reactions to locking these offenders up, there was considerable support for approaches related to improving mental health care and treatment to tackle drug addiction, rather than simply locking the offender up and throwing away the key.[16] This finding suggests that the public have a much more nuanced view about issues related to crime and punishment which can be traced over a number of years. An NOP poll following the riots at HMP Strangeways, for example, suggested that the general public thought that too many people were being sent to prison and that the majority were appalled by the squalid conditions in the jail.[17]

What is also striking about the general public, when they are asked their views in general surveys of this kind, is their lack of knowledge about crime and punishment. Most people underestimate the length of sentences which are routinely given to offenders, for example, and despite the fact that the British Crime Survey shows that crime rates have actually fallen by 42 per cent since 1997, only 4 per cent of those interviewed thought that it had decreased. Instead, 83 per cent of those interviewed thought that crime was rising. Significantly, 62 per cent of those people who thought that crime was rising said that this was a result of what they watched on TV, with many getting their information from soap operas. Indeed, research conducted in 2003 by the Open University (OU) suggested that TV crime stories are extremely popular and that 96 per cent of their sample watched crime programmes every week. This sample also agreed that television usually portrays community sentencing as a 'joke punishment that does not work' and that crime programmes 'make you think that prison is the only solution to most serious forms of crime'. The OU researchers concluded that through a discussion of the moral ambiguities of the crime stories that were being watched by their sample, their initially expressed, deeply punitive tabloid- or soundbite-inspired rhetoric disappeared. They also suggested that

> viewers' judgements of media crime stories indicate significant 'attitude sway' depending on the storyline, sometimes dramatic and sometimes minimal, between strong moral condemnation and a more understanding approach.[18]

All of this suggests a far different 'public' from the one that is usually evoked by the tabloid press – and then reacted to by our politicians – as well as the importance of taking seriously what it is that viewers watch about prisons and prisoners. Could popular, mainstream TV programmes and films about prisons and prisoners perhaps even have served a penal reform function?[19] Might television programmes and films about prisons, for example, help to set standards of what is and is not acceptable practice in prison and, by representing prisoners as people with hopes and values, dreams and ambitions – just like those of the public – help to counter processes of dramatic dehumanization, which often reduces prisoners to some sort of feral beast and 'super predators'? Perhaps popular television programmes have contributed towards these more subtle views about prisons and prisoners that are revealed in public opinion surveys.

Prison on Television: Prison Reform?

First aired in June 1999, ITV's prime-time women's prison drama *Bad Girls* was by the end of its second season regularly gaining audiences of more than 8 million viewers. In September 2003, as its fifth series came to a close – there were to be eight seasons of the drama in total before it ended in 2006 and then an opera – it was still achieving audiences of over 6 million viewers. The drama was set at the fictitious HMP Larkhall, a women's prison located somewhere in South London (although it was originally filmed at the old HMP Oxford before the prison was sold and turned into a luxury hotel), and in weekly episodes depicted the lives of prisoners and staff. The drama was set almost entirely within the prison, and eclectically combined aspects of soap opera, prime-time drama and cult television so as to deliver a variety of pleasures to its audience. However, over the duration of its existence, the series maintained a consistent, critical and informative perspective on prisons and prisoners and combined a number of strategies to ensure viewer pleasure with authorial purpose. As a result *Bad Girls* can be viewed as a more-or-less conscious attempt to 'speak the truth about prison' and as such ranks as one of the best, if not the best, prison drama series ever made. Without doubt it served a penal reform function.

Bad Girls is very self-consciously a women's prison drama – in two senses. First, the structure of the programme and the choice of topics for inclusion make it quite clear that the drama is attempting to make some comment on real-life experiences of prison. In addition, the producers and writers seem to be acutely aware that women's prison dramas

The Governor addresses her 'Bad Girls'.

have been done before, and that they are entering a field littered with the baggage of, most obviously, *Prisoner Cell Block H*. So the series develops an original and novel approach to dramatizing prison so as to achieve its aim of delivering a wide range of inclusive viewing pleasures to maintain the public's interest in a dramatic product that seeks to 'speak the truth' about prison. After all, speaking the truth about prison does not necessarily make interesting television or films and so *Bad Girls* bribes its viewers. In short, it does a deal with its viewers – we provide you with viewing pleasures in return for which you accept that we have some things that we want to say about prisons and prisoners. At any one time the show ran storylines that were intended to primarily engage viewer interest and entertain, and at the same time included scenes and storylines which were intended to carry a message. This separation of 'entertainment' and 'message' was never total, and frankly one of the show's greatest achievements was its ability to make 'message' elements as entertaining as those played for fun.

Bad Girls was a drama with a serious purpose, but its strategy for delivering that purpose was to produce an eclectic mix of the cartoonish, the camp and the serious. This is best understood when we consider the main characters within the series. Based on the first five seasons of *Bad Girls*, the show worked with four basic kinds of character types, although some characters inevitably fell – or moved – between them. We could identify: 'pantomime baddies' (such as Fenner and Shell) and 'goodies' (the two Julies); 'soap opera players' (such as Yvonne, Di Barker, Maxi);

players in a 'prime-time drama' (such as Helen Stewart, Nikki Wade); and finally 'dramatic approximations' (such as Zandra).

Shell and Fenner are easily identifiable as 'pantomime baddies', and their role within the series was as villains to motivate conflict. Bad Girls recognized that a women's prison drama needed a predatory 'screw' and bully. Fenner's consistently over-the-top evil is not intended as a comment on real-world prison officers and Shell's bullying of her peers is played mostly for dramatic entertainment, rather than as a comment on the violence within real-world prisons. Fenner also provides a foil for Helen Stewart – the idealistic governor – although it could be argued that this relationship is also played for entertainment not 'message', as Helen's real adversary within the jail is actually Sylvia Hollamby, whose constant carping and old-school approach to her prison officer duties create many of the problems that Helen has to deal with, which undermine her reformist intentions.

Hollamby is best thought of as a 'soap opera player'. Her character is played for fun, but not in the same way as Shell or Fenner. Sylvia's attitude towards her job is intended to carry more meaning than Fenner's deviousness or plotting. Sylvia's old-fashioned approach – which leads to the unsympathetic treatment of prisoners and causes problems within the prison (such as riots) – is meant to reveal one approach to prison work and how this is not only outmoded but also problematic. Hollamby is also different from another 'soap opera player', Yvonne Atkins. Yvonne's main function is as a locus for storylines. She is the primary instigator of scams and schemes and is the 'top dog' on the wing.

The characters of Helen Stewart and Nikki can be identified as players in a 'prime-time drama'. Through their appearance and behaviour they, and their story arcs, are connoted as characters to be taken more seriously than any other others – and in essence the early episodes of the series were built on the premise that they were in a relationship with each other. However, while it is clearly possible for prisoners and prison staff to enter into dubious relationships with one another, the love affair between Helen and Nikki was a device used to not only deliver viewer pleasure, but also to allow that relationship to carry a message. Through her on/off relationship with Helen, Nikki was able to act as an articulator of legitimate grievances about the management of the prison, and reform-minded Helen was able to respond to these within the constraints of the formal authority structure. By doing so the viewer is left in no doubt about what is fair and what is not in relation to the running of a prison.

In other words, Nikki articulates a standard of decency that should be encouraged and supported by Helen, and thus provides a benchmark for what it is that all prisons should be striving to achieve.

The last character type might be termed 'dramatic approximation'. The best example of this type of character from the first three seasons of the series is Zandra, who carried a major storyline from episode two of the first season, through to episode nine of the second season. Zandra entered Larkhall as a drug addict and briefly managed to kick her habit during her pregnancy. After losing custody of her baby, she briefly returned to drugs before stopping again, with the support and encouragement of her personal officer, Dominic McAllister. Just as she is beginning to get her life back in order it becomes apparent that she has a life-threatening illness, which eventually proves terminal. Zandra is portrayed as a minor offender who has taken the fall on a drugs rap for her boyfriend, and for whose problems prison is not really an appropriate response. Thanks to some good work by Dominic, she begins to sort out her life, although fate conspires to rob her of a happy ending. Zandra is intended to be a dramatic representation of the kind of person who can come to be inappropriately incarcerated in our penal system, and the viewer is asked to identify with her and her ultimate tragic end.

Through these characters *Bad Girls* attempted to give a voice to prisons and prisoners. What did it have to say on their behalf? Is prison a necessary and useful part of the criminal justice system? Who gets sent to prison and why? Is prison necessary to protect society from dangerous criminals? What is the trajectory of people who experience prison – in other words, will prison make a difference to their offending behaviour? *Bad Girls* consistently commented on these questions and generally concluded that, as far as women were concerned, for a surprising proportion of prisoners, prison was not a suitable response to their offending behaviour or their underlying problems, which in many instances had been the source of their offending behaviour.

Bad Girls had storylines devoted to suicide and self-harm, drug addiction, prison officer brutality and incompetence, racism, mental health, lesbianism, bullying, assault and murder – a storyline that brought its final season to an end. What about *Porridge* – the BBC comedy which ran for three series between 1974 and 1977 and was set in the 1970s when, as has been described, the penal system was known for corruption and unprofessional behaviour? *Porridge* – even if it was a situational comedy – used a number of aspects of real-world prisons, including a set featuring a

A still from 'New Faces, Old Hands', the first episode of *Porridge* (1974). One of the 'new faces' is Lennie Godber, played by Richard Beckinsale (left); Norman Stanley Fletcher, played by Ronnie Barker (second left), is an 'old hand'. The officer, Mr Mackay, has stereotypical views about prison discipline.

prison landing, cells and an association area, plus other readily identifiable prison features such as the governor's office, the prison farm and a hospital wing. Prisoners and prison staff wore uniforms, and the prisoners had to 'slop out' and were 'banged up' by the staff. The prison was shown as a hierarchy of authority, with a governor, chief officer (the rank that would disappear in 1987), senior officers and rank-and-file prison officers. There was a clear division between prison staff and prisoners, with further divisions within these two groups arising from an overall culture of 'us' and 'them'.

Through its inclusion of these and other features, *Porridge* constructed a view of prisons and prisoners which was intended to approximate what prison was actually like in some way. But in constructing this approximation, many issues related to real-world prisons and prisoners were ignored, and various other issues were modified in the process.

The criticism here is not that *Porridge* failed to show the 'reality of prison' but rather that the approximation that it constructed was selective and sanitized. Even recognizing that 'what prison is really like' is problematic – which prisons are we considering and whose account of them are we taking to constitute the reality? – we can still identify a number of ways in which *Porridge* either excluded or reworked elements which we would agree are aspects of prison. We might note, for example, that throughout three series and two Christmas specials, the show never featured a suicide. The use of solitary confinement is alluded to but never actually shown and the relationship between the 'screws' and the inmates is portrayed as structured, mild antagonism.

This is in marked contrast to the reality of the 1970s when British prisons were, as we have seen, affected by a wave of rooftop demonstrations, riots and disorder in protest against poor prison conditions, inflexible regimes and allegations of staff brutality. In *Porridge*, the inmate McLaren does indeed stage a rooftop protest and has to be talked down by the wily Fletcher, played by Ronnie Barker. But, as it turns out, the escapade is just a stunt cooked up by the two of them to wangle Fletcher a job in the library, and McLaren one in the hospital. So, too, when there is a riot, Fletcher manages to convince the governor that there is only one person who can end the disturbance – the hapless Officer Barraclough. 'Now, you men, just stop all of this and get this mess cleaned up', Barraclough implores. Much to his surprise the riot subsides and his instructions are followed. The disturbance had been staged to make 'soft screw' Mr Barraclough look good and prevent his transfer to another wing. Prison riots and *Porridge* riots are two very different things and that difference has contributed to a view of prison that still holds sway: that our prisons are too soft, and a bit of a laugh, or – as the tabloids might put it – a 'holiday camp'. In short, *Porridge*, unlike *Bad Girls*, did not serve a penal reform function and contributed to the general public's misunderstanding about what happens inside our prisons.

Banged Up

The suggestion that prison films and television series can perform a penal reform function by setting benchmarks for what is acceptable and unacceptable in our prisons, and the idea that we should take seriously the texts, audiences and industries that produce prison dramas, provide a context for considering the more recent Channel 5 reality television series *Banged Up*, which was set in a prison. This four-part series was made by the independent production company Shine North and was shown on Channel 5 in the United Kingdom between 7 and 28 July 2008.[20]

Banged Up saw the disused prison in Scarborough reconverted into a functioning jail – with suitably qualified prison personnel in attendance – into which ten young men aged between sixteen and seventeen, all of whom had offended (one or two persistently) were received as 'prisoners'. Later, adult former prisoners who had been trained as mentors were introduced into the jail as cellmates for the young prisoners. A specific device of having the young prisoners attend a 'parole board' hearing was introduced by the television production company as a means of both telling the young prisoners' stories and measuring their progress within the series. The Rt Hon. David Blunkett MP, the former home secretary (2001–2004), was recruited to chair the parole board hearing: here we have a perfect example of a politician using the media in a completely different way – albeit after he had left office. Throughout, the programme makers not only wanted to entertain viewers with this piece of reality television, but to have the young prisoners experience what prison was like in the belief that this could change their future behaviour. In short, the programme was seen as performing a penal reform function.

As might be inferred from this brief description of *Banged Up*, it is possible to uncover a number of rough groupings of participants in the series: prison staff, young prisoners, ex-offenders, other staff and staff from the television production company. However, dividing the participants into these rough groups does not capture the internal dynamics that were essential in creating the series, or reveal the overlapping and at times competing agendas which were to emerge. So, too, it is important to bear in mind that these groupings reflect only the filming process, and do not take into consideration other periods in the life of the series – either prior to the filming taking place, or afterwards during editing. However, as far as the filming process is concerned, there were three groups – irrespective of their established role – and at any given time each of these groups fought for ascendancy within the series and demanded that their agenda should have priority.

These three groups were production, moral guardians and contributors. Those in the production group were, in the main, from the production company and this group largely prioritized the needs of filming. However, this group could also include a psychologist – who was regularly on camera – the governor, parole board members and prison staff. In short, the need to produce a product – a reality television series – might involve those who saw their roles as outside of the production process and who would have prioritized other issues, become subsumed by the need to appear on camera, say something to camera or to one of the producers. Thus, even though the prison and the filming schedule were agreed in advance, there could still be tensions. For example, on the second day one member of the production group reminded the prison staff that 'I'm making a television programme here!' as a very clear reminder that a 'product' had to be produced.

The second group might be described as moral guardians. This group prioritized the needs of the young prisoners and ex-offenders and was particularly keen to emphasize the voluntary nature of the series, and, therefore, the ability of the participants to withdraw. In short, this group prioritized the issue of informed consent and guarded the ethical dimension of the project and it is a measure of the concerns of the production company that they insisted on the appointment of moral guardians. This group monitored the day-to-day physical and psychological welfare of the young prisoners and ex-offenders, and raised concerns if particular issues arose. While this group included the psychologist, the former home secretary, the governor and the on-site nurse, it also included members of the television production company who, for example, were keen to stress the various formal and informal assurances that had been given to the participants, as well as more bureaucratic procedures related to Health and Safety.

This group could also include the ex-offenders who balked at giving the young prisoners too much of a 'hard time', especially after they had bonded as the series wore on. As one ex-offender suggested: 'I wouldn't put up with bullying in a real nick and I won't put up with it in here either.' However, it is important to acknowledge that everyone involved in the making of the series was keen to ensure that no bullying or unethical behaviour took place.

The final group might be called contributors, and it included all of those who appeared in front of the camera. As such it included the young prisoners, ex-offenders, prison staff, parole board members, works staff and so forth, as well as those members of the television production company who had to take on front-of-camera, though not centre-stage, roles when the occasion demanded. For example, one of the female production team briefly became a prison officer, and it was common for the two main producers of the programme to wear prison uniforms too so as to monitor proceedings. However, the key point to grasp here is that those who belonged within this group were often pulled in different directions as the occasion demanded, especially when either the production or the moral guardians were ascendant, which would often result in them abandoning their contributors' role. For example, the governor and the psychologist were contributors to the making of the programme, and as such offered specialist advice and guidance as befitted that role. However, they also became part of production when the need demanded them to do so in the furtherance of the making of the series.

Overall it was the tension between these three groups – which often had overlapping interests as much as interests which competed – that ultimately created the product that became *Banged Up*. In order to illustrate this point and demonstrate how these groups operated in practice, I want to consider my own role in the first few hours of the series getting under way and which involved two of the young prisoners withdrawing from the series (for different reasons).

Here it should also be said that the casting of the series and the various logistical difficulties of getting ten young prisoners, contributors and a film crew to Scarborough, as well as the many problems with setting up the prison itself, meant that the first few days of filming were always going to be stressful. However, stress was added to these administrative difficulties when it became clear that on the first night – some three hours into the filming of the series – one of the young prisoners wanted to withdraw. His withdrawal meant that those who saw themselves as moral guardians prioritized this young prisoner's physical and psychological welfare – as well as practical problems such as trying to find him a place to stay that night, and arrange for his journey home – and the needs of production were consequently downgraded. Even so, these logistical and practical considerations – which clearly have a moral dimension – were organized by production. Nonetheless, his withdrawal was also filmed and production ensured that there was an appropriate narrative to explain this withdrawal. To that end I, as the governor – who had until that point been keen to stress the need to look after the young prisoner who was leaving the series – nevertheless explained to the young man that: 'You couldn't handle a pretend prison for three hours, how would you cope with a real prison for three days, three months, or even three years?' In this way my own role moved from moral guardian to contributor because of the needs of production.

In the example above – which came only hours after the experiment had started – the moral guardians could be viewed as being ascendant and the output of production characterized merely as a by-product of the action that was prompted by them. However, the withdrawal the following day by a second young prisoner saw a dramatic reversal of the relationship between production and moral guardians. In short, a second withdrawal seriously undermined the ability of the series to continue, especially as it was feared that this second withdrawal might have been merely the prelude to other young prisoners withdrawing too. So while every effort was again taken to ensure the physical and psychological well-being of this second young prisoner, it was also clear that the needs of production were becoming more pressing and would thereafter take priority. This became symbolized by the decision to allow the young prisoners to smoke in their cells.

The Smoke-free Legislation (Health Act 2006) took effect in prisons in England on 1 July 2007, at which time smoking was also banned in all prisons (or as they are known, Young Offender Institutions) holding prisoners under the age of eighteen years. This reality was enshrined in Prison Service Instruction 09/2007. As a result the young prisoners within *Banged Up* should not have been allowed to smoke. Indeed, as this would have been the situation in which they would have found themselves had they entered a real jail, enforcing this regulation created a sense of reality about the experience that the young prisoners were undergoing. However, when it became clear that the second young prisoner may have withdrawn from the experiment as a result of not being allowed to smoke (among other issues), and recognizing that all but one of the remaining prisoners smoked, a decision was taken by those within the production group to allow them to do so.

There is no way of knowing if more young prisoners would have withdrawn as a result of not being allowed to smoke in their cells, but as contributors, the young prisoners, in effect, conspired to overcome any objections that those who saw themselves as moral guardians might have had to keep the prison smoke-free. These glimpses of the industry behind the making of the series are clearly not comprehensive, but they do illustrate the tensions and opportunities that arose during the filming process. But how did the audience react to *Banged Up*?

Erwin James, writing in *The Guardian*, thought that 'David Blunkett's Banged Up is a sham'. His is one of the more negative views on the series. However, more positive and occasionally tangential comments are presented below as a way of understanding how *Banged Up* may have positively contributed to penal reform through setting a benchmark of what is acceptable and unacceptable practice in prison to the public, and by humanizing both the young offenders and their adult mentors.

Using LexisNexis, a search was made of UK newspapers on 14 August 2008 for the term 'banged up' in the previous three months. This yielded 42 stories over 24 newspapers in which the programme was mentioned. This mention might have been as brief as the programme being cited, with the return of *Superstars*, as evidence of Channel 5's commitment to new programmes in the summer of 2008; or as long as a 2,000-word interview with David Blunkett.

As might be expected, the majority of mentions were in television previews (twenty) and reviews (eight) and clearly the majority of other articles/profiles had been sparked by the series, or publicity for it. The setting of Scarborough's former jail ensured some coverage by local papers (four mentions in *Scarborough Evening News*, ranking them second) as did the participation of ex-offenders (*Birmingham Evening News*), offenders (*Liverpool Daily Echo*) and prison officers (*Western Mail*) from around the country, but it was the use of the former home secretary, David Blunkett, as the figurehead that created both coverage and criticism, as about half of the reports appeared to concentrate on him rather than the series.

The Guardian led with eight mentions (plus one in *The Observer*) with six different writers filing previews, reviews and a long profile. There was no party line on this, and thus Gareth McLean (7 August 2008) concentrated on Blunkett and was scathing on the lack of reality: 'without the random acts of violence, rape in the showers and being surrounded by people with mental illness. So nothing like prison, then.' On the other hand, Andrew Mueller also in *The Guardian* twice made it his 'pick of the day' (19 and 26 July 2008), remarking: 'it's astounding that, despite the uncountable permutations of reality television we've endured, nobody has done this before', describing it as 'dazzlingly simple, and arguably meaningful' and stating that 'The drama is compelling, the insight into prison life fascinating.'

On the other hand, Stuart Jeffries, reviewing the series, remarked: 'Like Big Brother, this had sociological justification lost in the mists of production meetings and probably similarly disappointing viewing figures.' So we have a 'Marmite' product – people either loved it or loathed it, although the Glasgow *Evening Times* seemed to do both. For example, the paper made the programme its 'pick of the day' while nonetheless remarking: 'television, the nation's self-appointed problem solver, has the answer. A reality show . . . to give weight to the social experiment, the series is fronted by David Blunkett.' The paper then selected this picaresque detail – 'Ex-con

Dave tells the guinea pigs: "In prison, you could lose your life over a piece of toast or a bit of custard."'

While much was made of the Blunkett connection (several stories in his local papers), the *Liverpool Daily Echo* (14 July 2008) merely noted in its preview: 'David Blunkett's documentary series continues.' On the other hand, Andrea Mullaney, writing in *The Scotsman* (29 July 2008), speaks of an 'experiment in rehabilitating David Blunkett as a television personality', and Alice Thomson in *The Times* (7 July 2008) allows Blunkett to insist: 'He was not playing the role of Davina McCall. "This was no Big Brother. It wasn't even The Apprentice. We didn't seek to humiliate anyone."' The *Western Mail* (14 July 2008) is more respectful and positive in claiming: 'unquestionably this summer's toughest reality show, and what's more, it serves a very serious purpose – which is probably why it's presented by a former Home Secretary'.

In addition to lengthy pieces (ranging from 585 to 2,450 words against an average word count of 277) in *The Guardian* (7 August 2008), the *Daily Telegraph* (5 July 2008) and *The Times* (7 and 8 August 2008) focusing on Blunkett, the *New Statesman* magazine (17 July 2008) allowed him 1,400 words to justify himself and the programme. In this he sets out very fully much of the material mentioned above, name-checks many of those involved front-of-camera and praises the ex-offender mentor, Bob Croxton, the young offender whom Bob helped and another who was to join the army. These mentions are by first name but some local papers did not give that level of anonymity. On 15 July 2008 the *Liverpool Daily Echo* focused on local 'DC', whose mother had started 'to lose hope for her son, who always seemed angry and barely spoke to her' but who 'has gone from lay about to full time office worker since taking part in the programme'.

BARB figures for the week ending 13 July show that *Banged Up* had 0.99 million viewers and was ranked 28th for the channel; in first place was *Neighbours* with 1.73 million. The numbers had dropped slightly for week two at 0.96 million viewers but it was ranked 25th. It suffered a slight further decline for week three to 0.87 million viewers and 29th rank and, regrettably had dropped out of the top 30 in its final week, in which *Myra Hindley: The Prison Years* was ranked 16th with 1.07 million. For comparison, BBC1's 30th ranked programme that week, the *Six O'Clock News*, attracted 3.59 million; BBC2's *Eggheads*, 1.36 million; ITV's *Trinny and Susannah Undress the Nation*, 2.93 million and Channel 4's *Richard and Judy*, 1.08 million. While Channel 5 cannot boast the public service pretensions of the BBC or Channel 4, its schedulers and audience have a taste for crime dramas and documentaries, so the use of a reality format to address this audience is particularly appropriate and will have reached more people than read this book.

In his discussion with Decca Aitkenhead (*The Guardian*, 7 July 2008) David Blunkett explained:

> We spent a lot of time making these four one-hour episodes, actually looking at the problem and being able to talk it through. You don't get that space to be able to articulate it when you're in government. You just don't.

Elsewhere he mentions the difficulties of being home secretary and of finding funding for what he calls 'experimental programmes'. Here he is referring to 'scared straight' and restorative justice or community interventions; one of the most dramatic scenes within the series related to a restorative justice initiative with two of the young offenders. In his autobiography, Blunkett complains of the 'hand-wringing' at liberal dinner parties when enthusing about a community justice initiative he wanted to import from Brooklyn. Released from the shackles of office, he could step back and consider other options; crucially one of these was to use the media to generate a very different view of prisons and prisoners. Finally we should note that James Rampton – writing in the *Daily Telegraph* (5 July 2008) – observed: 'It's a serious social experiment. Parents, schools or youth offending teams might record these programmes and use them as a tool', although perhaps we should stop short of Stephen Piles's suggestion – also in the *Telegraph* (12 July 2008) – that 'If all of them change their ways, the criminal justice system must be handed over to Channel Five immediately.'

Prisons and Privatization

Of course, our penal system hasn't been handed over to Channel 5, and nor should it be. However, that is not to say that large, multinational corporations are not trying to make a profit out of running prisons. In fact, Britain has the most privatized prison system in Europe – yet another example of 'English exceptionalism'. In England and Wales in 2012 nearly 11,000 prisoners were being held in fourteen privately run jails, almost 11 per cent of the total prison population. In Scotland there are some 1,400 prisoners being held in two privately run prisons, amounting to almost 20 per cent of the country's prison population. The Scottish Executive seems to want to have at least four privately run prisons.[21] More privatization is also inevitable in England and Wales, as a market testing programme of eight existing public prisons is currently under way, although the G4S-run HMP Wolds returned to the public sector in 2013. The estimated value of these contracts over fifteen years is £2.5 billion. The eight public prisons being market tested are HMPs Acklington, Castington, Coldingley, Durham, Hatfield, Lindholme, Moorland and Onley. It has been calculated that if the private sector wins the competition for all eight existing public prisons this could add approximately 5,700 prisoners to the privately run penal estate.

On 1 October 2011 HMP Birmingham – which we last encountered when Charles Wilson escaped from it in 1964 and Fred West committed suicide there in 1995 – became the first existing publicly run prison to be 'contracted out' to the private sector. The estimated value to the firm G4S of the contract over its fifteen-year life is £468.3 million. Contracts such as these are currently shared between just three companies. The largest is G4S – which failed to provide the required number of security staff during the London 2012 Olympics – and which runs HMPs Altcourse, Birmingham, Parc, Rye Hill and Oakwood. The other two companies are Serco, which runs HMPs Ashfield, Dovegate, Lowdham Grange, Doncaster and Thameside, and Sodexo Justice Services (which was formerly known as Kalyx), which runs HMPs Forest Bank, Bronzefield and Peterborough.[22]

How did we get to this state of affairs? In trying to answer this question we should bear in mind the abuses and corruption that we encountered being perpetrated by a previous generation of private contractors at Newgate and also remember that the state rejected Bentham's private prison – the Panopticon – in favour of the state-run Millbank. This process of state control, rather than private contractor control, of prisons was of course formalized by the Prisons Act of 1877, which was built on the failures of privatization to deliver a penal system that was transparent, effective and free from corruption. What has changed so dramatically in recent years to allow the running of prisons to become a multi-million-pound industry?

The origins of this new wave of prison privatization stems from a report by the Adam Smith Institute – a right-wing think tank – published in 1984.[23] In their report the Institute called for an extension of privatization into the social sphere, including the delivery of punishment. They suggested that privatizing prisons would overcome spiralling costs and increase penal capacity through the use of innovative managerial practices which were being held back by the unions. Their call was ideological and, at first, largely ignored. One home secretary – Douglas Hurd – even went as far as informing the House of Commons in 1987 that 'I do not think there is a case, and I do not believe that this House would accept a case, for auctioning or privatizing the prisons or handing over the business of keeping prisoners safe to anyone other than government servants.'[24] However, by this stage a number of other Conservative politicians were much keener than Hurd to extend the transfer of what had been a government function and responsibility to the private sector. In particular, the influential House of Commons Home Affairs Select Committee, chaired by Sir Edward Gardner (who would retire from the House of Commons in 1987 and then serve as chairman of a private firm called 'Contract Prisons'[25]), started to lobby hard for prison privatization.

Initially this lobbying focused on remand prisons, where overcrowding was at its most severe, which again suggests that privatization was seen as a solution to growing prison numbers. In other words, privatization would create more space. The end result of this lobbying was a policy u-turn. As a result, prison privatization became an acceptable government objective and thereafter that objective itself was extended beyond remand provision. Angela Rumbold, the Conservative prisons minister, for example, quietly supported an amendment to the Criminal Justice Bill of 1991 to allow privatization not only of remand prisons, but of prisons holding sentenced prisoners. Nonetheless, she assured the House of Commons that 'if, and only if, the contracted-out remand centre proves to be a success might we move towards privatization of other parts of the prison service'. The following year she told the *Financial Times* that as far as prison privatization was concerned she was going to take it 'step by step so that we can test it properly'. As Stephen Nathan, the foremost authority on the history of prison privatization in Britain, has put it, 'both of these statements turned out to be false.'[26]

Leaving these essentially party political matters to one side for the moment, it is important to note what prison privatization was seen as being able to deliver which the public sector could not. The key contributions from contracting out to the private sector were believed to be an ability to drive down costs while at the same rapidly increasing the numbers of prison spaces that were needed. This was why so much attention was focused on running remand prisons, at least at first. All of this was to be achieved through innovative management techniques which were seen to be spectacularly absent from the public sector. As we have seen, the public sector had hardly served as a particularly good prisons advert, with its 'Spanish practices', industrial relations problems, overtime costs, security and control failures. Private prisons were therefore also a means of providing competition to the public sector and, no doubt, a way of taming the growing power of the POA.

The test as to whether the private sector could deliver on the claims of its supporters would come through evaluating the work of HMP Wolds – the first contracted-out remand prison in the UK – which was under the management of a company known at the time as Group 4 (Remand Services) Ltd (now G4S). HMP Wolds was a 320-bed jail for unsentenced male prisoners, located near Everthorpe in Yorkshire. Invitations to tender to run HMP Wolds had been issued in May 1991, although the public sector was barred from tendering. The accompanying Home Office documentation emphasized that this was an opportunity to establish a constructive regime and to develop a new approach to the treatment of remand prisoners, as opposed to having prisoners locked in their cells for long periods of the day. HMP Wolds received its first prisoners in April 1992. Research into the performance of the prison began later that year, undertaken by Professor Keith Bottomley of Hull University, although this was not actually published until April 1996.[27] However, only a few months after HMP Wolds had opened, the government agreed that the next candidate for contracting out would be HMP Blakenhurst – which would also accept sentenced prisoners – and in September 1993 Michael Howard announced that he wanted 10 per cent of prisons in England and Wales (twelve prisons in total) run by the private sector. So much for taking things step by step.

Bottomley's evaluation suggested that Group 4 had succeeded in running the prison for its first two years with relatively few major incidents, none of which had involved a loss of control of the prison. He also suggested that both staff and prisoners identified the quality of staff–prisoner relationships as being one of the most important aspects of HMP Wolds, but that some prisoners felt isolated and vulnerable. Prisoners were unlocked for almost fifteen hours a day. However, there were concerns about staffing levels throughout the period of the research and it was suggested that 'higher staffing levels might have had a significant effect on the mainten-ance of order and helped to reduce staff concerns about their potential vulnerability.' Above all, Bottomley concluded that, despite all that had been achieved at HMP Wolds, there were comparable achievements in some of the new public-sector local prisons. There was therefore no evidence that Wolds' achievements were necessarily related to its contracted-out status.[28]

This conclusion is based on Bottomley's research team's analysis of the performance of HMP Woodhill in Milton Keynes, which was opened in July 1992 and was even at the time seen as the public sector's answer to HMP Wolds.[29] At HMP Woodhill many of the so-called innovative managerial techniques of the private sector were just as prominent within this publicly run jail, with similar benefits for prisoners in relation to their out-of-cell hours and the regime activities that they could engage in. Education and physical exercise were available throughout the day and also during the evening; visits were run on Wednesday evenings to allow working family members of the prisoners to attend without having to take a day off work; a charity-run Visitor's Centre processed visitors to the jail and offered one-to-one counselling; and a wide variety of community-based charities and NGOs were encouraged to come into the prison on a daily basis so as to start work with prisoners who might soon be released from court back into the community.

New Labour watched all of these developments in opposition and, perhaps because of the overtly ideological nature of the debate, took a very principled view about prison privatization. Jack Straw, while shadow home secretary in March 1995, for example, observed:

> It is not appropriate for people to profit out of incarceration. This is surely one area where a free market certainly does not exist [and] at the expiry of their contracts a Labour government will bring these prisons into proper public control and run them directly as public services.[30]

However, Straw performed a u-turn almost as soon as New Labour won the 1997 General Election, renewing old contracts for UKDS to run HMP Blakenhurst and signing new contracts for two new prisons to be privately financed, designed, built and managed. By 1998 – in a speech to the annual conference of the POA – he declared that all new prisons in England and Wales would be privately built and run.[31] In fact New Labour would eventually approve of more prison privatization than their Conservative predecessors.

Is this political support for private prisons justified? Does the private sector in fact, rather than in theory, drive down costs, increase prison capacity and develop better regimes for prisoners than their public sector competitors? The evidence to support these suggestions is at best mixed, although it is often difficult to compare private with public prisons in relation to the costs involved since much of the detail needed is not available, as this is deemed to be 'commercial in confidence'. However, a parliamentary written answer in 2007 revealed that the costs of private prison places were higher than public sector places, with the exception of those for Category C prisoners.[32] It is also significant that when the public sector was allowed to compete with private companies to run HMPs Buckley Hall and Blakenhurst in 2000 and HMP Manchester in 2001, they won these bids. Their success is indicative of the fact that privatization does not hold all the answers as far as running prisons are concerned. Perhaps more significantly, there were no private bids to run the so-called 'under-performing' HMP Brixton in 2001. Perhaps this lack of interest suggests that private companies do not see how they can make a profit out of the old Victorian prisons that still dominate some parts of the penal estate, which of course the public sector still have to manage and maintain.

There are also mixed results as far as a comparison of regime conditions between public and private prisons are concerned, as the original comparison between HMP Wolds and HMP Woodhill first indicated. Every year, for the past thirteen years, private prisons have held a higher percentage of their prisoners in overcrowded accommodation than in the public sector. HMPs Forest Bank, Doncaster and Altcourse have particularly high rates of overcrowding, with 48.9 per cent, 61.7 per cent and 72.9 per cent of prisoners held in overcrowded accommodation respectively. Prisoners in most privately run prisons are also spending more time locked in their cells. In 2009–10 prisoners spent an average of just over an hour more per day locked up than they did in 2007–8. In HMP Wolds prisoners are locked in their cells for nearly three hours a day more – a dramatic change since 1992 – and at HMP Bronzefield by nearly two hours a day more. Even so, the amount being paid to private companies has continued to rise, and it is now also clear that the profits that they make are related to reduced staff costs. The ratio of prison officers to prisoners is lower in privately run prisons and the pay of prison officers is some 30 per cent higher in the public sector.[33]

All of this suggests that privatization has not delivered on the promises that were made on its behalf by its supporters. In particular we should remember that when private prisons were first starting to be taken seriously as an option in our public policy in 1987, the prison population was just over 50,000. It is now over 87,000. In other words, two decades of privatization have not helped the number of new prison spaces to keep pace with the numbers of offenders being sent to prison. Worse still, the fact that there is a market for prison places may actually have contributed to this growth in prison numbers. After all, markets help to create as well as to service demands. And there is evidence from the United States to suggest that the private sector has worked out how to make even more money out of prisoners. In Santa Ana, California, and in a few other cities, non-violent offenders can pay for better accommodation. For $82 per night they can pay for a 'cell upgrade' – a clean, quiet cell away from those who cannot afford to pay.[34] It's almost as if we've returned to Newgate.

Endings and Beginnings;
Beginnings and Endings

Next Saturday night, we're sending you back to the future!
Dr Emmett Brown to Marty McFly in *Back to the Future* (1985)

The Hollywood movie *Back to the Future* has a young Michael J. Fox play the character Marty McFly, who travels back in time to 1955 and changes the circumstances of his then present, 1985. The movie deliberately toys with the idea that events in a person's past are what determines his or her present and therefore what the future will look like. By having Marty change his past, the movie suggested, he could change his destiny. The movie and its sequels enjoyed playing around with this theme of time, subtly altering small details so as to affect one character's success or failure and all the while suggesting to the audience the need to understand how the past influences the present, and therefore how the present might also influence the future.

This book has travelled much further back than 1955 and has been concerned with a seemingly permanent social institution rather than a fictional character in a movie. The events that it has described have been all too real, except where I have deliberately discussed how prisons and prisoners are portrayed in the media. However, as my example of paying for cell upgrades suggests, there is also a sense in which we have some 'back to the future' themes emerging too; continuities rather than changes, and restatements and refashionings of the past rather than a history of 'progress'. This is why I am so loath to use the word 'conclusion' to describe this final short chapter. Instead through my title I have suggested that what seems to have ended, as far as the organization and running of prisons is concerned, can regularly reappear and be given a new lease of life.

So how then do we make sense of this history? What continuities and changes can be detected when we look at the broad sweep of the history of prisons covered in the text? The most marked change to emerge over the last few centuries has been the steady and gradual disappearance of the prison from public view. By this I mean that the general public (rather than politicians, commentators, penal charities and NGOs) – one of, if not the key, audience to whom prison has to be legitimate – no longer seems to know very much at all about what happens inside our jails, even if what happens there is done in their name. Nor do they seem to know very much about punishment more generally and this provides a focus for how I believe we should pull together the various threads that have driven this history. Of course, whom we think of as the 'public' has also changed over the time frame of the book, but my comments here are about a 'general public' that we would all recognize – the men and women standing at bus stops, discussing the weather, or drinking in pubs and clubs, and watching television on a Saturday night. It is to this general public that these final remarks are addressed, for, as I hope has been shown, politicians and others involved with the criminal justice system seem to use their knowledge of prisons for their own ends, rather than for what might be appropriate, reasonable, just and beneficial. However, finding ways of re-engaging the general public into the realities of imprisonment – or at the very least explaining why this is so important – can be both an ending and a beginning in itself.

These issues seem to have had a very specific and common origin. The so-called 'civilizing' process which saw public hangings become private rituals from 1868 onwards – when state-sponsored execution literally disappeared behind the prison's walls – was the beginning of a more general public ignorance about prison and punishment. But, as a number of historians have explained, public executions did not disappear because they offended the public's sensibilities.[1] Rather, they were removed from the general public's view because the state found that it was no longer able to assert its power and authority over the crowds of people who wanted to attend an execution, and who had by 1868 turned these spectacles into bawdy carnivals of excess. Public executions had stopped being sites that served to flaunt state power, and instead had become occasions when the general public could judge state justice – punishment – as murder in itself.

There are other issues about this move from public execution to the private ritual of hanging that are also important to consider. First we should note how the condemned reacted to the reality that a crowd was going to observe their execution. Far from preferring their death to be hidden from public view, a crowd seemed to offer to the soon-to-be-executed prisoner an opportunity to engage in a range of behaviours that might allow them to protest or to display anger, terror, defiance or courage. By dying in public, the crowd was reminded that the prisoner was not so very different to themselves. More often than not, these prisoners (and their families) were as a consequence offered public support. Nor were public executions sanitized affairs, where the 'majesty of the law' was allowed to take its course and the condemned simply 'launched into eternity'. The scaffold was all too obviously a site of physical pain, where the condemned screamed, fought, kicked out and only then slowly 'choked to death', often pissing and shitting themselves in the process.[2] So public executions reminded those watching that punishment was terrifying, painful and often unjust, and, as such, was not something to be lightly wished on others. There, but for the grace of God.

The general public's connection to and understanding of punishment is something that has been lost over time. As a consequence there is understandably a greater willingness to accept what is claimed about punishment by those who are more intimately connected with the processes whereby people are punished – in various ways – and which can often then be presented to suit their own specific needs. Prisons can therefore become 'holiday camps', or alternatively sites where compulsory 'cognitive behaviour courses' promise to deliver changed offenders. Neither the descriptions nor the promised outcomes are necessarily accurate. However, the point is not their truth, but rather the fact that it would be very hard for the general public to come to any sort of judgement about what in fact might be true. Of course, as with these two examples, the state could simply issue a denial on the one hand, or perhaps a press release on the other, celebrating that the most recent 'target' has been achieved against the latest 'key performance indicator'. Which should we trust – the denial, or the press release? What if we distrust both?

Perhaps one way of understanding how to re-engage the general public in the process of punishment and penal reform would be to learn from examples of how this has happened, or at least been attempted elsewhere. Let me start by describing a short trip that I made north of the border before considering one last prison visit. Sadly, these Scottish efforts ultimately failed to re-engage the general public in the case for penal reform, and as a result the very noble attempt by the Scottish Prisons Commission has largely failed.

Scotland the Brave?

The Scottish Prisons Commission, chaired by Henry McLeish, the former first minister of Scotland, was convened in September 2007 to reconsider Scotland's use of imprisonment in the twenty-first century. The commission set out to raise the profile of this issue so as to provide the public with better information. The commission clearly hoped that this in turn would allow for a deeper understanding of the options, outcomes and costs of imprisoning so many of Scotland's people. Quite deliberately, it sought to engage the Scottish people in a rational debate about crime and punishment, and to provide the population with information about how and with what effect different forms of punishment work. The context for establishing the commission was also rather starkly put in its final report, *Scotland's Choice*. Acknowledging that Scotland imprisons more of its people than many other European countries, and that the numbers being sent inside had increased every year of the twenty-first century, the commission noted that this willingness to imprison 'is the result of using it for those who are troubled and troubling, rather than dangerous . . . [and] high prison populations do not reduce crime; they are more likely to drive reoffending than to reduce it'.[3]

Henry McLeish continued in this vein in his foreword, and deliberately appealed to a sense of Scottish patriotism. He noted that Scotland was at a crossroads, and therefore 'must choose which future it wants for its criminal justice system'. It imprisoned too many people on short sentences, 'where there is no real expectation of being able to punish, rehabilitate or deter', and so he wanted people to step back for just a moment and

> think about what future we want by asking: what might punishment in Scotland look like twenty or thirty years from now? Here's one possible future: Scotland's prisons have fewer people in them than now; they hold only the most serious offenders, and those who present the greatest threat of harm. Our prisons are regularly included in lists of the top international models of safety and security. Prison staff regularly and expertly deliver the kinds of programmes that are most effective at producing change and accountability. There is a widely used and well-respected system of community-based sentences, the effectiveness of which is demonstrated by low reconviction rates. Communities possess

high levels of hope and pride from smart investment in services that are both needed and desired locally. Scotland plays regular host to visitors from around the world who want to learn from our achievements.[4]

McLeish also warned that there was another possible and more negative future in which there were more overcrowded prisons and staff lacked support and suffered from low morale. Prisons at the time were regularly in some form of crisis. As a result the public distrusted what happened inside them, and already fragile communities became further weakened, ensuring that the next generation would almost inevitably find itself locked up. The report concluded that Scotland had to choose which future that it wanted, but for that positive future to become a reality, 'all of us – politicians, the judiciary, the media, professionals, communities, families and individuals – have to embrace the opportunity to change.'[5] In other words, each of our audiences (with the exception of prisoners) have to be satisfied at roughly the same time.

Unfortunately Scotland's prison population has continued to grow since the publication of *Scotland's Choice*, which largely failed to engage the public in the rational debate that had been hoped for. That failure means that we need to think about other ways of engaging people about what we should do with those offenders who are 'troubled and troubling' rather than dangerous. No matter how brave the Scottish Prisons Commission might have been, the rational debate that it wanted did not happen. Trying to engage the general public in some sort of broad policy debate about reducing the prison population does not seem to pay dividends. Simply stating that reducing prison numbers was a 'good thing' – and appealing to a sense of Scottish national identity – did not lead to the policy outcome that the Scottish Prisons Commission had hoped for. We therefore need to step back again, and above all must rethink how we can best explain, promote and campaign for that future. Above all, how can we make that future matter to the general public? Surprisingly, perhaps the lessons about how this might be achieved come from the USA, and in particular New York City. Let me recount here a trip to the Big Apple that I took in 2008 in my role as Chair of the Commission on English Prisons Today.[6]

Lessons from the Big Apple

New York City sends those offenders that it wants to lock up to a diverse collection of prisons located on Rikers Island. At one stage, the numbers being sent there threatened to reach 25,000, and then suddenly they began to fall dramatically. As a result, several prisons on the island had to be 'mothballed' – in other words, shut – because there simply weren't any offenders being sent there. Why? Michael Jacobson from the think-tank the Vera Institute summed it up to me best of all – 'in New York there is lower crime, safer communities *and* fewer people in prisons'. This seemingly impossible collection of public policy outcomes is almost irresistible, even if the fact that it first took place in New York City is, to put it mildly, very odd. After all, America in general does not appear to offer any hope to those who would like to see prison numbers fall. The USA has been in the grip of mass incarceration since 1970, and as a result is between five and ten times more likely to use imprisonment than similar Western-style democracies – a reality that falls disproportionately on the poor. As a result, one in three adult African Americans is now in some form of correctional supervision. More than 2.2 million Americans are currently in jail. Would we really want to choose that type of future? Perhaps even the Americans have come to conclusion that they don't want it either.

But how could New York, a city that famously adopted the 'broken windows' policy and 'zero tolerance policing', and which as a consequence saw the numbers on Rikers Island grow and grow, have achieved a reduction in its prison population while at the same time still generating support from the general public, who stated that they felt safer than they had ever felt before?

It soon became apparent that at the heart of this changing sensibility and policy approach was an attempt to reconcile two seemingly incompatible strategies. The first of these was taking low-level, 'quality of life' crimes seriously; the second was not over-relying on the use of prison as a means of combating those offenders who transgress in these ways. Of course, convincing the general public that it was better not to send these troubled and troubling offenders to jail, but instead to offer them other kinds of interventions to combat their low-level offending, was also necessary. As Greg Berman, director of the Center for Court Innovation and formerly the lead planner for the Red Hook Community Justice Center, put it, this was not 'jail or nothing' but 'problem solving justice that creates a space for punishment, help, services and accountability'.[7]

Allied to this desire to 'reconcile the irreconcilable' was the attitude that seemed to drive the various people and groups who work on these problems. They had a can-do approach and a willingness to take on big issues; they were 'success-orientated'; they believed that they could make a difference and that no issue – not even mass incarceration – was so intractable that it couldn't be overcome. They wanted to win the public's support and confidence, and were all able and persuasive advocates of the organizations that they had created, represented or managed. Inevitably, these very qualities often meant that they saw themselves in competition with other NYC organizations, and it was commonplace for one group to claim that what successes there had been were theirs alone, or that another approach was merely 'tinkering at the margins'. This was a marketplace for ideas, not prison spaces.

There were essentially three competing and/or overlapping approaches that can explain the reconciling of the irreconcilable in New York City, and that have served to fill the public policy gap between 'jail or nothing'. These are diverting offenders away from custody through 'problem solving courts', such as the Red Hook Community Justice Center; drugs courts, which might be viewed as a scaled-up version of Red Hook; and 'justice re-investment', which is based on detailed mapping techniques of where released prisoners will re-enter the community, and where, as a consequence, investment in that community's infrastructure can be viewed as a more effective means of combating recidivism.

Here we might note that none of these approaches are necessarily new, nor are they untried in England and Wales. There are drugs courts here, and the principles that guide Red Hook have been incorporated into the North Liverpool Community Justice Centre. However, what is different is the commitment to use these approaches to guide public policy rather simply seeing them as pilots or experiments. They have become embedded in the New York City justice system: systematized.

Part of this difference can be explained by the simple reality that these New York City approach(es) have garnered public and political support, and have therefore been allowed to guide, prompt and push public policy. One factor in all of this has been the development of a more 'techno-cratic' language to explain what is being done, or, as Berman characterized it to me, 'a move away from the language of social justice'. Indeed, the most obvious example of this technocratic approach was the detailed maps of the Justice Mapping Center – an organization that uses computer mapping and other graphical depictions of quantitative data 'to analyse and communicate social policy information'. In this way politicians from both the left and the right have been able to sign up to the approaches that have been outlined and which are worth considering in more detail.

The Problem-solving Court

The Red Hook Community Justice Center is situated in Red Hook, a low-income neighbourhood in southwest Brooklyn, where the majority of residents are African American or Latino. Red Hook has had an unenviable reputation as being an area characterized by drugs, crime and disorder. The Red Hook Community Justice Center opened in the spring of 2000. It was the country's first multi-jurisdictional community court, offering a co-ordinated approach to criminal, civil and family problems. In it a single judge will hear cases involving quality-of-life crimes, domestic violence cases and landlord–tenant disputes. Offenders and litigants are linked to a wide-range of on-site services – drug treatment, mental health screening, job training and education – and offenders are required to pay back to the community through highly visible restitution projects such as painting over graffiti and cleaning local parks.

From the beginning the Red Hook Community Justice Center has been presided over by Judge Alex Calabrese, who, in common with all of those people that the commission met, was enthusiastic, personable and committed to his work. On the day I visited I was allowed to participate in a List Meeting, where all the cases to appear before the judge on that day were discussed, and to attend Judge Calabrese's court. (The British are regular visitors at Red Hook, and we were informed that Jack Straw had been at Red Hook only a matter of months before our own trip.) This List Meeting is essentially a case management conference in which each individual offender's progress since their previous court appearance is monitored to ensure that they are still attending treatment meetings, going to classes, accessing mental health support and so forth. Here it should be noted that the case manager was court-appointed and was not a probation officer, and that many of the services that were offered were run by private organizations and companies. Indeed, they had been specifically developed to meet the needs of the court as a 'supplier'; so, for example, a drug treatment course might be tailored to the court's sentence.

In court itself, an array of offenders who had committed a variety of offences came before Judge Calabrese. The approach adopted was informal; the language used by Judge Calabrese was almost always colloquial and he was at pains to reward success as a means of encouraging compliance. He had everyone in the court applaud one offender who had nearly finished his treatment programme – and there would be a 'graduation ceremony' when he had finally finished with court. Calabrese showed the court the photograph of another offender when he had been arrested and asked us to compare that photograph with the man who stood before us today. 'This guy is scary', Calabrese observed about the arrest photograph, but 'now I hardly recognise you'. The offender beamed with pride.

The goal of the court was to divert 'quality-of-life' offenders, the 'troubled and the troubling', away from jail. It saw itself as the jail alternative by helping the offender to access services which would have a long-term impact on their lives, and which would reduce their likelihood of reoffending. As Calabrese put it to me, 'downtown I had only two tools – jail or no jail. Here I have a whole clinic.' Offenders were allowed to fail several times, but were still encouraged to stay on their treatment programmes. This was not a question of being given one or two chances, but several. 'I'm interested in promoting success,' was how Calabrese expressed it, 'not failure'.

The approach seems to work, and since 1993 crime has declined by over by 60 per cent in Red Hook. There were twelve murders in 1995, for example, but none in 2003; burglary has been reduced by just under 70 per cent in the same period and there have been equally impressive reductions in the numbers of robberies and sexual offences. However, it might be argued that these decreases were replicated citywide, and that some of the drop in crime predated the opening of Red Hook. There are other issues too. Red Hook is highly personalized – both on Calabrese and on pathologizing the individual offender. Some might even view it as paternalistic. Nonetheless, Red Hook is undeniably impressive; but how can this approach be scaled up?

Brooklyn Drugs Courts

Brooklyn has a series of drugs courts and my main interest in them was to see if these drugs courts were a way of scaling up the Red Hook Community Justice Center's approach, even if the latter also dealt with issues that were not simply drug-related. I was particularly interested in STEP – the acronym stands for Screening & Treatment, Enhancement Part – which is in effect a special programme in the Brooklyn Criminal Court where those who are arrested for non-violent offences and who abuse drugs are given a specially devised treatment programme which is closely monitored by a judge. In a section in their STEP literature entitled 'What's in it for me?' four issues are highlighted.

> Rewards – STEP acknowledges progress in the following ways – phase advancement certificates; recognition by the judge and your peers,
>
> Dismissal of your charges – if you successfully complete step, the Judge will dismiss your charges,
>
> STEP gives you the opportunity to – develop job skills or learn a trade; continue your education or get back in school; rebuild ties with family and the rest of your community; live a drug and crime-free life,
>
> A new Beginning – STEP offers you the chance to move forward in your life.

In 2006 4,583 defendants were referred to the drugs courts and 438 participants 'graduated'.

In all of this, the same principles that guided the work of Red Hook were evident, and again the approach was highly personalized. The same criticisms that might be voiced about Red Hook could be equally applied here. However, the goal – which has just as much relevance in Britain – was to divert those non-violent offenders who might have been sentenced to five or ten days in jail away from prison and to connect them with community-based facilities that might be able to make an impact on why these individuals had been offending in the first place. These are 'misdemeanour offenders' – those who abuse or sell drugs or alcohol or sell sexual services – who typically clog up the prison system. As Greg Berman described it, these offenders 'are serving a life sentence, but they are doing it 10 days at a time'. What Red Hook and the drugs courts are trying to do is find a way of ending that life sentence while overcoming an over-reliance on using prison as a means of combating these low-level offenders by dealing with the root cause of their offending behaviour. However, there was a third approach too, which was not focused on the individual but on the community that these individuals came from and would return to – or 're-enter' – after prison.

Million-dollar Blocks

As part of my visit to New York I met with Eric Cadora – the director of the Justice Mapping Center – and with Professor Todd Clear, author of *Imprisoning Communities: How Mass Incarceration Makes Neighborhoods Worse.* In this work Clear argues that imprisonment has been concentrated among poor, ethnic minority males who live in impoverished neighborhoods and that 'concentrated incarceration' in these impoverished communities has 'broken families, weakened the social control capacity of parents, eroded economic strength, soured attitudes toward society and distorted politics; even, after reaching a certain level, it has increased rather than decreased crime.'[8]

The Justice Mapping Center uses computer mapping and other graphic depictions of a variety of quantitative data to analyse exactly which impoverished communities experience this 'concentrated incarceration'. Further, it suggests that there are 'million-dollar blocks' in New York City, where the costs of incarceration could be 'realigned' to help rebuild and repair these communities and in doing so help to prevent future offending. This, it is argued, is 'justice reinvestment', and it involves a different way of thinking about how to combat crime and how to reduce the prison population by preventing future offending of prisoners re-entering the community.

I saw a number of maps produced by the Justice Mapping Center – not just those they had produced in New York City – and I heard from a number of people that these maps had made an impact on politicians of different political parties. In this respect the maps were another 'techno-cratic' way of communicating the desire to reduce the numbers of people going to prison, and reinvigorate a message that crime could be taken seriously by diverting funds away from incarceration and into community-based solutions.

Common to each of these approaches that I have described was a desire to promote and market what was being done, almost as if it was a form of salesmanship. I was offered glossy brochures, often containing newspaper stories about these approaches, wherever I went; I heard from 'graduates' in one project, and in another saw a specially commissioned video. Everyone had their own 'elevator pitch'. It was impressive how clearly these approaches had been reduced to media-friendly soundbites: 'million-dollar blocks'; 'justice re-investment'; 'problem solving courts'; 'the jail alternative'; 'the STEP programme'; and 'it's not about jail or nothing'.

These soundbites seem to allow the general public a way in to understanding what is being proposed, and I have already drawn attention to how the language used deliberately moved away from the language of social justice to that which was more technical. This in turn seems to have allowed politicians from both the left and the right to sign up to these approaches without the fear that they might be endorsing something which is ideologically inconsistent with their party, and which is not seen as being 'soft on crime'. There's no political outflanking to be done. This is no small matter, and undoubtedly this has helped to create the political and practical space to allow these approaches to flourish. These simple marketing descriptions were also a way of creating a narrative to describe change, or what needed to be done and why. In Scotland this narrative was linked to the Scottish character, but in New York City it was essentially about success. In short, what was being communicated to the general public was: 'These approaches work.'

But which approach has been the most successful in pushing down New York City's crime rate and in lowering its use of prison? The simple answer is that no one approach has delivered this dividend – and here I should also acknowledge that when on the same trip I visited the NYPD they also claimed to have contributed to this success. It seems rather to have been a combination of these approaches, although they were undoubtedly given impetus by the success of the Red Hook Community Justice Center. In one sense this operated as a market leader, since when it was shown to be successful and capable of garnering community support, it encouraged other approaches to develop accordingly.

What can we learn from what has happened in New York City? There are lessons both in terms of the ideas and systems and how they were promoted. Chief among these is that it is possible to reduce the prison population, create a safer community and reduce crime.[9] This has been done by diverting away from prison low-level, non-violent offenders – the troubled and the troubling – and investing heavily in a range of treatment to overcome their mental health, addiction, housing or other social problems. This has happened at both an individual and at a community level, and has in particular been driven by the courts. All of this is described in a variety of ways, but above all it has been about focusing on success, rather than failure.

Perhaps more than anything else, we should learn that mass incarceration is not inevitable – no matter what our government has planned, or may do in the near future – and that we can influence the policy debate on these matters to reduce an over-reliance on prison. There is no need to be pessimistic and celebrate successes such as when our crime rate falls, or alternatives to custody work. But we will only be able to choose that future if we encourage the general public to take an interest in what happens in our prisons, and repeat, as often as it is necessary, that it is perfectly possible to have less crime, safer communities and fewer people in prison.

Let's Do It!

Let me end with a description of yet another prison visit, undertaken in 2009 as part of a research trip to learn more about capital punishment. My visit was to HMP Wandsworth in South London, which we last encountered being governed by Major Grew during the Second World War. When Grew was in charge, HMP Wandsworth's gallows were located on E Wing, having been moved there from F Wing in the 1930s. Despite the fact that capital punishment had been abolished in the 1960s, these gallows at HMP Wandsworth were to remain in working order – just in case execution was reintroduced – and so they were not finally dismantled until the mid-1990s. As this brief outline of the purpose of my visit indicates, this was a research trip that would allow me to reflect on the history of our prisons, how they are currently run and the future direction that they might take. More unexpectedly, it also allowed me to put into a real prison context some of the people and ideas that have driven this history.

The guide for my visit was Stewart McLaughlin, the prison's local POA branch secretary, who had also become the official curator of a small museum dedicated to preserving the prison's history, located in the garage of the former governor's quarters, just outside the jail. This is no longer where the prison's governor lives and the house that Grew returned to after patrolling the landings during the Blitz is now a staff training unit. Stewart is a self-confessed 'history anorak', but he managed to convince managers at the prison to allow him to turn the garage into a museum. He raised the money himself to ensure that there are exhibits, brochures and books. However, only around three people a week bother to make an appointment to visit and Stewart's endeavours now rely on the sale of books and small donations. Three people – almost a perfect illustration of how much prison and punishment have disappeared. There were times during the visit that Stewart seemed to be running on empty – juggling too many balls in the air – and I wondered how long his museum would last after he had retired.

Even so, he still managed to have the museum opened officially by HRH Prince Michael, Duke of Kent, in 2008.

Stewart showed me around, pointing out old photographs of staff who worked at the jail; newspaper cuttings about celebrity prisoners; and the bric-a-brac of the life of an institution which most people in the community don't really want to acknowledge. I asked Stewart about the gallows on E Wing. There was really nothing to see. If you looked closely there was some slight discolouration to the brickwork, implying that the adjoining wall might have had some former use, but unless you knew, you would never have guessed that the cleaning store had once housed a gallows and that the staff rest room had once been the condemned man's cell.

Capital punishment had first disappeared from the public's view and was now fast fading from that of those who lived and worked inside our prisons. Slowly, but surely, it was also disappearing from history. Public execution had moved seamlessly into a private ritual of death in 1868 but now even the sites, architecture and memory of these rituals were becoming lost. Prisoner and staff turnover at HMP Wandsworth meant that no one, apart from Stewart, really knew anything about the prison's grisly role in the history of capital punishment and which was frankly only being kept alive – in view – by a local historian in a converted garage because of his passion for the subject. Is this not also a metaphor for prisons more generally?

Stewart produced for me the memorandum that had led to the gallows being dismantled and to E Wing gaining an extra cleaning store and a staff rest room. It was written by another of the characters that we have encountered in our history, Philippa Drew, whom we last met explaining to John Marriott that he was going to be replaced as governor of HMP Parkhurst in 1995. 'Let's do it!' she wrote, meaning let's dismantle the gallows. The phrase suggested glee, courage and enthusiasm. The exclamation mark was probably meant to encourage speed. It was almost as if she was saying 'let's get on with it'; do it quickly, now that the decision has been taken. Should we regard this as progress? Was this an indication of humanity and civilization, and of the progress that we are continuing to make?

I don't think so. In the same way that moving hanging behind the prison's walls did not lessen its horrors and may even have made those horrors worse, dismantling the gallows and finding a new use for the condemned cell does not mean that imprisonment – punishment – is no longer painful for those who are sent to prison today. Public executions stopped because the state no longer needed the general public to view the majesty and power of the state, especially when that very same public started to get in the way; when they started to question what was being done, and sometimes to take the side of the condemned. 'Leave it to us,' the public were effectively told, 'and the bureaucratic efficiency of state-sanctioned death will ensure that justice is done in your name, in a competent, practised manner. No need for you to be involved, nor worried; no need for you to view.' We have seen that this was not the case, even if I have often described punishments that were not as severe as execution.

So, too, the complete abolition of capital punishment does not mean that the state does not still rely on legitimized force, control and violence. Nor does it mean that prisoners do not die. At the same time that Drew was writing her memo, two people per week on average were taking their own lives in prison in England and Wales; others were murdered by their fellow inmates at a rate that surpassed the murder rate in the community; and an increasing number were getting ill, growing old or both, and then dying in prison. These trends continue today. In addition, a large, usually unreported number kill themselves shortly after release, often because they are so poorly equipped to face life on the outside having served a period in jail. In other words, prisons remain the primary sites of state-sanctioned violence.[10]

The vast majority of those we are sentencing to die in this way should not be in custody at all. Either suffering from mental disorders, addicted to drugs or both, any half-decent psychiatrist or social worker could predict that the sentence imposed on them by the state is likely to kill them. Yet the courts – at the behest of government – continue to fill up the penal production line with the socially disadvantaged without caring whether they survive incarceration or not. In short, our government regards the ever-rising prison population and the casualties that it spawns as a price worth paying for persuading the general public that they are being 'tough on crime'. After all, no one is going to shout too loudly if yet another prisoner dies while inside and some might secretly regard this unofficial death penalty as just deserts – a way of reducing crime and the prison population. What better way exists, they would reason, to save taxes and at the same time rid the streets of the undeserving and the disadvantaged; the poor; the troubled and the troubling?

As my trip to HMP Wandsworth revealed to me, the state and its prisons may appear to have become ever more civilized, but all that has happened is that the pain of punishment has become better camouflaged, more secret; it is now almost completely hidden. Few members of the general public will ever venture into a prison (or even to Stewart's museum), but if they did I have no doubt that they would be saddened and shocked by what happens there and which is done in their name. Meanwhile, the state continues to be bureaucratic – and to claim that it is competent and professional – but is it democratic? As far as prisons are concerned, the state no longer even feels the need to appeal to the general public at all about what happens within our jails. As a consequence, we are fed half-truths and tabloid headlines that have begun to masquerade as penal policy. This form of camouflage continues to mask the reality that our prisons remain, as they have always been, sites of pain and retribution. That is why we need to learn lessons from the past so that we can choose a future that will deliver less crime, safer communities and fewer people in prison. Endings and beginnings; beginnings and endings.

REFERENCES

Introduction

1 See especially M. Cavadino and J. Dignan, *The Penal System: An Introduction* (London, 1992).
2 This was also noted by the French-American criminologist Loic Waquant, who questions why social scientists have stopped visiting prisons, and thus forced academics to 'turn to the writings of journalists and inmates to learn about everyday life in the cells and dungeons of America'. See his 'The Curious Eclipse of Prison Ethnography in the Age of Mass Incarceration', *Ethnography*, III/4 (2002), pp. 371–97, at p. 385. This is a trend which is perhaps less evident in the UK, although we should also consider *why* some British prisons allow criminologists to conduct research behind their walls, and who pays for this research to be done.
3 For example, there are only three books about the history of Scottish prisons in the Radzinowicz Library in the Institute of Criminology at Cambridge University – each of which I make use of in this text – and the most recent of these was published in 1991. Indeed, in discussing which books I should use as background reading, a friend and colleague – who is a professor of criminology at a Scottish University – admitted that there 'wasn't much' on the history of Scottish prisons, and suggested two of the three titles held in Cambridge. Of these three titles, the most recent is Andrew Coyle's *Inside: Re-thinking Scotland's Prisons* (Edinburgh, 1991). Coyle, a former prison governor in Scotland and later in England, also maintains that a 'comprehensive history of imprisonment in Scotland remains to be written' (p. 15), and suggests that there were three distinct phases in the development of Scottish prisons: 1835 to 1877; 1877 to the demise of the Prison Commission for Scotland in 1929; and finally 1929 to 'the present day', when the Scottish Prison Service became more fully located within the civil service rather than the criminal justice system. I do not use this periodization in what follows, and fear that the distinctiveness that Coyle suggests for the Scottish prison system is much less marked than he imagines.

ONE Grand Castles and Thieves' Holes

1 J. Cameron, *Prisons and Punishment in Scotland from the Middle Ages to the Present* (Edinburgh, 1983), p. 2. Cameron also advises that it was a 'matter of course' to pay compensation for offences such as murder, theft, assault and most other crimes.

2   See B. Dolman, 'Prisoners of the Tower', in J. Ashbee et al., *Prisoners of the Tower: The Tower of London as a State Prison, 1100–1941* (Surrey, n.d.), pp. 41–2.

3   E. Impey and G. Parnell, *The Tower of London: The Official Illustrated History* (London, 2000), p. 92. All further references to prisoners located in the Tower are taken from this book, or from Dolman, 'Prisoners of the Tower'. I also visited the Tower on a number of occasions so as to get a taste of the 'dark tourism' experience that I discuss in the text.

4   This is the advice of Colonel Adam Williamson to his men, and the quote is taken from Dolman, 'Prisoners of the Tower', p. 34.

5   Impey and Parnell, *The Tower of London*, p. 94. Those executed within the grounds of the Tower included Lady Jane Grey in 1554 and the Earl of Essex in 1601, probably because popular sympathy would have made a public execution too difficult to control and therefore would not be in the state's interests. On the other hand, the rebel Scottish peers Lord Balmerino and the Earl of Kilmarnock, who had taken part in the 1745 Jacobite rebellion, were very publicly executed on Tower Hill in 1746. Contemporary prints of their execution show how popular this event must have been, as specially erected viewing stands had to be built around the Tower's moat.

6   Quote taken from J. Ashbee, 'Torture in the Tower', in Ashbee et al., *Prisoners of the Tower*, p. 66.

7   For an account of Anne Askew's torture and execution see K. Grovier, *The Gaol: The Story of Newgate, London's Most Notorious Prison* (London, 2008), pp. 36–8.

8   Impey and Parnell, *The Tower of London*, p. 92.

9   All figures ibid., p. 98.

10 A photograph of the miniature rack, the painting by O'Neill and the photograph of the Yeoman Guard at the supposed 'scaffold site' are reproduced in Impey and Parnell, *The Tower of London*, p. 111.

11 The Tower would not be the last prison to be turned into a tourist attraction. For example, Inverary Jail is now 'Scotland's top visitor attraction', having been opened to the public in 1989. The prison itself was formerly the principal jail for the County of Argyll (see www.inveraryjail.co.uk). Four years later, Buckingham Old Gaol – which dates from 1748 – was also turned into a museum and tourist attraction, having previously been used as a police station, a fire station, an antiques shop and a public toilet after having been decommissioned as a prison (see Milton Keynes Heritage Association, www.mkheritage.co.uk). Both venues offer the opportunity to be locked up in the cells, and at Inverary staff wear period costumes to add to the authenticity. More recently a museum dedicated to recreating the history of crime and punishment in Nottingham opened in 1995, located in the city's old courthouse and gaol. The museum promises to 'capture and explain this grim and gruesome reality [by] using actors, audio guides, guide sheets & boards, lighting, sounds, set dressing and exhibitions'. There is even a 'villainous Sheriff' who can be hired to host your child's birthday party (see www.galleriesofjustice.org.uk). As with the Tower, I visited all three attractions – plus the dungeon at Dunvegan Castle on the Isle of Skye which was also used as a prison – to try to make sense of how punishment has become a commodity and the various uses that that commodity has within our culture.

12 Quote taken from Cameron, *Prisons and Punishment*, p. 35.

13 Quoted in A. Coyle, *Inside: Re-thinking Scotland's Prisons* (Edinburgh, 1991), p. 22.

14 Figures taken from Cameron, *Prisons and Punishment*, pp. 28–40.

15 The story of the pebble-dropping parishioners and of the Caithness debtor are described ibid., pp. 32–3.

16 Coyle, Inside, p. 24.

17 The use of terminology about prisons and those staff who work there is always of interest. Consider, for example, the change of description and what it implies when we move from having 'jails', 'keepers', 'turnkeys' and 'guards' – where the role being performed seems to be simply custodial – to 'penitentiaries', or closer to the present day when we have prisoners described as 'inmates' or 'offenders' and have 'corrections' staff, all of whom are controlled by a 'National Offender Management Service'.

18 Dickens would write about his visit in Sketches by Boz; Johnson would use his prison experiences in Newgate as the backdrop to his comedy The Devil is an Ass, in which we meet an archetypal keeper called 'Shackles'; and Defoe, who was imprisoned in Newgate in 1703, used memories of the prison to best effect in the novel Moll Flanders. Published under a pseudonym, Moll Flanders was supposed to be an authentic journal chronicling the life of the eponymous heroine who had been born in a prison.

19 For a discussion of the role of the Newgate ordinary, and of some of the language related to capital punishment and the 'neck verse', see H. Potter, Hanging in Judgement: Religion and the Death Penalty in England from the Bloody Code to Abolition (London, 1993).

20 Grovier, The Gaol. There are a number of other useful books about Newgate. I found S. Halliday, Newgate: London's Prototype of Hell (Stroud, 2006) and D. Rumbelow, The Triple Tree: Newgate, Tyburn and the Old Bailey (London, 1982) especially helpful.

21 Grovier, The Gaol, p. 100. We should not imagine that this irony of prison space being disreputable and also desirable has disappeared. The Malmaison (literally 'sick house') Hotel in Oxford is now a 'different kind of boutique hotel' having been converted into 95 rooms and suites out of the old Oxford gaol. Rates for one of the more luxurious of its suites can cost over £350. The hotel's entertaining website makes clear 'this time we're taking no prisoners – imagine a prison that's suddenly a luxury boutique hotel in Oxford, destination brasserie and hang-out for high-life hoodlums. Pinch yourself. You're doing time at the Mal.' While I did not stay in the hotel, I did walk round it and, having twenty years previously known this space as a prison, I quickly found myself noting how the segregation unit had become a bar, and how cells that once no one had wanted to be locked up in were being eagerly snapped up by young couples and wealthy businessmen.

22 The smell associated with prisons is an issue which has persisted over the years. For example, writing in 2008 about his career at HMP Pentonville – which would take over many of the functions of Newgate after its closure – Tony Levy remembered that in the 1980s 'my most lasting impression of the Ville will always be the stench. The whole place stank of stale tobacco, body odour and rotting human excrement. Its walls wept the smell; it got on your clothes, in your hair, and on your skin'; T. Levy, A Turnkey or Not? (Clacton-on-Sea, 2011). We should also note the title of Levy's book – and see endnote 18 – given that he was clearly upset to be thought of as simply a 'turnkey'.

23 Langley's An Accurate Description of Newgate, With the Rights, Privileges, Allowances, Fees, Dues, and Customs thereof, which Alone Offers a Detailed Tour of the Famous Premises

is discussed at some length by Grovier, *The Gaol*, pp. 96–101.

24 See Grovier, *The Gaol*, pp. 98–103.

25 Ibid., p. 30.

26 Ibid., p. 100.

27 V.A.C. Gatrell, *The Hanging Tree: Execution and the English People, 1770–1868* (Oxford, 1994), p. 32.

28 Potter, *Hanging in Judgement*, p. 20; Grovier, *The Gaol*, p. 184.

29 Gatrell, *The Hanging Tree*, p. 7. These 7,000 executions represent just a small fraction of the 35,000 people who were sentenced to death; most were transported or pardoned. Gatrell calculates that 75,000 people had been executed in England between 1530 and 1630, and so the eighteenth century – despite its association with the Bloody Code – was actually less brutal than earlier times. Gatrell also notes that there were few hangings in Scotland, with only five per year between 1805 and 1814, while there were 67 per year during the comparable period in England and Wales.

30 Grovier, *The Gaol*, at p. 270.

31 Potter, *Hanging in Judgement*, at p. 24.

32 T. West, *The Curious Case of Mr Howard: Legendary Prison Reformer* (Winchester, 2011). West's impeccably researched and fascinating biography concludes that this 'legendary prison reformer's' 'obsession' with visiting prisons and improving their conditions was 'driven partly by personal distress and by duty' (p. 353). Indeed, it is in attempting to understand this strange obsession which helps to explain the use of the adjective 'curious' in her title, as well as the more immediate sense of Howard's curiosity to see what went on behind the prison's walls. The 'distress' that West describes relates to Howard's reactions to the deaths of his mother while he was still an infant and later his two wives, but also to the strange relationship that he had with his son Jack, whom he very rarely saw, and who would ultimately end up in a Leicester asylum. However, West – rightly in my view – remains slightly sceptical about research which has previously suggested that Howard was suffering from Asperger's syndrome, as it is extremely difficult to telescope backwards and infer illnesses – mental or otherwise – from contemporary descriptions about ailments, symptoms or indeed second-hand accounts of an individual's personality. The 'duty' that she describes will be more familiar to those who understand a little of Howard and his well-known Christian, Nonconformist religious beliefs.

33 Quoted in Cameron, *Prisoners and Punishment in Scotland from the Middle Ages to the Present*, pp. 49–50.

TWO Prisons, Penitentiaries and the Origins of the Prison System

1 M. Ignatieff, *A Just Measure of Pain: The Penitentiary in the Industrial Revolution* (Harmondsworth, 1978), p. 1.

2 P. Priestley, *Victorian Prison Lives: English Prison Biography, 1830–1914* (London, 1999).

3 N. Morris, *Maconochie's Gentlemen: The Story of Norfolk Island and the Roots of Modern Prison Reform* (Oxford, 2002). This is a very interesting but largely ignored work which shows what happened to those who were transported to Australia but then committed further crimes: they were transported again, but this time to Norfolk Island.

4 Lord Justice Woolf, *Prison Disturbances, April 1990: Report of an Inquiry* (London, 1991).

5 J. Rose, *The Intellectual Life of the British Working Classes* (New Haven, CT, 2001), p. 114.

6 There are a number of accounts about Dickens and his interest in crime generally and prisons specifically. See P. Ackroyd, *Dickens* (London, 1990); P. Collins, *Dickens and Crime* (Basingstoke, 1962); E. Johnson, *Charles Dickens: His Tragedy and Triumph* (London, 1977); M. Slater, *Charles Dickens* (New Haven, CT, 2009). I have also written more extensively about this subject in my 'Millbank, the Panopticon, and their Victorian Audiences', *The Howard Journal of Criminal Justice*, XLI/4 (2002), pp. 361–81.

7 J. Cameron, *Prisons and Punishment in Scotland from the Middle Ages to the Present* (Edinburgh, 1983), p. 93.

8 A. Coyle, *Inside: Re-thinking Scotland's Prisons* (Edinburgh, 1991), p. 29.

9 For example, when Fry visited a prison in Dundee in 1818, with her brother Joseph Gurney, there was not one prisoner in it – despite the fact that Dundee was a city of some 35,000 inhabitants. James Neild visited more than 30 Scottish prisons in 1812, and records in his *State of the Prisons in England, Scotland and Wales* that in five of these prisons there were no prisoners at all, and of the rest, only the jails and bridewells of Edinburgh, Glasgow and Aberdeen held more than a dozen inmates. Howard, Fry, Gurney and Neild suggested that this lack of prisoners could largely be explained by the better system of Scottish schooling and religious instruction.

   Howard – who visited Scottish prisons in 1779, 1782 and 1783 – may have found the buildings old, dirty and unsatisfactory, but he nonetheless commented favourably on the fact that female prisoners were not put in irons, and that prisoners were released without having to pay a fee to their gaolers. These were reforms that had still to be won south of the border.

10 S. McConville, 'The Victorian Prison: England, 1865–1965', in *The Oxford History of the Prison: The Practice of Punishment in Western Society*, ed. N. Morris and D. J. Rothman (Oxford, 1998), p. 120.

11 R. McGowen, 'The Well-ordered Prison: England, 1780–1865', in *The Oxford History of the Prison*, ed. Norris and Rothman. See figures on p. 76.

12 R. Evans, *The Fabrication of Virtue: English Prison Architecture, 1750–1840* (Cambridge, 1982), p. 199.

13 Ibid., p. 198.

14 Ibid., p. 247.

15 A. Griffiths, *Memorials of Millbank and Chapters in Prison History* (London, 1884), pp. 56, 61.

16 Evans, *The Fabrication of Virtue*, p. 250.

17 Quoted in Griffiths, *Memorials of Millbank*, p. 106

18 Ibid., p. 29.

19 Ibid., p. 62.

20 S. Bryans and D. Wilson, *The Prison Governor: Theory and Practice* (Leyhill, 2001), pp. 117–20.

21 Quoted ibid., pp. 117–18.

22 Griffiths, *Memorials of Millbank*, pp. 47–50.

23 Ibid., p. 58.

24 Ibid., pp. 63–5, 170.

25 Ackroyd, *Dickens*, p. 248.
26 Ibid., p. 168
27 All of this is recounted by Griffiths, *Memorials of Millbank*.
28 See Ackroyd, *Dickens*, pp. 357–8, 493.
29 Griffiths, *Memorials of Millbank*, p. 160.
30 Ibid., pp. 41, 46.
31 Ibid., pp. 178, 179.
32 A. Liebling, *Suicide in Prison* (London, 1992), p. 59.
33 Griffiths, *Memorials of Millbank*, pp. 93–6, 128.
34 Liebling, *Suicide in Prison*, p. 171.

THREE The Prisons Act of 1877 and the Gladstone Report of 1895

1 The name lives on and HMP Wormwood Scrubs can still be found in Du Cane Road.
2 S. McConville, 'The Victorian Prison: England, 1865–1965', in *The Oxford History of the Prison: The Practice of Punishment in Western Society*, ed. N. Morris and D. J. Rothman (Oxford, 1995), p. 154.
3 The Gladstone Committee Report, quoted in R. Cross, *Punishment, Prison and the Public* (London, 1971), p. 6.
4 The Gladstone Committee Report, quoted in L. Radzinowicz and R. Hood, *A History of the English Criminal Law and Its Administration from 1750*, vol. V: *The Emergence of Penal Policy* (London, 1986), pp. 577–8.
5 See G. Pearson, *Hooligan: A History of Respectable Fears* (London, 1983).
6 R. Hughes, *The Fatal Shore: A History of the Transportation of Convicts to Australia, 1787–1868* (London, 1987), p. 70. Hughes describes the First Fleeters as a 'Noah's ark of small-time criminality' (p. 74) and notes that the majority had been convicted of minor theft. Thomas Hawell, for example, had been sentenced to seven years' transportation at the Stafford Assizes for stealing a live hen which had the value of 2d (4 pence) and a dead hen worth the same; William Rickson had stolen a wooden box which had contained some linen and five books; and fifteen-year-old John Wisehammer had stolen a packet of snuff from an apothecary's counter in Gloucester.
7 C. Emsley, *Crime and Society in England, 1750–1900* (Harlow, 2005), p. 275.
8 Quoted ibid., p. 276.
9 For an account of the journey of the First Fleeters, see Hughes, *The Fatal Shore*, pp. 67–77.
10 The correspondence can be found in J. Cameron, *Prisons and Punishment in Scotland from the Middle Ages to the Present* (Edinburgh, 1983), pp. 117–23.
11 I am thinking here of how certain bands – especially during the punk era – were quickly viewed, and in some senses deliberately portrayed, in apocalyptic terms, as a means to convey their rebellion and danger to the status quo. All of this merely served to create even greater interest in punk music. But what was true for punk can equally be seen at work in the fashion industry, literature, cinema and even design.
12 S. Cohen, *Folk Devils and Moral Panics* (London, 1972). The idea of 'deviancy amplification' comes from the work of the brilliant but rather forgotten British criminologist Leslie Wilkins in his *Social Deviance: Social Policy, Action and Research* (London, 1964). This was in turn part of what is known as 'labelling theory',

and is most associated with the work of Howard Becker, *Outsiders: Studies in the Sociology of Deviance* (London, 1963).

13 L. Radzinowicz and R. Hood, *A History of English Criminal Law* (London, 1982), p. 248.

14 Pearson, *Hooligan*, p. 130. Pearson's book remains a classic sociological examination of how the media have used certain crimes and certain types of offenders throughout British history, although curiously he does not employ the concept of moral panic. The quotes from newspapers that I use within the text come from Pearson, pp. 128–42, where reproductions of the various cartoons which I mention can also be found.

15 Quotes ibid., pp. 147–8.

16 V.A.C. Gatrell, *The Hanging Tree: Execution and the English People, 1770–1868* (Oxford, 1994), p. 5. Gatrell also states that Scotland had fewer hangings. For example, he notes that between 1805 and 1814 there was an average of 67 hangings per year in England, while over the same period in Scotland there was an average of five hangings per annum.

17 A. Stokes, *Pit of Shame: The Real Ballad of Reading Gaol* (Winchester, 2007). Stokes was a prison officer at the time when he wrote his book, and it is clear that he used his unique access to the place and to some of the records kept within the prison to good effect. He also reproduces the whole of Wilde's 'The Ballad of Reading Gaol' within his text, and offers a commentary on various issues within the poem.

18 Stokes advises that these turrets were in fact occupied by staff until 1969, prior to their being demolished.

19 Stokes, *Pit of Shame*, pp. 34–5.

20 This account of Wilde's trial, arrest and term of imprisonment is largely culled from Stokes, *Pit of Shame*, and from R. Ellmann, *Oscar Wilde* (London, 1987). I was also interested in an article written by William Payne – a former governor of HMP Reading – called 'Oscar Wilde's Imprisonment', *Prison Service Journal* (1998), pp. 30–32, in which Payne reflects on the two very different types of prison governors that Wilde encountered. He writes, 'there is a sense that prison governors today have the choice of being either an Isaacson or a Nelson.'

21 This is not meant to imply that prisoners more generally, or Wilde specifically, might not masturbate in their cells. A wonderful autobiography from our own day – F. Owens, *The Little Book of Prison: A Beginners Guide* (Winchester, 2012), pp. 63–4 – describes masturbation as 'personal time'. He goes on: 'self-abuse . . . you know knocking one out . . . spanking the monkey . . . flogging the dolphin might be your thing but this is a tricky one if you don't have a single cell . . . Even when you have the place to yourself you are still chancing getting caught.'

22 Quoted by Stokes, *Pit of Shame*, p. 83.

23 Quoted by Ellmann, *Oscar Wilde*, p. 476.

24 A copy of the table of drops from 1913 is reproduced in Stokes, *Pit of Shame*, p. 58. Tables such as these clearly indicate a desire to professionalize the mechanics of executions as a way of avoiding some of the scandals of the earlier era, when either the drop was too long – so that the head of the person being executed might literally be pulled off – or too short, which would leave the victim slowly strangling to death.

25 For example, Albert Pierrepoint used to claim that he could complete an execution in seven seconds, and a recent autobiography of a former prison officer, Robert

Douglas's *At Her Majesty's Pleasure* (London, 2007), also brings this idea of the speed and efficiency of capital punishment closer to our own day. *At Her Majesty's Pleasure* is the last part of a trilogy which traces Douglas's life, starting in Glasgow after the Second World War and afterwards describing his National Service.

26 The idea of prisons being built with 'bricks of shame' became the title of a best-selling book about prisons written by Baroness Vivien Stern in 1987.

27 Stokes, *Pit of Shame*, p. 117, advises that he has now identified where Wooldridge was buried and placed there a small brass plaque on the prison wall giving his name and date of execution.

FOUR Decarceration and the Interwar Years

1 Perhaps a couple of examples will reveal the enduring appeal of Churchill's aphorism. Lord Ramsbotham, former Chief Inspector of Prisons, uses Churchill's words in *Prisongate: The Shocking State of Britain's Prisons and the Need for Visionary Change* (London, 2003), pp. 66–7, while on the back cover Sir John Mortimer uses exactly the same quote to endorse Ramsbotham's argument. The same quote is used on the back cover of Louis Blom-Cooper's *The Penalty of Imprisonment* (London, 2008).

2 N. Elias, *The Civilizing Process* (Oxford, 1963).

3 Z. Bauman, *Modernity and the Holocaust* (Cambridge, 1989); N. Christie, *Crime Control as Industry* (London, 1993), p. 117.

4 These issues are discussed well in D. Garland, *Punishment and Modern Society* (Oxford, 1990), and J. Pratt, *Punishment and Civilization: Penal Tolerance and Intolerance in Modern Society* (London, 2002).

5 Most importantly within A. Rutherford, *Prisons and the Process of Justice: The Reductionist Challenge* (London, 1984). Rutherford was writing at a time when there was yet another 'deepening crisis' in English prisons related to increased numbers of people being sent to jail, which he characterized as 'a new and virulent form of gaol fever', p. x.

6 Ibid., p. 47.

7 E. Sutherland, 'The Decreasing Prison Population of England', *Journal of Criminal Law and Criminology*, 24 (1934), p. 800.

8 Stokes, *Pit of Shame*, p. 139.

9 See N. Mandela, *Long Walk to Freedom* (London, 1994), and V. Havel, *Letters to Olga: June 1979–September 1982* (London, 1988).

10 S. Hobhouse and F. Brockway, *English Prisons Today: Being the Report of the Prison System Enquiry Committee* (London, 1922), p. 593. This title was deliberately used by the Commission on English Prisons Today set up by the Howard League for Penal Reform, which reported in 2009.

11 S. Webb and B. Webb, *English Prisons Under Local Government* (London, 1922), p. 249.

12 T. Royle, *The Flowers of the Forest: Scotland and the First World War* (Edinburgh, 2006), p. xiii.

13 D. Kirkwood, *My Life of Revolt* (London, 1935), p. 108.

14 Ibid., p. 130.

15 Ibid., p. 149

16 Ibid., p. vi.

17 Royle, *The Flowers of the Forest*, p. 240.

18 Ibid., p. 244.

19 Ironically it costs about the same to send a young offender to prison as it would to send him to Eton or Harrow.

20 Home Office, *Report of the Departmental Committee on Persistent Offenders* (London, 1932); W. N. East and W. H. de B. Hubert, *Report on the Psychological Treatment of Crime* (London, 1939).

21 W. N. East, *Medical Aspects of Crime* (London, 1936), and *Society and the Criminal* (London, 1949).

22 V. Bailey, *Delinquency and Citizenship: Reclaiming the Young Offender, 1914–1948* (Oxford, 1987).

23 H. Scott, *Your Obedient Servant* (London, 1959).

24 A. Brown, 'Class, Discipline and Philosophy: Contested Visions in the Early Twentieth Century', *Prison Service Journal*, 194 (2009) pp. 3–5, quotation at p. 3.

25 Quoted L. Fox, *The English Prison and Borstal Systems* (London, 1952), pp. 70–71.

26 Quoted S. K. Ruck, ed., *Paterson on Prisons* (London, 1952), p. 2.

27 W. J. Forsythe, *Penal Discipline, Reformatory Projects and the English Prison Commission, 1895–1939* (Exeter, 1990), p. 189.

28 See, for example, Ruck, ed., *Paterson on Prisons*; G. F. Clayton, *The Wall Is Strong* (London, 1958); J. E. Thomas, *English Prison Officer: A Study in Conflict* (London, 1972); and G. Dendrickson and F. Thomas, *The Truth About Dartmoor* (London, 1954).

29 A. Brown, 'The Amazing Mutiny at the Dartmoor Convict Prison', *British Journal of Criminology*, 47 (2007), pp. 276–92, quotation at p. 278.

30 See, for example, the accounts provided by two ex-Dartmoor inmates: J. Phelan, *Jail Journey* (London, 1940), and R. Sparks, *Burglar to the Nobility* (London, 1961).

31 N. Milkins, *Every Mother's Nightmare: Abertillery in Mourning* (Abertillery, 2008).

32 I have written about Jones before with a colleague – see D. Wilson and M. Brookes, 'Making Sense of the Sexual Sadist Between the Wars: The Case of Harold Jones', *Journal of Forensic Psychiatry and Psychology*, XXII/4 (2011), pp. 535–50.

33 Milkins, *Every Mother's Nightmare*, p. 49.

34 Ibid., p. 51.

35 C.E.F. Rich, *Recollections of a Prison Governor* (London, 1932), p. 17.

36 Ibid., p. 49.

37 Ibid., pp. 46–7.

38 Ibid., pp. 97–100.

39 Ibid., p. 105.

40 A. Paterson, *Across the Bridges; or, Life by the South London River-side* (London, 1911), p. 1.

41 Ibid., p. 167.

42 Ibid., p. 187.

43 Ibid., p. 130.

44 Forsythe, *Penal Discipline*, p. 201.

45 P. Bowden, 'Pioneers in Forensic Psychiatry: William Norwood East: The Acceptable Face of Psychiatry', *Journal of Forensic Psychiatry and Psychology*, II/1 (1991), pp. 59–78, quoted at p. 69.

46 Quoted in Ruck, ed., *Paterson on Prisons*, pp. 12–13.

FIVE From World War to World Cup, 1945–1966

1 A. Rutherford, *Prisons and the Process of Justice: The Reductionist Challenge* (London, 1984), p. 24.

2 R. Croft-Cooke, *The Verdict of You All* (London, 1955), pp. 83, 119.

3 Ibid., p. 115

4 P. Wildeblood, *Against the Law* (London, 1955), p. 181.

5 Quoted in J. Muncie, 'Failure Never Matters: Detention Centres and the Politics of Deterrence', *Critical Social Policy*, 28 (1990), pp. 53–66.

6 For comparison's sake, in England and Wales in 2011 the average time spent in prison by someone who has committed one murder is sixteen years.

7 The most extraordinary example of this trend is the Netherlands, which saw its prison population fall between 1950 and 1975 from over 6,500 to under 2,500, or from 66 prisoners per 100,000 of the general population to seventeen. For a discussion as to why this took place see Rutherford, *Prisons and the Process of Justice*, pp. 136–45.

8 All quotes are taken from Major B. D. Grew, *Prison Governor* (London, 1958). Chapter 13 – titled 'Blitzed' – deals specifically with Grew's wartime memories.

9 It has always been a curious irony that prisons adopt rather rural names, which at one time might have suggested their comparative distance from the centre of urban areas in the Victorian era, but does not explain 'HMP Woodhill' in Milton Keynes, which was opened in the 1990s, 'HMP Lancaster Farms' or 'HMP Moorland'. In any event, supposedly isolated areas can quite quickly become swallowed up by the steady march of suburban house building, as was the case for HMP Wormwood Scrubs.

10 Ibid., p. 134.

11 Ibid., p. 128.

12 H. Potter, *Hanging in Judgement: Religion and the Death Penalty in England from the Bloody Code to Abolition* (London, 1993).

13 S. Morgan, 'Prison Lives: Critical Issues in Reading Prisoner Autobiography', *Howard Journal of Criminal Justice*, XXXVIII/3 (1999), pp. 328–40.

14 P. Baker, *Time Out of Life* (London, 1961).

15 Two excellent exceptions would be N. Smith, *A Few Kind Words and a Loaded Gun* (Harmondsworth, 2004), and E. James, *A Life Inside: A Prisoner's Notebook* (London, 2005).

16 Grew, *Prison Governor*, pp. 141, 79.

17 The Prison Act recognized the role of the secretary of state, the Prison Commission, the governor, medical officer, chaplain and officers, although the Prison Commission was abolished in 1963 and nothing was put in its place. As a result the Prison Act of 1952 does not recognize the director general of the Prison Service, or indeed any of the senior civil servants or area managers who manage individual prison governors.

18 For an overview of the work and role of the prison governor see S. Bryans and D. Wilson, *The Prison Governor: Theory and Practice* (Leyhill, 2008), and B. Abbott and S. Bryans, 'Prison Governors', in *Prisons and the Prisoner: An Introduction to the Work of Her Majesty's Prison Service*, ed. S. Bryans and R. Jones (London, 2001), pp. 182–92. For a recent autobiography of a former prison governor see J. Podmore, *Out of Sight, Out of Mind: Why Britain's Prisons are Failing* (London, 2012).

19 S. McConville, *A History of English Prison Administration, 1750–1877* (London, 1981), p. 307.

20 Home Office, *Report of the Committee on Remuneration and Conditions of Service of Certain Grades in the Prison Service (Wynn-Parry Report)* (London, 1958).

21 S. Bryans, 'Governing Prisons: An Analysis of Who is Governing Prisons and the Competencies which they Require to Govern Effectively', *Howard Journal of Criminal Justice*, XXXIX/1 (2000), pp. 14–29.

22 J. Pratt, *Punishment and Civilization: Penal Tolerance and Intolerance in Modern Society* (London, 2002), p. 151

23 Quotes taken from Rutherford, *Prisons and the Process of Justice*, p. 78.

24 There are a variety of accounts related to Blake and his escape from prison, including Blake's own autobiography, *No Other Choice* (London, 1991), as well as S. Bourke, *The Springing of George Blake* (London, 1970). Bourke undertook much of the organization of the escape. He was aided by two CND activists named Michael Randle and Patrick Pottle, who wrote an account of their part in Blake's escape, *The Blake Escape: How We Freed George Blake – and Why* (London, 1989). Despite this confession to their role in helping Blake to escape from the prison, they were actually acquitted at their subsequent trial in 1991.

25 BBC News, 'How the Great Train Robbery Unfolded', www.bbc.co.uk/news, 1 July 2009.

26 Podmore, *Out of Sight, Out of Mind*, p. 24.

27 Rutherford, *Prisons and the Process of Justice*, p. 77.

28 Thus this was actually an 'abscond' rather than an escape, given that Mitchell was working outside the prison, but the public was in no mood to acknowledge such technicalities.

six Custody, Security, Order and Control, 1967–1991

1 There is a lively debate about these issues, and I do not ignore the fact that 'order' for some criminologists is more wide-ranging, and would include 'any long-standing pattern of social relations (characterised by a minimum level of respect for persons) in which the expectations that participants have of one another are commonly met, though not necessarily without contestation': R. Sparks, A. Bottoms and W. Hay, *Prisons and the Problem of Order* (Oxford, 1996), pp. 70–79, 118–26. This is close to what Ian Dunbar described as 'dynamic security', which is discussed more fully in this chapter. For a very general introduction to this subject see E. Tullett, 'Maintaining Security and Order', in *Prisons and the Prisoner: An Introduction to the Work of Her Majesty's Prison Service*, ed. S. Bryans and R. Jones (London, 2001), pp. 270–88. See A. Liebling, ed., *Security, Justice and Order in Prison: Developing Perspectives*, report published by University of Cambridge, Institute of Criminology (1997), and more recently *Prisons and their Moral Performance: A Study of Values, Quality and Prison Life* (Oxford, 2004).

2 Home Office, *Report of the Inquiry into Prison Escapes and Security (The Mountbatten Report)* (London, 1966). Also see D. Price, 'The Origins and Durability of Security Categorisation: A Study in Penological Pragmatism or Spies, Dickie and Prison Security', *British Criminology Conference: Selected Proceedings*, vol. III: *Papers from the British Society of Criminology Conference, Liverpool, July 1999*.

3 Ibid., p. 3.

4 The issues related to dispersal versus concentration are all well covered by
A. Rutherford, *Prisons and the Process of Justice: The Reductionist Challenge* (London,
1984), pp. 79–82. Radzinowicz's report is more formally known as *Advisory
Council on the Penal System* (1968), and Leo Abse – a member of the advisory
council – wrote about their deliberations in the strangely titled *Private Member*
(London, 1973).

5 For a recent discussion see Peter J. Leonard, 'High-Security Prisoners', in *Prisons
and the Prisoner*, ed. Bryans and Jones, pp. 96–107.

6 Home Office, *Statement on the Background, Circumstances and Action taken Subsequently
Relative to the Disturbance in 'D' wing at* HM *Prison, Wormwood Scrubs on 31 August
1979; together with the Report of an Inquiry by the Regional Director of the South East
Region of the Prison Department* HC 199 (London, 1982), p. 44. Training for staff
dealing with major incidents, such as riots, has increased significantly since
the introduction of MUFTI (Minimum Use of Force Tactical Intervention) and
is now called Control and Restraint (C&R). Staff are given basic C&R training,
then further specialized training and annual refresher training to allow them
to work as part of a squad of officers who might be deployed during a riot.

7 D. Callan, *Gartree: The Story of a Prison* (Leyhill, 2005), p. xv. I have used Callan's
work to construct this account of the prison in its first twenty years, but where
I quote directly from his text I will acknowledge it by the usual convention. This
is a very useful and well-researched account of the prison – partly helped by the
fact that Callan worked at the jail and had access to the governor's journals and
POA minutes while constructing his history.

8 Ibid., p. 24.

9 Ibid., p. 29.

10 Rutherford, *Prisons and the Process of Justice*, p. 81.

11 Callan, *Gartree*, p. 31

12 Ibid., p. 32.

13 Ibid., pp. 44–9, for an account.

14 My first job as the new assistant governor at HMYOI Huntercombe in 1984 was
to sign – on a weekly basis – the cheques that were to be paid to the various
prison officers who worked in the young offender institution. It was not until
a few years later that staff began to be paid on a monthly basis with their money
directly credited to their bank accounts. Thus I know only too well how their
salary compared to my own. As a result of the Fresh Start initiative in 1987,
my own salary doubled.

15 Home Office, *The Report of the Committee of Inquiry into the* UK *Prison Service (chaired
by Mr Justice May)*, Cm 7673 (London, 1979).

16 Callan, *Gartree*, p. 36.

17 As a result, prison slang for governors is 'suits'.

18 Callan, *Gartree*, p. 64.

19 See BBC News, 'Bridgewater Pair have Awards Cut', www.bbc.co.uk/news,
24 July 2004.

20 Callan, *Gartree*, p. 75.

21 Ibid., p. 82.

22 Quoted by D. MacDonald and J. Sim, *Scottish Prisons and the Special Unit* (Glasgow,
1978), pp. 23–4.

23 R. Jeffrey, *The Barlinnie Story: Riots, Death, Retribution and Redemption in Scotland's
Infamous Prison* (Edinburgh, 2009).

24 See in particular J. Boyle, *A Sense of Freedom* (London, 1977), and H. Collins, *Autobiography of a Murderer* (London, 1997).

25 For a general introduction to the work of HMP Grendon see E. Genders and E. Player, *Grendon: A Study of a Therapeutic Prison* (Oxford, 1995) and more recently R. Shuker and E. Sullivan, *Grendon and the Emergence of Forensic Therapeutic Communities: Developments in Research and Practice* (Oxford, 2010).

26 Quoted in Jeffrey, *The Barlinnie Story*, pp. 204–5.

27 Ibid., p. 180.

28 See for example A. Coyle, *The Prisons We Deserve* (London, 1994), about his time as a prison governor in Scotland and England; D. Lewis, *Hidden Agendas: Politics, Law and Disorder* (London, 1997), who writes about his brief tenure as director general of the prison service; and D. Ramsbotham, *Prisongate: The Shocking State of Britain's Prisons and the Need for Visionary Change* (London, 2003), which outlines his views about prisons after retiring as Chief Inspector of Prisons. The Prison Inspectorate had been re-established as a result of recommendations contained within the May Report of 1979. I have previously cited John Podmore's *Out of Sight*.

29 A. Leibling and D. Price, *The Prison Officer* (Leyhill, 2001), p. 191.

30 Quite apart from ibid., see also E. Crawley and P. Crawley, 'Understanding Prison Officers: Culture, Cohesion and Conflict', in *Understanding Prison Staff*, ed. J. Bennett, B. Crewe and A. Wahidin (Cullompton, Devon, 2008), pp. 134–52, and J. E. Thomas, *The English Prison Officer since 1850: A Study in Conflict* (London, 1972).

31 Crawley and Crawley, 'Understanding Prison Officers', p. 134.

32 J. Sim, '"An Inconvenient Criminological Truth": Pain, Punishment and Prison Officers', in *Understanding Prison Staff*, ed. Bennett, Crewe and Wahidin, pp. 187–209, quotation at p. 189.

33 T. Levy, *A Turnkey of Not? My 25 Years as a Prison Officer in Her Majesty's Prisons* (Clacton-on-Sea, 2011), p. 206.

34 R. Thompson, *Screwed: The Truth About Life as a Prison Officer* (London, 2008), p. 24.

35 J. Dawkins, *The Loose Screw* (Clacton-on-Sea, 2005), quote taken from p. 12.

36 Thompson, *Screwed*, p. 56, and Dawkins, *The Loose Screw*, p. 108.

37 D. Scott, 'Creating Ghosts in the Penal Machine: Prison Officer Occupational Morality and the Techniques of Denial', in *Understanding Prison Staff*, ed. Bennett, Crewe and Wahidin, pp. 168–86, quotation at p. 168.

38 Control and Restraint – C&R – is the officially approved means by which staff can physically control prisoners, or indeed break away from a dangerous situation. C&R was developed from Tai Chi and has a number of different techniques which are taught to staff during their basic training and then throughout the rest of their career. It can be used by an individual member of staff, or as part of a three-person team and is often used to remove a prisoner from one cell to another location. This form of training is very popular with prison staff.

39 Thompson, *Screwed*, p. 230; Dawkins, *The Loose Screw*, p. 127; Robert Douglas, *At Her Majesty's Pleasure* (London, 2007), p. 144.

40 Douglas, *At Her Majesty's Pleasure*, p. 26.

41 This idea is taken from S. Cohen, *States of Denial* (Cambridge, 2001).

42 G. Sykes and D. Matza, 'Techniques of Neutralization: A Theory of Delinquency', *American Sociological Review*, XXII/6 (1957), pp. 664–70.

43 Douglas, *At Her Majesty's Pleasure*, pp. 8–9; Thompson, *Screwed*, pp. 90–99; and Dawkins, *The Loose Screw*, pp. 73–5.

44 Thompson, *Screwed*, pp. 74–5.

45 Douglas, *At Her Majesty's Pleasure*, p. 107.

46 I have written about Charles Bronson – a prisoner with whom I had some regular dealings while he was located at HMP Woodhill – in 'Bronson and Me', *The Guardian*, 16 March 2009. The quotes from Dawkins are taken from *The Loose Screw*, p. 178.

47 Quotes taken from Dawkins, *The Loose Screw*, p. 80; Thompson, *Screwed*, pp. 253–5, 259.

48 Douglas, *At Her Majesty's Pleasure*, p. 8; Dawkins, *The Loose Screw*, p. 55; and Thompson, *Screwed*, p. 69.

49 The Howard League for Penal Reform, *Turnkeys or Professionals? A Vision for the 21st Century Prison Officer* (London, 2009).

50 Thompson, *Screwed*, p. 80; Dawkins, *The Loose Screw*, p. 55; and Douglas, *At Her Majesty's Pleasure*, p. 229, and 196–7.

51 Thompson, *Screwed*, p. 8.

52 Levy, *A Turnkey or Not?*, p. 216.

53 Ibid., pp. 46, 51–2.

54 Thompson, *Screwed*, p. 119.

55 Leonard, 'High Security Prisoners', p. 103.

56 J. Woodcock, *Report of the Enquiry into the Attempted Escape from HM Prison Whitemoor on 9 September 1994* (London, 1994), p. 1.

57 Price, 'The Origins and Durability of Security', p. 2. Also see Home Office, *Review of Prison Service Security in England and Wales (The Learmont Report)* (London, 1995).

58 Lord Justice H. Woolf and Judge S. Tumim, *Prison Disturbances, 1900: Report of an Inquiry Presented to the Home Office by Lord Justice Woolf and Judge Stephen Tumim* (London, 1991).

59 Sim, 'An Inconvenient Criminological Truth', p. 56.

60 E. Carrabine, *Power, Discourse, Resistance: A Genealogy of the Strangeways Riot* (Aldershot, 2004), p. 190

61 John Bowden cited in N. Jameson and E. Allison, *Strangeways 1990: A Serious Disturbance* (London, 1995), p. 157.

62 I remember this fall in prison numbers all too clearly, as I was a governor at the soon to be opened, newly built and costly prison in Milton Keynes called HMP Woodhill. In 1992 we were so concerned that we would not have enough prisoners to fill the jail that we took the unusual step of actually advertising facilities within Woodhill to prisoners at other jails in the hope of encouraging them to apply for a transfer. In the end the prison was opened with sufficient numbers by Kenneth Clarke in July 1992. As he stepped out of his official car to survey the most cutting-edge prison in the penal estate, the home secretary commented: 'Fuck me, it looks like Sainsbury's.'

SEVEN Politicians, the Public and Privatization, 1992–2010

1 For a very moving and perceptive account of the murder of James Bulger see B. Morrison, *As If* (Cambridge, 1988). Here we should also note that in some ways the impact of the murder of James Bulger was the culmination of popular

concerns about young people and criminality. See, for example, T. Newburn, 'Back
to the Future? Youth Crime, Youth Justice and the Rediscovery of "Authoritarian
Populism"', in *Thatcher's Children? Politics, Childhood and Society in the 1980s and
1990s*, ed. J. Pilcher and S. Wagg (London, 1996), and B. Campbell, *Goliath:
Britain's Dangerous Places* (London, 1993).

2   For the influence of Clinton on the 'New Labour project' and Tony Blair see
J. Silverman, *Crime, Policy and the Media: The Shaping of Criminal Justice, 1989–2010*
(London, 2012). I have also written about this influence in D. Wilson and J. Ashton,
What Everyone in Britain Should Know About Crime and Punishment (Oxford, 2001).

3   Quoted in D. Green, *When Children Kill: Penal Populism and Political Culture*
(Oxford, 2008).

4   B. Richards, *Emotional Governance: Politics, Media and Terror* (Basingstoke, 1997).

5   For a more developed account of the reaction to Sonje's murder and how this
compares with the reaction to the murder of James Bulger, see Green, *When
Children Kill*.

6   By the summer of 2006, for example, New Labour had created 3,023 new
offences since coming to power in 1997, including making it a criminal offence
to impersonate a school inspector, carry potatoes in the hold of a ship without
a licence or cause a nuclear explosion. I wrote about all of this in *The Independent*
on 16 August 2006 in an article called 'Seduced by the Politics of Penal Populism'.
I suggested that this legislative zeal 'reflects the desire of a government to
legislate first and think later – if they think at all. For, what matters most to
them is not to carefully assess the evidence that they have, but rather to be seen
to have "done something" – anything – in the face of each new moral panic that
bubbles up from the pages of the tabloids.' I concluded this piece by asking
'So where will it all end? 4,000 new offences? Perhaps 5,000? Would perhaps
10,000 new offences make us all feel safer and, by implication keen to re-elect
New Labour? Ironically with the "fear of crime" still as high as it ever was, and
despite all the sound and fury of each new criminal justice act, it might be that
the best way to convince the electorate that "something is being done" is to do
nothing at all.'
     Silverman, *Crime, Policy and the Media*, in conducting the research for his book,
asked for copies of every press release from the Home Office between 2001 and
2009. He was sent a box containing 3,214 documents. Silverman comments that
he thinks that the number would have been greater had not the Home Office
given responsibility for prisons to the new Ministry of Justice in May 2006.

7   M. Crick, *In Search of Michael Howard* (London, 2005), p. 297.

8   Quoted in Silverman, *Crime, Policy and the Media*, p. 62.

9   D. Lewis, *Hidden Agendas: Politics, Law and Disorder* (London, 1997), p. 172.

10 Obituary of John Marriott, *The Independent*, 19 June 1998.

11 'Monsters' Ball', *The Sun*, 12 September 2008.

12 For an overview see L. Caulfield and D. Wilson, 'The Role of the Arts as
an intervention with Offenders in Prison', in *Interventions in Criminal Justice:
A Handbook for Counsellors and Therapists Working in the Criminal Justice System*,
ed. Peter Jones (Brighton, 2012)

13 *The Guardian*, 12 July 2008. Also see James's contribution to the 'public
acceptability test' debate in *The Guardian*, 3 February 2009.

14 Nacro used to be called the National Association for the Care and Resettlement
of Offenders. It now is simply known as 'Nacro – the crime reduction charity'.

It run until 2013 by Paul MacDowell, former governor of HMP Brixton. See www.nacro.org.uk.

15 Silverman, *Crime, Policy and the Media*, p. 60.

16 Prison Reform Trust, *Public Want Offenders to Make Amends*, Briefing Paper (London, 2011).

17 Quoted in M. Cavadino and J. Dignan, *The Penal System: An Introduction* (London, 1992), pp. 307–8.

18 M. Gillespie and E. McLaughlin, *Media and the Shaping of Public Knowledge and Attitudes towards Crime and Punishment* (London, 2003).

19 See D. Wilson and S. O'Sullivan, *Images of Incarceration: Representations of Prison in Film and Television Drama* (Winchester, 2004).

20 I acted as an advisor to the production company and subsequently appeared in the programme as the prison's 'governor'. As such, I was able to see in a very direct way not only how the programme was made, but also how the various messages that the programme hoped to carry to its audience were constructed. I have written about all of this more academically in D. Wilson and N. Groombridge, 'I'm Making a TV Programme Here!: Reality TV's *Banged Up* and Public Criminology', *Howard Journal of Criminal Justice*, XLIX/1 (2009), pp. 1–17.

21 Scottish Consortium on Crime and Criminal Justice, *Prison Privatisation in Scotland: A Briefing Paper of the Scottish Consortium on Crime and Criminal Justice* (Glasgow, 2006).

22 Bromley Briefings, *Prison Factfile* (London, 2012).

23 Adam Smith Institute, *Justice Policy* (London, 1984).

24 House of Commons Debates, vol. CXIX, col. 1299, 16 July 1987.

25 See Cavadino and Dignan, *The Penal System*, p. 156. Cavadino and Dignan also draw attention to a 'revolving door' between Conservative politicians and private prison companies. For example, Sir Norman Fowler, the Tory Party chairman, was a non-executive director of Group 4 until he resigned in September 1993.

26 S. Nathan, 'Prison Privatization in the United Kingdom', in *Capitalist Punishment: Prison Privatization and Human Rights*, ed. A. Coyle, A. Campbell and R. Neufeld (London, 2003), pp. 162–78, quotation at p. 163.

27 K. Bottomley, A. James, E. Clare and A. Liebling, *Wolds Remand Prison: An Evaluation*, Research Findings No. 32 (London, 1996).

28 Ibid., p. 3.

29 I know these pressures only too well, as I was a governor at the prison and had to personally deal with many of the personnel and training issues that would allow these seemingly innocuous regime changes to take place.

30 *The Times*, 8 March 1995.

31 See Nathan, 'Prison Privatization in the United Kingdom', p. 169.

32 Bromley Briefings, p. 73.

33 All figures taken from Bromley Briefings, pp. 71–3.

34 M. Sandel, *What Money Can't Buy: The Moral Limit of Markets* (London, 2012), p. 3.

Endings and Beginnings; Beginnings and Endings

1 V.A.C. Gatrell, *The Hanging Tree: Execution and the English People, 1770–1868* (Oxford, 1994), and H. Potter, *Hanging in Judgement: Religion and the Death Penalty in England from the Bloody Code to Abolition* (London, 1993).

2 I am paraphrasing Gatrell here, who urges us that we have to 'move closer to the

choking, pissing and screaming than taboo, custom, or comfort usually allows'
so as to get a better understanding of public executions. Gatrell, *The Hanging Tree*, p. 29.

3 The Scottish Prisons Commission, *Scotland's Choice: Report of the Scottish Prisons Commission* (Edinburgh, 2008).

4 Ibid., p. 1.

5 Ibid.

6 The Commission on English Prisons Today, *Do Better Do Less* (London, 2009). This final report of the commission also shows how we interpreted the lessons from New York City and suggested how they could be used within a British context.

7 All quotes are taken from my field notes of this trip.

8 T. Clear, *Imprisoning Communities: How Mass Incarceration Makes Disadvantaged Neighborhoods Worse* (New York and Oxford, 2007), p. 12.

9 The Howard League for Penal Reform has subsequently adopted this phrase as a motto which they use on their website and in written communications.

10 I have written about this state-sanctioned violence in our prisons in my *Death at the Hands of the State* (London, 2005). I opened that book with an account of the murder of Zahid Mubarek at HMYOI Feltham in March 2000. Zahid Mubarek shared Cell 38 on Swallow Unit with Robert Stewart, his killer. Nineteen-year-old Zahid had been sentenced to 90 days in custody for shoplifting £6 worth of razor blades and interfering with a motor vehicle – a perfect example of behaviour that is troubling but not dangerous. These petty misdemeanours turned out to be a capital offence.

BIBLIOGRAPHY

Abse, L., *Private Member* (London, 1973)

Ackroyd, P., *Dickens* (London, 1990)

Adam Smith Institute, *Justice Policy* (London, 1984)

Bailey, V., *Delinquency and Citizenship: Reclaiming the Young Offender, 1914–1948* (Oxford, 1987)

Baker, P., *Time Out of Life* (London, 1961)

Bauman, Z., *Modernity and the Holocaust* (Cambridge, 1989)

Becker, H., *Outsiders: Studies in the Sociology of Deviance* (London, 1963)

Bennett, J., B. Crewe and A. Wahidin, *Understanding Prison Staff* (Cullompton, Devon, 2008)

Blake, G., *No Other Choice* (London, 1991)

Blom-Cooper, L., *The Penalty of Imprisonment* (London, 2008)

Bottomley, K., A. James, E. Clare and A. Liebling, *Wolds Remand Prison: An Evaluation*, Research Findings No. 32 (London, 1996)

Bourke, S., *The Springing of George Blake* (London, 1970)

Boyle, J., *A Sense of Freedom* (London, 1977)

Bryans, S., and David Wilson, *The Prison Governor: Theory and Practice* (Leyhill, 2008)

Callan, D., *Gartree: The Story of a Prison* (Leyhill, 2005)

Cameron, J., *Prisons and Punishment in Scotland from the Middle Ages to the Present* (Edinburgh, 1983)

Campbell, B., *Goliath: Britain's Dangerous Places* (London, 1993)

Carrabine, E., *Power, Discourse, Resistance: A Genealogy of the Strangeways Riot* (Aldershot, 2004),

Cavadino, M., and J. Dignan, *The Penal System: An Introduction* (London, 1992)

Christie, N., *Crime Control as Industry* (London, 1993)

Clayton, G. F., *The Wall Is Strong* (London, 1958)

Clear, T., *Imprisoning Communities: How Mass Incarceration Makes Disadvantaged Neighborhoods Worse* (New York and Oxford, 2007),

Cohen, S., *Folk Devils and Moral Panics* (London, 1972)

Collins, H., *Autobiography of a Murderer* (London, 1997)

Collins, P., *Dickens and Crime* (Basingstoke, 1962)

The Commission on English Prisons Today, *Do Better Do Less* (London, 2009)

Coyle, A., *Inside: Re-Thinking Scotland's Prisons* (Edinburgh, 1991)

——, A. Campbell and R. Neufeld, eds, *Capitalist Punishment: Prison Privatization and Human Rights* (London, 2003)

Crick, M., *In Search of Michael Howard* (London, 2005)

Croft-Cooke, R., *The Verdict of You All* (London, 1955)

Cross, R., *Punishment, Prison and the Public* (London, 1971)

Dawkins, J., *The Loose Screw* (Clacton-on-Sea, 2005)

Dendrickson, G., and F. Thomas, *The Truth About Dartmoor* (London, 1954)

East, W. N., *Medical Aspects of Crime* (London, 1936)

——, *Society and the Criminal* (London, 1949)

——, and W. H. de B. Hubert, *Report on the Psychological Treatment of Crime* (London, 1939)

Elias, N., *The Civilizing Process* (Oxford, 1963)

Ellmann, R., *Oscar Wilde* (London, 1987)

Emsley, C., *Crime and Society in England, 1750–1900* (Harlow, 2005)

Forsythe, W. J., *Penal Discipline, Reformatory Projects and the English Prison Commission, 1895–1939* (Exeter, 1990)

Fox, L., *The English Prison and Borstal Systems* (London, 1952)

Garland, D., *Punishment and Modern Society* (Oxford, 1990)

Gatrell, V.A.C., *The Hanging Tree: Execution and the English People, 1770–1868* (Oxford, 1994)

Genders, E., and E. Player, *Grendon: A Study of a Therapeutic Prison* (Oxford, 1995)

Gillespie, M., and E. McLaughlin, *Media and the Shaping of Public Knowledge and Attitudes towards Crime and Punishment* (London, 2003).

Green, D., *When Children Kill: Penal Populism and Political Culture* (Oxford, 2008).

Grew, Major B. D., *Prison Governor* (London, 1958)

Griffiths, A., *Memorials of Millbank and Chapters in Prison History* (London, 1884)

Grovier, K., *The Gaol: The Story of Newgate, London's Most Notorious Prison* (London, 2008)

Halliday, S., *Newgate: London's Prototype of Hell* (Stroud, 2006)

Havel, V., *Letters to Olga: June 1979–September 1982* (London, 1988)

Hobhouse, S., and F. Brockway, *English Prisons Today, Being the Report of the Prison System Enquiry Committee* (London, 1922)

Home Office, *Report of the Departmental Committee on Persistent Offenders* (London, 1932)

——, *Report of the Inquiry into Prison Escapes and Security (The Mountbatten Report)* (London, 1966).

——, *Report of the Committee on Remuneration and Conditions of Service of Certain Grades in the Prison Service (Wynn-Parry Report)* (London, 1958)

——, *Statement on the Background, Circumstances and Action taken Subsequently Relative to the Disturbance in 'D' wing at HM Prison, Wormwood Scrubs on 31 August 1979; together with the Report of an Inquiry by the Regional Director of the South East Region of the Prison Department* HC 199 (London, 1982)

——, *The Report of the Committee of Inquiry into the UK Prison Service (chaired by Mr Justice May)*, Cm 7673 (London, 1979)

——, *Review of Prison Service Security in England and Wales (The Learmont Report)* (London, 1995)

The Howard League for Penal Reform, *Turnkeys or Professionals? A Vision for the 21st Century Prison Officer* (London, 2009).

Hughes, R., *The Fatal Shore: A History of the Transportation of Convicts to Australia, 1787–1868* (London, 1987)

Ignatieff, M., *A Just Measure of Pain: The Penitentiary in the Industrial Revolution* (Harmondsworth, 1978)

Impey, E., and G. Parnell, *The Tower of London: The Official Illustrated History* (London, 2000)

James, E., *A Life Inside: A Prisoner's Notebook* (London, 2005)

Jameson, N., and E. Allison, *Strangeways 1990: A Serious Disturbance* (London, 1995)

Jeffrey, R., *The Barlinnie Story: Riots, Death, Retribution and Redemption in Scotland's Infamous Prison* (Edinburgh, 2009)

Johnson, E., *Charles Dickens: His Tragedy and Triumph* (London, 1977)

Jones, P., ed., *Interventions in Criminal Justice: A Handbook for Counsellors and Therapists Working in the Criminal Justice System* (Brighton, 2012)

Kirkwood, D., *My Life of Revolt* (London, 1935)

Liebling, A., *Suicide in Prison* (London, 1992)

——, *Prisons and their Moral Performance: A Study of Values, Quality and Prison Life* (Oxford, 2004)

——, and D. Price, *The Prison Officer* (Leyhill, 2001)

Levy, T., *A Turnkey of Not? My 25 Years as a Prison Officer in Her Majesty's Prisons* (Clacton on Sea, 2011)

Lewis, D., *Hidden Agendas: Politics, Law and Disorder* (London, 1997)

McConville, S., *A History of English Prison Administration, 1750–1877* (London, 1981)

MacDonald, D., and Joe Sim, *Scottish Prisons and the Special Unit* (Glasgow, 1978)

Mandela, N., *Long Walk to Freedom* (London, 1994)

Milkins, N., *Every Mother's Nightmare: Abertillery in Mourning* (Abertillery, 2008)

Morris, N., *Maconochie's Gentlemen: The Story of Norfolk Island and the Roots of Modern Prison Reform* (Oxford, 2002)

——, and D. J. Rothman, eds, *The Oxford History of the Prison: The Practice of Punishment in Western Society* (Oxford, 1995)

Morrison, B., *As If* (Cambridge, 1988)

Owens, F., *The Little Book of Prison: A Beginners Guide* (Winchester, 2012)

Paterson, A., *Across the Bridges; or, Life by the South London River-side* (London, 1911)

Pearson, G., *Hooligan: A History of Respectable Fears* (London, 1983)

Phelan, J., *Jail Journey* (London, 1940)

Pilcher, J., and S. Wagg, eds, *Thatcher's Children? Politics, Childhood and Society in the 1980s and 1990s* (London, 1996)

Podmore, J., *Out of Sight, Out of Mind: Why Britain's Prisons are Failing* (London, 2012)

Potter, H., *Hanging in Judgement: Religion and the Death Penalty in England from the Bloody Code to Abolition* (London, 1993)

Pratt, J., *Punishment and Civilization: Penal Tolerance and Intolerance in Modern Society* (London, 2002)

Priestley, P., *Victorian Prison Lives: English Prison Biography, 1830–1914* (London, 1999)

Prison Reform Trust, *Public Want Offenders to Make Amends, Briefing Paper* (London, 2011)

Radzinowicz, L., and R. Hood, *A History of English Criminal Law* (London, 1982)

Ramsbotham, D., *Prisongate: The Shocking State of Britain's Prisons and the Need for Visionary Change* (London, 2003)

Randle, M., and P. Pottle, *The Blake Escape: How We Freed George Blake – and Why* (London, 1989)

Rich, C.E.F., *Recollections of a Prison Governor* (London, 1932)

Richards, B., *Emotional Governance: Politics, Media and Terror* (Basingstoke, 1997)

Rose, J., *The Intellectual Life of the British Working Classes* (New Haven, CT, 2001)

Royle, T., *The Flowers of the Forest: Scotland and the First World War* (Edinburgh, 2006)

Ruck, S. K., ed., *Paterson on Prisons* (London, 1952)

Rumbelow, D., *The Triple Tree: Newgate, Tyburn and the Old Bailey* (London, 1982)

Rutherford, A., *Prisons and the Process of Justice: The Reductionist Challenge* (London, 1984)

Sandel, M., *What Money Can't Buy: The Moral Limit of Markets* (London, 2012)

Scott, H., *Your Obedient Servant* (London, 1959)

The Scottish Prisons Commission, *Scotland's Choice: Report of the Scottish Prisons Commission* (Edinburgh, 2008).

Shuker, R., and E. Sullivan, *Grendon and the Emergence of Forensic Therapeutic Communities: Developments in Research and Practice* (Oxford, 2010)

Silverman, J., *Crime, Policy and the Media: The Shaping of Criminal Justice, 1989–2010* (London, 2012).

Slater, M., *Charles Dickens* (New Haven, CT, 2009)

Smith, N., *A Few Kind Words and a Loaded Gun* (Harmondsworth, 2004)

Sparks, R., *Burglar to the Nobility* (London, 1961)

——, A. Bottoms and W. Hay, *Prisons and the Problem of Order* (Oxford, 1996)

Stokes, A., *Pit of Shame: The Real Ballad of Reading Gaol* (Winchester, 2007)

Thomas, J. E., *The English Prison Officer since 1850: A Study in Conflict* (London, 1972)

Thompson, R., *Screwed: The Truth About Life as a Prison Officer* (London, 2008)

Webb, S. and B., *English Prisons Under Local Government* (London, 1922)

West, T., *The Curious Case of Mr Howard: Legendary Prison Reformer* (Winchester, 2011)

Wildeblood, P., *Against the Law* (London, 1955)

Wilkins, L., *Social Deviance: Social Policy, Action and Research* (London, 1964)

Wilson, D., *Death at the Hands of the State* (London, 2005)

——, and J. Ashton, *What Everyone in Britain Should Know About Crime and Punishment* (Oxford, 2001)

——, and S. O'Sullivan, *Images of Incarceration: Representations of Prison in Film and Television Drama* (Winchester, 2004).

Woodcock, J., *Report of the Enquiry into the Attempted Escape from HM Prison Whitemoor on 9 September 1994* (London, 1994)

Woolf, Lord Justice H., and Judge S. Tumim, *Prison Disturbances, 1900: Report of an Inquiry Presented to the Home Office by Lord Justice Woolf and Judge Stephen Tumim* (London, 1991)

ACKNOWLEDGEMENTS

One of the greatest pleasures in finishing a book is being able to publicly acknowledge all of those people who have in some way helped in the book's completion. Chief among those who have helped me on this occasion were colleagues at the Centre for Applied Criminology at Birmingham City University, especially Dr Elizabeth Yardley, Professors Craig Jackson, John Clibbens and Michael Brookes, who is also Director of Therapeutic Communities at HMP Grendon, and Visiting Professor Donal MacIntyre. Michael kindly read an early draft of the text, and contributed towards my thinking about penal policy between the wars. Also within the Centre, Charlotte Wasilewski kept the numerous drafts of the book in some form of order, the ever reliable Barbara McCalla helped with some crucial word processing, and Drs Lyndsey Harris, Sarah Pemberton and Laura Caulfield regularly offered some insight from their own academic backgrounds which made me think more critically about what I was writing. The tireless Rory Wheeler suggested the title of the book to me, in between producing and directing four documentaries for Channel 5.

Dr David Scott, Dr Jamie Bennett, Erwin James and Noel 'Razor' Smith also read drafts of the text and all provided me with excellent commentary which improved immeasurably on what I had written.

The librarians and staff of the university libraries of Birmingham City University, Cambridge University and the Institute of Criminology at Cambridge were tireless in their willingness to track down books for me, for which I am extremely grateful. I would also like to thank the librarians of the Newcastle City Library.

At the Howard League for Penal Reform, Andrew Neilson and Anita Dockley were both very generous with their time and assistance and, of course, the Howard League does also have a repository of books, articles and documents which I regularly consulted. I should also acknowledge that the conclusion to the book was informed by a trip to New York financed by the Howard League in my role as Chair of the Commission on English Prisons Today.

I have, of course, acknowledged my greatest debt at the Howard League within the dedication to this book.

PHOTO ACKNOWLEDGEMENTS

The author and publishers wish to express their thanks to the below sources of illustrative material and/or permission to reproduce it:

From Rudoph Ackermann, *The Microcosm of London* (London, 1808): p. 70; from Thomas Bayly, *Herba Parietis, or the Wall Flower as it Grew out of the Stone-Chamber belonging to the Metropolitan Prison of London, called Newgate* (London, 1650): p. 24; from *The Works of Jeremy Bentham . . .*, vol. IV (Edinburgh, 1842): p. 39; photos © The Trustees of the British Museum, London: pp. 12, 21, 28 (foot), 29, 30, 33, 44, 66, 67, 68, 69, 70; from E. W. Cooke, *Fifty Plates of Shipping and Craft Drawn and Etched by E. W. Cooke* (London, 1828): p. 66; from Charles Gordon, *The Old Bailey and Newgate* (London, 1902): p. 27; reproduced courtesy of the Howard League: pp. 35, 160, 165; from *The Illustrated London News*, 7 January 1843: p. 46; from Thomas Malton, *A Picturesque Tour through the Cities of London and Westminster: Illustrated with the most Interesting Views . . .* (London, 1792–1801): p. 28 (top); from Henry Mayhew and John Binney, *The Criminal Prisons of London . . .* (London, 1862): pp. 28 (top), 71.

INDEX

Page numbers in *italics* refer to illustrations